EXPERIENCING THE LIFE CYCLE

A Social Psychology of Aging

By

DAVID A. KARP

Boston College
Chestnut Hill, Massachusetts

and

WILLIAM C. YOELS

Wayne State University
Detroit, Michigan

For m

For D

CHARLES C THOMAS • PUBLISHER
Springfield • Illinois • U.S.A.

W
des
qu

PREFACE

IN recent years the study of gerontology has become an increasingly popular area of concern for social scientists. Courses have proliferated in sociology, psychology, and social work curriculums. Most of the full-length treatments now available focus on the *aged* rather than on *aging as a social process*. In so doing, they concentrate on a specific group of persons rather than on general social processes that affect us continually throughout our lives. In addition, current studies deal nearly exclusively with the "objective" correlates of aging—with matters such as health, poverty, unemployment, housing, social security status, and retirement.

Our aim in this volume is to deal with the more subjective, personal responses that persons make to aging in the course of their daily lives. Our focus is on the *social psychology* of aging rather than on the aged as such. Society's response to the body is not simply a result of biological functioning; it is also the product of cultural, historical, and structural conditions. To comprehend the aging process, we need to examine how persons occupying different locations in social space interpret and respond to repeated social messages about the meanings of age. For this reason, our concern is with such matters as the role of historical factors in definitions of aging, the significance of the general values of the larger society, the importance of work careers, the structure of family life, and the role of gender in the aging process.

The perspective maintained throughout this book is that of symbolic interaction. A major strength of the book lies in the theoretical continuity followed from chapter to chapter. Readers will shortly see the salience of such interactionist concepts as self, impression management, role taking, and symbolic behavior in directing attention and providing insights into the study of the aging process. Our emphasis throughout is on the continual, ongoing efforts of persons to give meaning and significance to their lives.

Chapter 1 surveys the theoretical literature in the field of aging.

We describe disengagement, activity, developmental, and sub-culture theories and analyze them from a social psychological per-spective. Here we stress the importance of viewing aging as a *socially constructed* phenomenon. Having presented the essentials of an inter-actionist view of aging in Chapter 1, we then illustrate the manner in which aging may be viewed as a *symbolic* phenomenon. As such, we should expect the meanings of aging to vary from culture to culture. In Chapter 2 we draw on the work of historians to illustrate the changing meanings of *childhood, adolescence, middle age*, and *old age* throughout recent history. We also employ the work of anthropolo-gists to demonstrate the cultural components of the aging process. Chapter 2 enlarges upon the theoretical themes raised in the pre-vious chapter. We continue to stress the argument that the "mean-ings" of aging are a function of both the general values of the larger society and the more specific values of the groups with which we interact and identify.

The way we think about ourselves is plainly a function of the evaluations and responses we get from "significant others." In general, our conceptions of aging cannot be understood apart from the networks of intimate relations we sustain. The central concern of Chapter 3 is with typical *family careers* and their influence on aging. This discussion leads us into Chapter 4, where we consider how work careers influence the meanings persons give to their several aging statuses.

A tradition of sociological research illustrates the centrality of work to personal identity. Occupation is a "master status" that often supersedes other personal attributes in forming our self-definitions and others' views of us. Certainly, our work lives constitute one very significant source of the aging messages we hear. In most societies the work career and the aging career overlap. Career curves struc-ture the way we think about aging. Different career patterns involve varying conceptions of what it means to be early, on time, or late. The way persons evaluate their own life progress, and so the ex-perience of growing older, is, in large measure, a function of where they are "supposed to be" occupationally at any given point in time. Chapter 4 examines a number of work situations with special em-phasis on contrasts between professional, white collar, and unskilled workers.

Social scientists have always understood that gender is not merely a biological phenomenon, that "maleness" and "femaleness" are culturally produced. Every society socializes men and women differently. Cultural definitions are imposed on nature, creating very different male and female roles, attitudes, feelings, aspirations, and behavior patterns. Men and women look at themselves and define themselves differently. Very importantly, their life chances are directly affected by these social definitions. In Chapter 5 we show how men and women undergo very different aging experiences. We describe and anlyze the nature of these experiences with special emphasis on the role of power differentials and the importance of physical appearance.

In the last chapter we illustrate how a number of major social trends influence our conceptions of aging. We explore the relationships between the growth of experts in the modern world, the development of a "therapeutic state," and the shaping of our age consciousness. We argue that aging has increasingly come to be viewed as a troublesome, problematic aspect of identity for many persons in contemporary society. Under the influence of medical and psychiatric experts, the process of aging has been transformed into a *problem* to be *solved*.

As in our previous books and articles, this volume is the result of a truly joint effort and the listing of the authors' names in alphabetical order should be interpreted as emphasizing the fact of equal authorship.

DAK
WCY

ACKNOWLEDGMENTS

THIS manuscript has benefited from the criticisms of several colleagues. We would like to thank Professor Norval Glenn of the University of Texas and Professor Russell Ward of the State University of New York at Albany for their cogent and constructive reviews of our work. Marshall Graney, Darleen Karp, Sharon Leveque, and John Williamson also contributed to the improvement of this book through their plentiful insights and their emotional support. Alice Close, Terri Krutell, Shirley Urban, and Sara White typed several drafts of this book in their typically thoughtful and expert fashion. We also thank Lorraine Bone for her careful editorial assistance.

While writing this book Gregory P. Stone, a close friend and colleague of ours for many years, died suddenly in Costa Rica. Our thoughts on sociological matters have been heavily influenced by both his writings and our conversations with him. We are proud to be part of an intellectual tradition that has produced scholars of Greg Stone's caliber. We hope that this manuscript lives up to those demanding standards of intellectual craftsmanship that Greg embodied in his writing and teaching.

The authors are also grateful for permission to use material from the following sources:

"Age and the Satisfaction from Work," by R. Cohn, *Journal of Gerontology*, Vol. 34, 1979. Copyright 1979 by The Gerontological Society. Used by permission of The Gerontological Society.

"Dimensions of Widowhood in Later Life," by R. Atchley, *The Gerontologist*, Vol. 15, 1975. Copyright 1975 by The Gerontological Society. Used by permission of The Gerontological Society.

"Life Cycle Squeeze and the Morale Curve," by R. Estes and H. Wilensky, *Social Problems*, Vol. 25, 1978. Copyright 1978 by The Society for the Study of Social Problems. Used by permission of The Society for the Study of Social Problems and the authors.

Death of a Salesman, by Arthur Miller. Copyright 1949 by Arthur

CONTENTS

EXPERIENCING
THE LIFE CYCLE

SOCIAL THEORIES OF AGING

A T age eighty-eight, Colonel Sanders, of fried chicken fame, told a reporter: "I'm real interested in old folks because I guess maybe someday I'll be old myself." In another occupational context, Willie Stargell and Willie McCovey, at ages thirty-eight and forty-one respectively, are considered among the "grand old men" of baseball. Another sport provides an example of someone who is young and old at the same time. A Boston newspaper described thirty-six-year-old Dave Cowens, former player–coach of the Celtics basketball team, as the "boy" coach and the "middle-aged" player. Professional athletes, it appears, are considered old by those around them as they approach forty years. Many businessmen, working for large companies, on the other hand, are viewed as "in their prime" at forty but approaching retirement in their mid-50s. Contrast this with the village of Vilcabamba in Ecuador where reportedly a high proportion of the population lives beyond 100 years. In this agrarian community there is no retirement age and all able-bodied persons are expected to contribute to the well-being of the community. Here, also, increased age brings with it increased social status (Leaf, 1973). These examples illustrate the deep connection between general cultural values, values particular to specific social contexts, and the meanings attached to chronological age.

Meanings accorded to age are contextual; they are tied to the societies and situations in which we act. Since we all move through and participate in many social circles during the course of our daily lives, we are responded to in terms of different age categories. As we move from situation to situation we are defined differently by those around us and are required thereby to behave in accordance with quite different age conventions. Our colleagues at work consider us one age, our superiors another, and the members of our family yet another. Of course, even within each of these contexts we need to be responsive to a number of age definitions. Our parents may define us throughout life as their "little boy or girl," a definition we may seek to avoid; our children may define us as too old to understand their problems, while brothers, sisters, cousins, and spouses respond to each other as still only "kids." In some contexts our age requires that we adopt a subordinate position, in others a dominant position. Different situations involve varying expectations concerning age-appropriate behaviors. What we can say, the attitudes we can safely express, the respect we believe is due us, and the responses we predict others will make to us, all relate to age expectations. In short, our age is a critical factor in determining how others define us, how we define ourselves, and so, the "performances" we put on in front of given audiences.

What does it mean to grow old? What, in fact, do we mean when we speak of childhood, adolescence, early adulthood, the middle years, and old age? How do age-related expectations emerge, govern behaviors, and often change? What is the relationship between individuals' age and the status, prestige, and power accorded them? Are there developmental stages in adulthood comparable to those social scientists have described as part of childhood? What happens to intelligence, memory, creativity, and sexuality as we grow older? Do individuals with different personality types adapt differently to the passage of time? The questions just stated are among those posed by an increasingly large number of social scientists who study the aging process. Although age has always been a significant factor or variable in social scientists' explanations of human conduct, only in recent years has the aging process become an area of inquiry in its own right. To this point social scientists have gone some distance in answering these questions we have framed. At the same time, efforts to answer these questions reveal the complexity of the aging process. The questions imply an obvious biological/chronological aspect to the way human beings age. Yet, to document only those physiological changes neglects the psychological, social, cultural, and historical dimensions of the process. Aging is a multidimensional phenomenon.

In this book we shall argue that full comprehension of the aging process requires analysis of the interrelationships of the biological, psychological, and cultural aspects of aging. In this respect, our focus is on the *social psychology* of aging. The task of the social psychologist studying aging is to make clear the intersection of the predictable, patterned biological life changes we all experience, with the specific cultural milieus in which persons live their daily lives. [1]

In this first chapter we will provide an expanded rationale for analyzing aging from a social psychological viewpoint. We will also outline the theoretical perspective in sociology—*symbolic interaction*—that we consider especially valuable in guiding our inquiry. In the broadest sense, we will argue that age, as such, has no intrinsic meaning. In concert with others we assign meanings, and often quite arbitrary meanings, to age. Such a view implies that there are *many* aging processes. To comprehend the complexities of growing older, we must consider the subjective responses persons make to their own aging. We must examine how persons occupying different locations in social space interpret and respond to the social messages they hear about the meanings of age. Although stressing the interpretive process underlying the meanings conferred on aging, we can not be blinded to the ways in which society "structures" our behaviors. An adequate explanation of any life situation must see human behavior as an ongoing interchange between freedom and constraint.

POPULATION TRENDS AND AGE NORMS

Each day approximately 4,000 Americans turn sixty-five while approximately 3,000 persons over sixty-five die. There is, then, a net increase of 1,000 persons older than sixty-five each day, and so an absolute increase of 3,500,000 persons per year in that age category (Davis, 1979). Moreover, if the birth rate continues at its current low rate (nearly zero population growth), a likely event according to most projections, and if mortality rates continue their slight decline, just over 16 percent of the population will be sixty-five or older by the year 2030. This represents a sharp increase from the current 11 percent of the population older than sixty-five (Neugarten, 1975). Further estimates are that by the turn of the century the median age of the population will have risen from twenty-nine to thirty-five years. For the first time in history, the older population is increasing in size while the population under age thirty-five is decreasing.

What are some of the consequences of this changing age struc-

---

[1]Vern Bengston's (1973) brief treatment of the social psychology of aging is one of the very few efforts in this direction. This work sensitizes us to important issues for elaboration in this volume.

ture? It is not surprising that much of the political rhetoric in the 1980s centers on what the respective parties and political candidates will be able to do for the elderly. Plainly, as an age category increases in size, its political importance, as a voting block whose collective interests must be considered, also increases. Table 1-I below, which shows actual and projected changes in voting age population from 1900 to 2030, indicates the shifting balance of political power in America.

Table 1-I Voting Population of the United States, 1900 - 2030, By Age Group

	1900	1940	1970	2030 (Projection)
18-44	70.1%	61.6%	54.1%	46.3%
45-64	23.1%	28.6%	31.1%	29.5%
65+	6.8%	9.8%	14.9%	24.2%
Total	100%	100%	100%	100%

Sources: U.S. Bureau of the Census, <u>Historical Statistics of the United States</u>, Colonial Times to 1970, bicentennial edition (Washington, D.C.: U.S. Government Printing Office, 1975), and "Projections of the Population of the United States: 1977 to 2050," <u>Current Population Reports</u>, Series P25, no. 704 (Washington, D.C.: U.S. Government Printing Office, 1977).

From the statistics in Table 1-I, we see that those between the ages of eighteen and forty-four, although still the largest category of voting-aged persons, have steadily declined since 1900 in size and potential influence. The percentage of those between forty-five and sixty-four has remained essentially stable during the same period. However, the over sixty-five population, which was only 6.8 percent of the over-eighteen population in 1900, will constitute 24.2 percent by the year 2030; nearly one-fourth of those eligible to vote. The potential power generated by the sheer numbers of elderly persons may stimulate major changes in governmental health and economic policies. The likelihood of such changes occurring, of course, depends upon the elderly's ability to achieve a unity of purpose through effective political organization.

The political clout of an elderly population will also be the basis for a general change in younger persons' conceptions of the aged. As older persons gain greater autonomy and visibility through the exercise of political power, many of the negative attitudes now held about the aged as a category and about aging as a process may begin to dissipate.

Given the demographic changes we have been describing, one central concern of scientists has been to predict how the changing age structure of the society will alter other social patterns. For example, most gerontologists expect individuals to be retiring earlier and earlier. One can even find predictions that mark forty years old as a future average retirement age. A more accepted estimate is that by the year 2000, the average age of retirement will drop to fifty-five years old (Neugarten, 1975). Along with an anticipated slight increase in life expectancy, the postretirement period of the life span for men will rise from the present thirteen years to between twenty-five and twenty-eight years. Based on these projections, Bernice Neugarten believes that the age of fifty-five will become a new symbolic marker in the life cycle, which then gives rise to a meaningful distinction between the group she terms the "young-old" (those between fifty-five and seventy-five) and the "old-old" (those older than seventy-five).

In an article on the subject she speculates on some of the demands that the young-old might be making and consequently some of the changes they might bring about in the society. At one point she remarks, "The young-old are likely to want greater options for what might generally be called an "age-irrelevant" society, one in which arbitrary constraints based on chronological age are removed, and in which all individuals have opportunities consonant with their needs, desires and abilities, whether they be young or old" (Neugarten, 1975:9).

Since its first mention, the idea of an age-irrelevant society has generated controversy. Neugarten argues that with the "graying of America," our perceptions concerning the behaviors appropriate at given ages have loosened up considerably. The norms that regulate what we can and ought to do at different points in our lives have become less effective regulators of behavior. Beyond adolescence especially, chronological age is becoming a poorer predictor of the way people will behave. In one interview Neugarten (1980) was asked whether we are becoming a less rigid society in terms of the way persons live their lives. She responded this way:

> Yes, I think so. Lives are more fluid. There is no longer a particular year—or even a particular decade—in which one marries or enters the labor market, or goes to school or has children.... It no longer surprises us to hear of a 22-year old mayor or a 29-year old university president—or a 35-year old grandmother or a retiree of 50. No one blinks at a 70-year old college student or at the 55-year old man who becomes a father for the first time—or who starts a second family. I can remember when the late Justice William Douglas, in old age, married a young wife. The press was shocked and hostile. That hostility would be gone today. People might smirk a little, but the outrage has vanished (Neugarten, 1980:66).

The notion of age irrelevancy is certainly intriguing. Imagine how different society and our personal relationships would look if age no longer dictated our behaviors. While we can agree that the constraints on individual behavior based on age seem to be loosening up, we think the word *irrelevancy* is far too strong, too strident, too overstated. We cannot conceive of a social structure in which age would be truly irrelevant.

As social psychologists, we will maintain throughout this volume that the meanings of age are socially constructed, the products of the interactions between persons. In later chapters we will illustrate how age-appropriate behaviors vary from culture to culture. The prospect, therefore, that persons living longer lives will "negotiate" the meanings of age and attempt to free themselves from certain age-related constraints seems perfectly plausible. We can easily entertain the idea that categories of similarly aged persons who feel oppressed by age norms will seek each other out, raise their collective consciousness, and then decide to challenge the dominant reality impinging on them. Sometimes these challenges to established reality will be successful and new expectations for behavior will, over time, become institutionalized. As the age structure of the society changes, we can expect modifications in the "time clocks" that govern, order, and make our lives predictable. It is, however, difficult to imagine a functioning society without age-related conventions to regulate behavior. We agree with the sociologist Glen Elder when he says: "We have to have age norms to anchor and structure our lives. An age-irrelevant society is a rudderless society" (Elder, 1980). A society in which age was truly irrelevant would be psychologically impossible and institutionally chaotic. To see how this is so, we need only to examine our everyday conduct.

AGE NORMS AND EVERYDAY LIFE

Once we begin to think about it, we realize just how much our daily lives are circumscribed by age-related norms. Indeed, the distinctions we make are often very finely grained. We have, for example, quite different expectations of a three-year-old than a five-year-old. A matter of even a few years can influence our judgments about what a person can and cannot or ought and ought not do. Persons in many states cannot legally frequent bars at seventeen, but may at eighteen. In some social circles, persons at eighteen or nineteen are thought too young to marry. By the time individuals reach the late twenties, however, parents, relatives, and friends may come to define them as "problems" if they remain unmarried. Popular culture images make the distinction between under and over thirty an important one. There is a consensus concerning the ages at which persons are expected to engage in specific activities. Data indicate, for example, that the early to mid-twenties are thought to be the best times for American men and women to marry. By twenty-four to twenty-six men should be settled in careers. Most people should finish their schooling by their early twenties and then go to work (Neugarten et al., 1965).

Intimacy is an area of social life obviously bounded by clear age norms. We expect to "fall in love," have sex, and get married within well-recognized time frames. Adults typically define teenagers' first attempts at establishing an intimate relationship as infatuation or "puppy love." Teenagers are, after all, too young to experience the "real thing." We should again acknowledge that the conventions we are naming, deeply embedded in our consciousness and apparently "natural" to us, are arbitrary social constructions. We shall see in later chapters that the specific requirements attached to age will be quite different in other societies and historical eras. The arbitrary, socially constructed nature of age norms is also revealed in a society's laws. Consider recent attempts in New Jersey to reduce the age of consent for sexual relationships to thirteen years old. Another interesting case involves changes in appropriate ages for marriage in Iran. With the recent takeover of the government by the religious patriarch, the Ayatollah, the appropriate age of marriage was lowered several years for both males and females. This legal change in conformance with Islamic tradition nicely illustrates how a society's religious values shape age expectations.

In American society, we generally share fairly rigid ideas concerning who may have an intimate sexual relationship with whom. Here, the age of persons is deemed critically important. Discrepancies in age between sexual partners is frequently a premise for humor. Some of you, for example, might have seen the comedy *Harold and Maude* in which a young man pursues an intimate relationship with a very old woman. Humorous scenes are constructed around the attempts of Harold's mother to distract him by providing women nearer his age as "suitable" replacements for the elderly Maude.

Sexual relations between "inappropriate" couples are not always viewed with humor. Our language contains many phrases derogating relationships between persons with a large age gap. We speak of some persons as "robbing the cradle"; other romances are negatively labelled "May–December" romances. All of us have heard the phrase "dirty old man." Although we do not refer to dirty old women, the portrayal of Mrs. Robinson in *The Graduate* would fit such a description. The audience is sympathetic when Benjamin rejects middle-aged Mrs. Robinson for her daughter, a more appropriate, "natural" partner. Of course, many do not expect elderly persons to have any sexual activity, even with partners of the same age. Proposals that nursing homes set aside "privacy rooms" in which aged residents could engage in handholding, petting, or sexual intercourse have elicited widespread and heated debate. Many find it hard to reject the image of old persons as asexual, white-haired cookie dispensers (Hess, 1974).

The last example concerning the sexuality of older persons is especially useful because it displays so dramatically the relationship between cultural norms, biological processes, and aging experiences. We might believe that biological processes occur independently of social forces. Yet, here is a case where persons' involvements in a biological activity is regulated by the messages they hear from those around them concerning that activity. The available evidence suggests that there are no known biological factors precluding a vigorous and active sex life into old age (Masters and

Johnson, 1966; Pfeiffer, Verwoerdt, and Davis, 1972), and yet there is a substantial decrease in sexual activity among the elderly. Our definitions of appropriate sexuality are symbolic constructions. They derive from general social values and the more specific values of those groups and persons with whom we frequently communicate. In the case under discussion, old persons hear negative communications concerning extensive sexual activity among the elderly. Our definitions of appropriate sexuality are symbolic constructions. They derive from general social values and the more specific values of those groups and persons with whom we frequently communicate. In the case under discussion, old persons hear negative communications concerning extensive sexual activity among the aged. The result is an actual dimunition in their sexual activity and a corresponding belief that the decreased activity is the *inevitable* result of biological changes. This is a classic example of a self-fulfilling prophesy and attests to the validity of William I. Thomas' famous dictum that "What persons define as real is real in its consequences."

The way women experience menopause in American society affords another interesting example of the social basis for behaviors often thought to have biological origins. It is a widespread belief that menopause is a central cause of increased depression among middle-aged women. Under closer scrutiny, the one-to-one connection made between the biological experience of menopause and depression begins to fall down. Pauline Bart's (1977) cross-cultural study of female menopause and middle age in a number of different societies underscores the importance of looking at aging from a broad social psychological perspective. Her study of non-Western cultures led her to state that "...middle age was not usually considered an especially stressful period for women. Consequently, purely biological explanations for stress felt at this time by Western women can be rejected. Middle age need not be fraught with difficulty." (Bart, 1977:282).

Bart's study also displays the necessity of looking at aging from a cross-cultural perspective. We often create our explanations of human conduct from a culturally provincial point of view. We cannot assume that because persons experience the aging process in a particular way within the United States that this is a *universal* human experience. Further, when cross-cultural data show substantial variation between societies, social scientists are forced to specify just how cultural factors intervene to create unique behavior patterns. In this instance, Bart has helped to clarify the specific relationship between mental depression and age in the United States.

It is no accident, as Bart has previously noted (1970), that in our society mental depression often occurs among middle-class married women, after the children have been "launched." For men, mental depression often coincides with retirement. Bart is suggesting, then, that the presumed causal relationship between menopause and depression is spurious. Rather, mental depression results from persons being denied the opportunity to play socially valued and rewarding roles after having previously been involved in such activities. Her study also alerts us to the ways in which a society's work and family structures influence how persons will experience the passage of years. Critical in this respect are differences in the meaning of aging for men and women who traditionally have had different levels of involvement in work and family life.

Although the women's movement has wrought central changes in women's perceptions of work and family relationships, compared to men, most women still invest a larger proportion of their time in home-related roles. As the marriage continues the husband's options are often increasing while the wife's are being restricted. Just as Jessie Bernard (1972) suggests that there is a "his" and a "her" marriage, so also is there a "his" and a "her" aging. This is a point to be explored and elaborated on in Chapter 5 of this book.

EXPERIENTIAL AGE

We have been commenting on the fact that to understand human behavior in terms of the aging process, we must identify the *meanings* attached to chronological ages. In addition, we note that in some instances persons' chronological age is deeply significant in the way they relate to each other, and in other cases it is far less important. Here we should comment on the connection between age in years, the life worlds that persons occupy, and the meaning of age for interaction. It might be especially useful to distinguish chronological age from what we term *experiential age*. Again let us stress the interconnections of age norms and specific social contexts.

Consider for a moment the meanings attached to slight chronological age differences by children.[2] Children make sharp distinctions concerning who may be friends with whom. During their early years, of course, children are flooded with new experiences, rights, and obligations. Because of their short biographies and limited life experiences, children are constantly learning and experiencing seemingly endless novelty. Differences between children of even a few months carry with them substantial knowledge differences. Six-year-olds believe themselves infinitely wiser than five-year-olds and in a class totally separate from anyone younger still. This belief is in some measure appropriate since during these early ages children who are separated by only one chronological year truly do inhabit quite different social/experiential/symbolic worlds. That being so, a difference of only one year assumes great subjective value.

Parents with young children are constantly setting rules limiting their behavior. Based largely on communications with other parents like themselves, they define the rights, expectations, duties, and freedoms appropriate to their different-aged children. Often these judgments are made in terms of parents' perceptions of the physical and emotional readiness of their children to assume certain tasks or engage in certain behaviors. In that sense, there is a correspondence between the stages of childhood and the norms surrounding children's behaviors. Parents' decisions, however, about age-related behaviors for their children are also emergent and made on an individual *ad hoc* basis. In this regard, the production of age norms, like the production of any norms, has an arbitrary quality to it. As an example, one of the author's children, a seven-year-old, is allowed to play in the neighborhood at large. His four-year-old, on the other hand, is told not to leave the yard surrounding the house. The point here is that the ecological or territorial freedom provided the older child expands his world enormously. Remember your own forays as children. Once in the neighborhood you discovered short cuts, explored the undersides of porches, formed a club in bushes "far" from your own house. As the example suggests, the restriction of territorial movement separates the four-year-old from her brother by much more than a few hundred yards; it keeps her in a wholly different world. Lacking his "street wisdom," she remains a baby in her

---

[2]For interesting discussions of the meanings of age differences for children, *see* Denzin (1972, 1975).

own eyes and in her brother's.

Not only children attach great value to small chronological age differences in choosing appropriate friends and acquaintances. From a number of papers submitted to the authors on the topic of the socialization of students to college life, it becomes clear that college sophomores typically have few freshmen among their close friends. Here again, it seems that a one-year age difference is given considerable significance. We suggest that at this point in the students' lives, the slight one-year difference corresponds to a very large status difference. The difference, of course, is that the sophomores already know their way around, they "know the ropes," they are "wise" about the customs, mores, and norms of college life. Sophomores have, in short, experienced a set of events that sharply discriminates them from freshmen, and so perceive themselves, in a subjective way, as much older. We hypothesize that the wearing of high school letter jackets by college students sharply decreases after the freshman year. Since the primary period of socialization to college life is in the freshman year, we would guess that another one-year difference, say that between juniors and sophomores, carries far less salience than the freshman/sophomore distinction.

As a last example concerning the relationship between chronological and experiential age, we have observed women of quite different ages meeting and befriending one another in public parks. In this case the women's ages appear generally irrelevant to the production of a friendship. What does seem critical as the basis of friendship, however, is *the age of the women's children*. Two women aged twenty-two and thirty-five, both with three-year-old children, respond to each other as equals. Because the two women are experiencing a similar point in their family life cycles despite a thirteen-year age gap, they consider each other suitable friends. In this context at least, the salience of chronological age diminishes. We acknowledge, however, that these same two women might find each other unsuitable talk partners in a different situation.

Perhaps the line of thinking in the last paragraph or two helps to explain why, in contrast to childhood, chronological age differences become less critical in limiting adult interactions. There are, of course, limits to associations in adulthood along age lines. Twenty-year-olds only irregularly have sixty-five-year-olds as "friends." However, a few years difference in age is easily tolerated and not an obstacle to friendship. Perhaps this is so because the number of uniquely "new" experiences persons have as adults become fewer and fewer as they grow older. We might say that the pace of socialization has greatly slowed down, and there is therefore an ever-expanding overlap of the life worlds of different-aged persons. This is why, for example, young persons can be friends on the job with persons often twice or more their age. The shared work context minimizes the subjective sense of age difference *in that work context*.

In the last few pages we have described only a small number of the familiar age-related expectations that guide our everyday interactions. Since our concern in this book is with the life-long process of aging and the factors involved in shaping our experiencing of that process, we have not restricted our examples to any one point in the life cycle. Our perspective leads us to examine how the members of various age groups experience aging. The experiences of the elderly, for example, are best viewed in the larger context of their associations with other age groups.

It would, of course, be quite impossible to cite all the age conventions in a society since they number well into the thousands and are constantly changing. At this moment we want you to appreciate the number and variation of cultural prescriptions around age that circumscribe our daily encounters. In addition, our several examples should have sensitized you to our theoretical interests and concerns.

Researchers always make decisions about the concepts and questions they deem most useful in extending their insight into social affairs. The authors of this book have decided to adopt a specific theoretical perspective. By the questions we have so far raised, the examples offered, and the emphasis maintained, we have touched upon the particular version of social psychology that will give impetus and unity to this enterprise. Throughout this work we will show the value of a perspective in sociology called *symbolic interaction* for analyzing aging. Since this perspective guides much of what follows, we should briefly acquaint the reader with its key concepts and root images.

AGING AND THE PERSPECTIVE OF SYMBOLIC INTERACTION

The perspective of symbolic interaction is based on the uncomplicated idea that the social world is composed of acting, thinking, defining, interpreting human beings in interaction with one another. Unlike the image of humankind offered by some social scientific theories, symbolic interactionists do not see persons as puppets pushed around by forces over which they have no control. Interactionists hold a picture of social life in which persons are to a great degree the architects of their worlds. Unlike atoms, molecules, or other elements of the physical universe, persons think, construct meanings, and respond creatively to their environments. Reality, then, is "socially constructed" and to understand human behavior, we must inquire into those processes through which persons do create and transform their social worlds. According to the sociologist Herbert Blumer (1969:2), there are three central premises underlying the symbolic interaction perspective:

1. Human beings act toward things or situations on the basis of the meaning that the things or situations have for them.
2. The meaning of things is derived from or arises out of the interaction one has with his or her fellows.
3. These meanings are handled or modified through an interpretive process used by persons in dealing with the objects or situations that they encounter.

These three premises, and the first in particular, call our attention to the fact that objects, events, situations, or processes (including aging) have no fixed meanings. Whatever meanings they have derive from the responses that persons make to them. As obvious as this view may seem, it has been neglected by several explanations of human behavior and, as we shall see, by some current theories of aging. The interactionist perspective, which locates meaning as an emergent property of interaction, avoids the position of some psychologies that conceive of meaning as inherent in phenomena. Models of explanation such as that offered by behavioral psychologists who see human behavior as "determined" by environmental circumstances disregard the interpretations that human beings with self-consciousness are able to make.

Another way to communicate the substance of the propositions above is to see human beings as living in a world of *symbols*. Humans, we are arguing, live in a world where they alone have assigned meanings to things. That is the definition of a symbol. It is "an object to which any meaning can be assigned. Its meaning is derived from its (socio-historical) context, and cannot be derived from either its physical qualities or the sensory experiences it may cause" (Hartung, 1969:237). That is, the physical characteristics of symbols are irrelevant to their meaning. Symbols, we are arguing, mobilize our responses to the world. They help us bring together or conceptualize aspects of the world. In contrast to humans, animals are limited to responding to their environments in terms dictated by their physiology. Humans alone, through symbolic behavior, are able to transform their environment through the meaning that they, in concert with others, confer on it. As Ernest Becker (1962:20) nicely puts it: "Nature provided all of life with H_2O, but only man could create a world in which 'holy' water generates a special stimulus."

There are two other features of symbolic behavior that require mention here. First, through symbolic behavior we in effect "liberate" ourselves from the constraints imposed by time and space. Having created the word (i.e. verbal symbol) *house*, for example, to refer to the actual physical object called a house, we are now free to talk about, think about, and refer to houses without the necessity of having a house physically present in our sight. We can refer to houses that existed in the past as well as conjure up houses that might exist in the future, not just in the United States, but elsewhere — indeed, possibly on other planets! It is the human ability to engage in symbolic behavior that "culminates in the organism's ability to choose what it will react to" (Becker, 1962:20).

Second, through the use of symbols we can not only step outside the particular physical setting in which we find ourselves, but, more important, step outside ourselves. We can look at ourselves from the standpoint of others; put ourselves in their place and anticipate how they are going to react to us. We can, in effect, look at ourselves as if we were objects and then anticipate how others are going to respond to those objects. Verbal symbols (language) are critical here since it is the character of the spoken word that it is heard simultaneously by both the speaker and those to whom it is addressed. Speakers thus react to the word at the same time that they are monitoring the responses of others to what they are saying.

The ability to evaluate objectively our own behaviors from the perspective of others is necessary for becoming a "normal," functioning member of society. Once we acquire that ability, we possess what George Herbert Mead, a major formulator of the interactionist perspective, called the *self*. From the interactionist perspective, the self is formed and transformed through interaction with others. One is not born with a preformed self. Through the use of symbols one learns to take on the attitudes, values, and moods appropriate to the particular social circles to which one belongs. Through the reflected appraisals of others, we come to define ourselves as certain kinds of persons.

Definitions of self, of course, extend to our personal sense of age. Persons' awareness of middle age, for example, comes about through their recognition of others' definitions of them as middle-aged. In a study on this subject Bernice Neugarten (1968:96) comments that "men...perceive the onset of middle age...often from the deferential behavior accorded them in the work setting. One man described the first time a younger associate held open a door for him; another, being called by his official title by a newcomer in the company; another, the first time he was ceremoniously asked for advice by a younger man." It is as though others become mirrors in which we see ourselves reflected, and through these reflections we come to have certain subjective definitions of ourselves. One woman in Neugarten's study used exactly this metaphor in describing the origins of her own sense of age: "It is as if there are two mirrors before me, each held at a partial angle. I see part of myself in my mother who is growing old, and part of her in me. In the other mirror, I see part of myself in my daughter. I have had some dramatic insights, just from looking in those mirrors... It is a set of revelations that I suppose can only come when you are in the middle of three generations." These examples cause us to amend the old saying that "you are as young as you feel." The interactionist conception of self implies more precisely that "you are as young or old as *others* make you feel."

The purpose of any theoretical perspective in the social sciences is to guide the direction of research, to raise distinct and insight-yielding questions about aspects of the social world. However, it would be a mistake to claim that the questions and emphases suggested by an interactionist framework are the only valuable ones. Those who study aging would do well to look at the process from a number of different perspectives. It is too complicated a process to be understood by any one vantage point alone. In this book, however, our goal is to look at aging from a social–psychological viewpoint. We think that the significance of such key interactionist concepts as symbols, the nature of human selves, role taking, and impression–management lies in their capacity to sensitize us to certain aspects of the phenomena we investigate. The major concern of our approach is to establish the relationship between the meanings persons attach to their environments and the consequences of those "definitions of the situation" for their behavior.

Now, we should consider how the broad principles we have named apply to our thinking about age and aging. Recalling the three central propositions of symbolic interaction, we must seriously consider the ideas that (1) age like any other symbol submits to a multiplicity of meanings; (2) those meanings attached to age emerge out of our interactions with others; and (3) the meanings of age are likely to be modified and reinterpreted depending upon definitions of the situations in which we act. Beyond these points, we think that an adequate social psychology of aging must be attentive to the following broad dimensions of the process:

- While the aging process certainly involves regular, predictable biological changes, understanding of the process requires knowledge of the cultural definitions given to the process.
- The meanings given to chronological age categories are not constant. They vary from context to context and with different audiences. In interactionist terminology, different groups respond to age in terms of quite different inventories of symbols and thereby create among their members quite different aging selves.
- The meanings attached to age will vary with persons' social attributes such as their gender, race, ethnic affiliation, occupation, social class, and marital status.
- In a larger sense, our conceptions of aging and our experience of the process will be shaped by our place in history, by the historical epoch in which we live.
- Although there are, as we have seen, age norms, the aging experience is also a subjective one and must be viewed from the perspective of persons moving through the experience.

Throughout this book, we will elaborate on and illustrate the importance of the concepts, ideas, and dimensions of social life we have been describing for the last few pages. By now, you have become acquainted with the contours of an interactionist approach to aging. In the next section of this chapter we will describe the types of theories that currently dominate social scientists' conceptions and explanations of the aging process. It is not our intention to disprove or reject current and traditional theorizing. Rather, we shall consider how the social–psychological perspective we are advancing extends insight into the aging process by complementing existing viewpoints.

CURRENT THEORIES OF AGING

It is a well documented idea that theory development in science follows a patterned career (Kuhn, 1969; Mullins, 1975). Until recently, work in gerontology, a "young" area of social science inquiry, was primarily descriptive. Researchers saw it as their central task to "get the facts," especially about the status of the elderly. Although much contemporary research still seeks basic statistical information, social scientists presently show a more active concern with the construction of theories to order and explain the now available facts. Some of these theories refer only to the social experience of the elderly while others are more comprehensive, dealing with change and regularity over the whole life cycle.

We shall not provide a description of all aging theories in this section. Rather, we will broadly characterize the "types" of theories current in the aging area. For purposes of clarity and organization these theories can be grouped under three general categories: *integration theories, developmental theories* and *subculture theories*. We will deal with these theory types in turn. We will consider how each complements the symbolic interaction perspective and can be complemented by it.

Integration Theories

Throughout the early 1960s a theoretical perspective called *structural functionalism* dominated sociological thinking about the nature and structure of societies. Talcott Parsons (1937, 1951), the major American formulator of this theory, argued that every element of a society persisting over a long period of time serves some distinctive function in maintaining the society as a whole. As Parsons conceived it, society is like any living organism. Just as the several parts of an organism, e.g. heart, lungs, and liver, are interconnected to maintain its biological equilibrium, so also are the parts of society, e.g. religious, economic, and political institutions, related in a complementary way to maintain social equilibrium. The stress of structural–functional theory is on the way that the various social elements are integrated with each other to produce and sustain order in society. It follows that much structural-functional thought emphasizes the means through which persons learn social roles and are, thereby, fitted into the life of an ongoing society. The theory stresses the harmonious integration of persons into society and the manner in which adoption of culturally prescribed roles contributes to overall order in society.

Considering the pervasive influence of structural-functional thinking in American social science, it is not surprising that initial theorizing in gerontology would employ its imagery and assumptions in explaining particularly the role of the aged in society. One influential theory deriving from functionalism attempts to explain the changing nature of persons' integration into society as they grow old. *Disengagement theory* proposes that there is an inevitable withdrawal of older persons from active involvement in the society. According to Cumming and Henry (1961), originators of disengagement theory, such a withdrawal process is universal, governed by cultural norms, and participated in voluntarily by older persons who, faced with diminishing physical abilities, choose to withdraw from social roles previously held.

From a functionalist point of view, the disengagement process is perfectly sensible since it ultimately contributes to society's equilibrium. Those with diminished abilities sever social ties, reduce their integration into society before dying, and simultaneously provide space for younger persons who are conveniently beginning to "engage" themselves with the social positions being vacated by the elderly. Disengagement, according to the theory, represents a happy and complementary relationship between the needs of old persons and the needs of an ongoing, functioning society. The theme of society/individual complementarity is expressed in this statement of the theory:

> (There is) an inevitable mutual withdrawal or disengagement resulting in decreased interaction between the aging person and others in the social system he belongs to. The process may be initiated by the individual or by others in the situation. . . . When the aging process is complete, the equi-

librium which existed in middle life between the individual and his society
has given way to a new equilibrium characterized by a greater distance
and an altered type of relationship (Cumming and Henry, 1961).

Immediately there seem to be flaws in disengagement theory. If
withdrawal from the social roles of middle age is a natural, inevitable, universal, and voluntary process, why do some persons
resist it, and why are there certain categories of persons who seem
exempt from it? For example, there is no age limitation for serving
in the United States Senate and the age distribution of persons in
that position suggests the desire to retain it for as long as possible.
One study (Roman and Tailetz, 1967) of an occupational role in
which persons are allowed continued engagement after formal
retirement, that of "professor emeritus," indicates that most professors want to continue working. Thus, both casual observation and
empirical investigation indicate, contrary to Cumming's and
Henry's thesis, that disengagement is not necessarily universal, inevitable, or voluntary.

Partly as a response to the apparent problems we have named,
some have proposed an explanation quite the reverse of disengagement theory. Advocates of *activity theory* claim that successful adjustment to old age requires active and continued integration into society through the performance of valued roles. Here the claim is that
"the older person who ages optimally is the person who manages to
resist the shrinkage of his social world. He maintains the activities of
middle age as long as possible, and then finds substitutes for work
when he is forced to retire and substitutes for friends and loved ones
whom he loses by death" (Havighurst, 1968:21).

Should we maintain a functionalist stance toward the operation
of society, with emphasis on integration, equilibrium, and the complementary meeting of individual and social needs, the picture looks
murky at this point. With disengagement and activity theories we
have two opposed explanations of the nature of the relationship between social systems and their older members. When advocates of
two contradictory theories can provide evidence for their respective
positions, we seem caught on the horns of a difficult theoretical
dilemma. But, do we have to choose between these theories?

In one attempt at resolution (Reichard, Livson, and Peterson,
1962), researchers tried to explain different patterns of adaptation in
old age by introducing personality variables. Their data collected
from eighty-seven elderly men, revealed five "types," some of whom

were satisfied with disengagement and others not. As illustrations, those called "mature" took a constructive rather than defensive approach to old age and were high on adjustment. Those labelled *rocking chair* types by the researchers also adapted well by "taking life easy" and depending on others. At the other extreme, those described as *angry* or *self-hating* types adjusted badly. We question such explanations that have, we think, a circular quality to them. These explanations effectively argue that persons with adaptive personalities adapt well to old age. Now, let us consider how the interactionist perspective leads us to evaluate the theories we have been discussing.

We should not be surprised by the apparently contradictory findings that some persons seek disengagement while others seek continued activity. Indeed, such variation in response to "role loss" might be *precisely* the prediction an interactionist would make. Rather than asking whether disengagement is functional or not, we ought to ask about the meaning of role loss to different groups of persons. That is, role loss is not an inherently positive or negative event for persons, but depends rather on the value they place on the roles lost. We simply do not evaluate in the same way all of the roles we are obliged to perform throughout our lives. Work, for example, does not carry the same meaning for all persons in the society. For some occupational groups, such as college professors, the work role is highly valued and central to persons' conceptions of self. In other cases work may be defined only as a necessary sacrifice one must make for one's family (*see* Sennett and Cobb, 1973). Holding this latter definition, disengagement from work roles is more likely to be anticipated with relief. In an extensive critique of disengagement theory, Arlie Hochschild (1976) comments on the importance of the interpretive process:

> ...The disengagement theorists...have detached social and psychological behavior from the meanings people ascribe to it....What is missing is evidence about the *meaning* of the daily acts that constitute engagement or disengagement. Lacking this phenomenological level of inquiry, we cannot see how two individuals with identical "role counts" apply different meanings to these roles, or how two people psychologically disengaged see the world and themselves differently as a result (1976:66).

Rather than focusing on disengagement or activity as complete explanations of adaptive behavior in old age, it better fits the complexity of things to analyze why persons easily disengage from certain of their life roles and seek to continue others. As previously, we maintain that individuals' responses to social situations (including retirement) are not uniform. Instead, retirement will carry quite different meanings for persons depending upon the values and attitudes of those with whom they are normally in communication. We expect that persons whose lives have been guided by different symbol systems concerning the meaning of work, leisure, family, friendship, and so on will interpret a reduction of role performance in these spheres quite differently. These points imply that theories of adaptation in old age require greater specification than is allowed by theories flatly claiming that withdrawal from social roles either is or is not functional. Such theories do not consider seriously enough how persons' adaptations to situations vary with their subjective definitions of those situations.

Developmental Theories

One of the most persistent challenges in social psychology is to construct a conception of human development that accounts for the ways humans both change and exhibit stability over the life course. Our theories should account for both the uniqueness of individuals' responses to situations and the regularities we all exhibit as we move through the life cycle. While persons display enormous variability in their responses to situations, such variability can still be viewed within a broader framework of consistency and predictability.

As an example, think of the formation of love relationships. On the one hand, it is correct to say that every single human relationship has its own unique properties. No two persons relate to each other in quite the same way as do some other couple. Having said this, we should not miss the point that persons still construct their love relationships within a tightly circumscribed network of social expectations. We must not dismiss the fact that the overwhelming proportion of persons "fall in love" and marry between the ages of twenty and twenty-four. This is not simply some kind of statistical anomaly. These are the years when you are *expected* to fall in love and marry! Most of us abide by a "social clock" regulating the "proper" timing of life events. Falling in love is only one example. There is similar consistency attached to a large number of life events—when to change jobs, become a parent, buy a home, and the like. Developmental perspectives on aging postulate universal and patterned sequences to the human life cycle. As previously, we will acquaint you with some of the most prominent developmental theories and then evaluate them.

Students of aging have sought out regularities over the life course in a number of areas of human life. Psychologists have produced an enormous amount of research, too voluminous to treat in detail here, on the relationships between chronological age and various human functions: sensory processes, e.g. vision and hearing; psychomotor performance, e.g. reaction time and speed of movement; mental functioning, e.g. intelligence, learning and memory; and drives, e.g. hunger and sex. Although the findings of such research (*see* Birren and Schaie, 1976) remain somewhat unclear because of enormous individual variability in the processes mentioned, certain general patterns do emerge. For instance, there is now general consensus that aging brings with it decreases in sensory acuity and memory. Equally important are findings that explode certain myths about the aged. Evidence now challenges the widespread belief in age-related declines in intelligence and the capacity to learn (Schaie, 1975).

Whatever the findings of this literature, one of our repeated caveats is necessary. It would be a serious error to explain findings like those above *only* in biological terms. As before, we maintain that increases or decreases in creativity, intelligence, sexual functioning, and so forth must be understood in terms of the interaction of inevitable age-related changes and the range of cultural expectations dictating how we view and interpret those changes. If we want to appreciate the behavioral consequences of certain biological changes for persons, we need to know more about the meanings persons give to such changes (Kastenbaum, 1965, 1968). Theorists tell only half the story if their work begins and ends with a description of patterned changes in human functioning. This is so because members of different groups will respond quite differently to the changes we have mentioned. We must complete the story by noting the variety of responses that can be made to the same objective conditions.

A slight decrease with age in such a psychomotor capacity as reaction time (defined as the period that elapses between the presentation of a stimulus and the beginning of our response to that stimulus) will be assigned great importance by a major league shortstop whose career is ended when he loses a step or two in quickness while fielding a ground ball. However, the same decrease may even go unnoticed by those with more sedentary occupations. Because of the meaning of this particular change for the ballplayer, it may have a range of behavioral consequences unique to his occupational status. We could imagine the player trying to hide the change from coaches by playing back a few steps in order to allow more reaction time. Perhaps he also tries to renegotiate his contract before his diminished ability is discovered by coaches, or he begins to explore seriously alternative career options. In short, like the ballplayer, our subjective feelings and actual behaviors will depend on the interpretations we give to inevitable, predictable changes in our bodily functions.

Additional work in developmental psychology attends to issues of change and stability in personality attributes throughout the life cycle. This research raises basic questions about the nature of human selves. Earlier we described George Herbert Mead's conception of the self as a process in which persons evaluate their behaviors from the perspective of others. This notion, you will recall, implies that persons present quite different selves in different situations. You might properly be asking yourself, however, whether the self is always discrete, called forth only by the situation and the audience. Isn't there an order and stability to the self that transcends the particular normative structure of settings? Those of you who have studied the writings of personality theorists such as Sigmund Freud, Abraham Maslow, Harry Stack Sullivan, and Erik Erikson know that they argue for the development of a personality structure that coordinates or controls situational presentations of self; a personlity structure that has continuity through time.

Developmental aging theories emphasize stages through which all persons are assumed to pass as they grow older (Freud, 1933; Piaget, 1932; Erikson, 1950; Kolhberg, 1964; Gould, 1978; Levinson, 1978). While such theories may differ on a number of points, they are united in their focus on the inevitability of one's passage through various universal life stages. In a popularized version of these approaches, Gail Sheehy (1977) argues that crises regularly confront persons in predictable ten-year cycles. No doubt, part of the popularity of works such as Sheehy's derives from the influence that developmental theorists have had in shaping our consciousness of expectations about the "normal" life cycle. The popular appeal of these works also reflects the ahistorical character of thinking predominant in American behavioral science. This historical naivete creates serious problems for scholarly disciplines, which ought to be concerned with developing historically sophisticated, broadly based theories of human development.

In Chapter 2 of this volume we shall see how the life stages occurring in any society are products of history and culture. To briefly anticipate our argument there, consider the following: Childhood was "discovered" in seventeenth century Western Europe; the emergence of adolescence as an age category was associated with the "invention of juvenile delinquency" in late nineteenth century America; middle age is a very recent age associated with profound demographic changes in mortality rates and marriage patterns. Kenneth Keniston succinctly conveys this point in his following statement:

> Some societies may "create" stages of life that do not exist in other societies; some societies may "stop" human development in some sectors far earlier than other societies "choose" to do so. If, therefore, a given stage of life or developmental change is not recognized in a given society, we should seriously entertain the possibility that it simply does not occur in that society. And if this is the case, then in societies where adolescence does not occur many of the results of an adolescent experience should be extremely rare... (1971:342).

Finally, we have reservations about the existence of universal life stages even *within* the same society. Every society contains within it a multiplicity of cultural value systems. While persons may move through regular stages, we question whether such movements apply equally to *all* segments of a society. For example, we are hard pressed to imagine those from upper-class social circles in the United States moving through the same life stages as those encountered by the "dispossessed" members of this society. Our concern here, it should be emphasized, is not to deny the idea of *passages*, but rather to claim that whatever passages persons do in fact experience will relate to their *places* within the larger social structure.

Subculture Theories

A final group of theories for discussion in this chapter may broadly be labelled *subculture theories*. Of the theories discussed thus far, these come closest to an interactionist view. Arnold Rose (1965) has argued that the aged form themselves into a subculture with its own distinctive norms, values, and life-styles. The emergence of such an age solidarity group, according to Rose, is facilitated by several factors. First, the size of the elderly population and their increasing segregation into retirement communities and urban neighborhoods put them in close contact with one another. Retirement practices make it difficult for the elderly to continue identifying with the larger society. As a result, they begin to shift their orientation to those who are their age peers. Finally, it is argued that their treatment by representatives of social service agencies creates a consciousness among the elderly of being placed in a common situation.

Rose's theory that, through interaction, persons create their own distinctive symbolic worlds generally appeals to us. Available evidence, however, raises serious questions about the validity of the assumptions put forth by Rose. For example, the elderly interact more frequently with their children than with each other. A very small percentage of the elderly live in retirement communities. The notion of a life-style common to the elderly is also not demonstrated by the literature in gerontology (Atchley, 1972:252). Thus, we see, contrary to Rose's viewpoint, that there is no consistent and uniform aging consciousness among the elderly. Like members of all other age categories, the elderly, too, experience their chronological age in manifold ways. Like all of us, the elderly, in trying to make sense of their lives, must negotiate and interpret the world around them (Marshall, 1978; Strauss, 1978).

One of the most influential of recent theories to explain how chronological age structures and patterns the social roles we perform is termed *age stratification theory*. The general issue of social stratification, or the process by which individuals socially place and differentiate one another, has long been of concern to social scientists. The very term stratification is revealing, calling to mind a conception of social ordering modeled on the "strata" found in geological studies. American sociologists studying the phenomenon of stratification have typically viewed it in terms of an hierarchical continuum in which persons are ranked from high to low on the basis of possessing a certain "amount" of things such as education, income, or occupational prestige.

Studies of stratification have most usually centered on the concept of social class. However, race, ethnicity, religion, and gender are also dimensions along which persons and groups are differentially ranked in terms of their power, prestige, status, and wealth. In traditional studies of stratification the interest has been in documenting exactly how possession of various configurations of social attributes affects individuals' experiences in the world, their values, their attitudes; indeed, as the famous sociologist Max Weber has put it, their very "life chances."

Age is yet another critical dimension along which persons may be ranked and in terms of which roles and resources are distributed. Matilda White Riley, Marilyn Johnson, and Anne Foner (1972) have elaborated on the implications of one's membership in particular age groups or *age strata* for creating ditinctive life-cycle roles, expectations, and opportunities.

Age strata may be created in a number of ways. For example, we will discuss throughout this volume how persons' perceptions and behaviors are related to such life periods as childhood, adolescence, middle age, and old age. Each of these periods may be considered an age stratum. In later chapters we also describe how the meanings of work and family life change as we grow older. Thus, different points in work and family life cycles may also comprise age strata. The basic point of age stratification theory, however we conceptualize age strata, is that location in one or another stratum is a major factor according to which social roles are allocated. Moreover, a person's movement from one age stratum to another is continuous and unavoidable. Unless we die, there is no way to avoid successive movement from childhood, to adolescence, to adulthood, and eventually to old age. The manner in which we are treated by society and the behaviors we are expected to enact are related to our movement from one age category to another.

Age stratification theory also calls attention to the fact that we move through the life cycle with a cohort of persons who experience each major life period at the same time we do. Every person born in 1980, for instance, becomes part of a cohort that will travel through life together in so far as they simultaneously pass through childhood, adolescence, adulthood, and old age. From a social–psychological perspective this is important because each cohort enters successive life stages with a unique set of historical experiences. Each cohort, therefore, brings distinctive values, ideas, and consciousnesses to these life periods.

The cohort of persons who were children during The Great Depression, for example, were greatly shaped by that historical event and, consequently, interpret much of the remainder of their lives in light of that experience. Compared to earlier and later generations (cohorts), they confer quite different meanings on adolescence, midlife, and old age. Among other things, they place a great deal of interpretive emphasis on the financial contingencies posed by each major point in their life passage (Elder, 1974). In similar fashion, such formative historical events as World War II, the McCarthy era, the emergence of rock and roll music, the black revolution of the 1960s, and the Vietnam War have greatly influenced the way different age cohorts view themselves and the world.

There are two interrelated ideas, both very much in conformity with our point of view in this book, that age stratification theory magnifies for us. First, our experience of aging cannot be understood apart from the particular historical contexts in which we live out our lives. Second, since different cohorts of persons bring different attitudes, values, and world views to such categories as middle age or old age, the meanings attached to these categories cannot remain fixed. The meanings of being middle age or old are constantly undergoing transformation as each new cohort comes to occupy these statuses. In later chapters of this book we will further elaborate on some of the structural and social–psychological processes described as part of age stratification theory. We will particularly be concerned with how human beings constantly construct and reconstruct the meanings of various age categories.

CONCLUSION

The major goal of this first chapter has been to lay out some of the essential dimensions of a social–psychological view of aging. We have described, more particularly, some of the questions that a symbolic interactionist social psychology requires us to ask about the aging process. Informed by this theoretical perspective, we argued that aging is a social construction taking place within the confines of history and culture: In proposing the concept of experiential age we have sensitized the reader to the idea that chronological age can carry multiple meanings, depending upon one's location in the life course. In addition, subjective age meanings correspond to and arise out of our interactions with others who occupy similar social structural positions. In taking this point of view we have previewed the conceptual focus of this work. Our task throughout will be to elaborate on the connections between persons' movement through the life cycle, their places in society, and their subjective senses of age.

As part of our effort to explain this book's approach to aging, we examined current aging theories. We noted that such theories tend to slight the significance of the range of interpretations we give to age and the processual elements in human development. In describing three dominant theory types — integration, developmental, and subculture theories — we find too great an emphais on efforts to name universal, unvarying aspects of the aging process. Although we surely ought to document regularities in human behavior and perception, we need equal appreciation for the diversity of aging experiences humans can create. Our perspective cautions us against treating specific life periods as isolated and autonomous "things," divorced from earlier constructed meanings. Thus, our concern in this book will be the life-long process of aging.

In Chapter 2 we will enlarge on the theoretical themes introduced in this chapter. Historical evidence affirms our position that age categories are humanly constructed and rooted in particular cultural milieus. We question the apparent timelessness of such contemporary age groupings as childhood, adolescence, middle age, and old age. We shall see how these taken-for-granted categories emerged out of specific demographic, social structural, and value changes that substantially predate our own lives.

REFERENCES

Atchley, R.: *The Social Forces In Later Life.* Belmont, CA, Wadsworth Publishing Co., 1972.

Bart, P.: Mother Portnoy's complaint. *Transaction, 8 (November-December):* 69-74, 1970.

Bart, P.: The loneliness of the long-distance mother. In P. Stein et al. (Eds.): *The Family.* MA, Addison-Wesley, 1977.

Becker, E.: *The Birth and Death of Meaning.* Glencoe, IL, The Free Press, 1962.

Bengston, V.: *The Social Psychology of Aging.* Indianapolis, Bobbs-Merrill, 1973.

Bernard, J.: *The Future of Marriage.* New York, Basic Books, 1972.

Birren, J., and Schaie, K.: *Handbook of the Psychology of Aging.* New York, Van Nostrand, Reinhold, 1976.

Blumer, H.: *Symbolic Interactionism: Perspective and Method.* New Jersey, Prentice-Hall, 1969.

Cumming, E., and Henry, W.: *Growing Old: The Process of Disengagement.* New York, Basic Books, 1961.

Davis, R.: Aging: Prospects and issues. In Richard H. Davis (Ed.): *Aging: Prospects and Issues.* CA, University of California Press, 1979.

Denzin, N.: The genesis of self in early childhood. *Sociological Quarterly, 13*: 291-314, 1972.

Denzin, N.: Play, games, and interaction: The contexts of childhood socialization. *Sociological Quarterly, 16*:458,472, 1975.

Elder, G.: *Children of the Great Depression.* Chicago, University of Chicago Press, 1974.

Elder, G.: Quoted in *Time Magazine, (August) 11*:75, 1980.

Erikson, E.: *Childhood and Society.* New York, Norton, 1950.

Estes, C.: *The Aging Enterprise.* San Francisco, Jossey-Bass, 1979.

Freud, S.: *New Introductory Lectures on Psycho-Analysis.* London, Hogarth Press, 1933.

Gould, R.: *Transformations.* New York, Simon and Schuster, 1978.

Hartung, F.: Behavior, culture, and symbolism. In G.E. Dole and R.L. Carneiro (Ed.): *Science of Culture.* New York, Thomas Crowell, 1960.

Havighurst, R., et al.: Disengagement and patterns of aging. In B. Neugarten (Ed.): *Middle Age and Aging.* Chicago, University of Chicago Press, 1968.

Hess, B.: Stereotypes of the aged. *Journal of Communication, 24*:76-85, 1974.

Hochschild, A.: Disengagement theory: A logical, empirical, and phenomenological critique. In J. Gubrium (Ed.): *Time, Roles, and Self In Old Age.* New York, Human Sciences Press, 1976.

Kastenbaum, R.: Theories of human aging: A search for a conceptual framework. *Journal of Social Issues, 21*:13-36, 1965.

Kastenbaum, R.: Perspectives on the development and modification of behavior in the aged. *Gerontologist, 8*:280-284, 1968.

Kenniston, K.: Psychological development and historical change. *Journal of Interdisciplinary History, 2*:329-345, 1971.

Kohlberg, L.: Development of moral character and moral ideology. In M. Hoffman (Eds.): *Review of Child Development Research.* New York, Russell Sage Foundation, 1964.

Kuhn, T.: *The Structure of Scientific Revolutions.* Chicago, The University of Chicago Press, 1962.

Leaf, A.: Getting old. *Scientific American, 229*:44-52, 1973.

Levinson, D.: *The Seasons of a Man's Life.* New York, Knopf, 1978.

Marshall, V.: No exit. *Aging and Human Development, 9*:345-357, 1978.

Masters, W.H., and Johnson, V.E.: *Human Sexual Response.* Boston, Little, Brown and Co., 1966.

Mullins, N.: *Theories and Theory Groups in Contemporary American Sociology.* New York, Harper and Row, 1973.

Neugarten, B., Moore, J., and Lowe, J.: Age norms, age constraints, and adult socialization. *American Journal of Sociology, 70*:710-717, 1965.

Neugarten, B.: The awareness of middle age. In B. Neugarten (Ed.): *Middle Age and Aging.* Chicago, University of Chicago Press, 1968.

Neugarten, B.: Acting one's age: New rules for the old. *Psychology Today, April*: 66-74, 77-80, 1980.

Parsons, T.: *The Structure of Social Action.* New York, The Free Press, 1937.

Parsons, T.: *The Social System.* New York, The Free Press, 1951.

Pfeiffer, E., Verwoerdt, A., and Davis, G.: Sexual behavior in middle life. *American Journal of Psychiatry, 128*:1262-67, 1972.

Piaget, J.: *The Moral Judgment of the Child.* New York, Harcourt, Brace, and World, 1932.

Reichard, S., Livson, F., and Peterson, P.: *Aging and Personality.* New York, Wiley, 1962.

Riley, M., Johnson, M., and Foner, A.: *Aging and Society, Volume 3: A Sociology of Age Stratification.* New York, Russell Sage, 1968.

Roman, P., and Taietz, P.: Organizational structure and disengagement: the emeritus professor. *Gerontologist, 7*:147-152, 1967.

Rose, A.: The subculture of aging: A framework for research in social gerontology. In A. Rose and W. Peterson (Eds.): *Old People and Their Social World.* Philadelphia, F.A. Davis, 1965.

Schaie, K.: Age changes and age differences. *Gerontologist, 7*:128-132, 1967.

Sennett, R., and Cobb, J.: *The Hidden Injuries of Class.* New York, Random House, 1973.

Sheehy, G.: *Passages.* New York, E.P. Dutton, 1977.

Strauss, A.: *Negotiations.* San Francisco, Jossey-Bass, 1978.

Chapter 2

THE SOCIAL CONSTRUCTION OF AGING

O UR everyday lives involve us in continual daily contacts with
persons whose ages differ considerably from our own as well
as those whose ages approximate ours. In our families, for example,
we encounter parents who are much older than we and perhaps
brothers and/or sisters who may be older or younger. At school, we
meet teachers and classmates whose ages correspond to ours in varying degrees. These dealings with older and younger persons serve as
constant reminders of our own age situation. When young, we can't
wait to get older so as to enjoy certain freedoms and privileges.
Often when older, we wish we were younger so that we could slough
off nagging social responsibilities and burdensome financial obligations. Whatever our specific life situation may be, we become aware
of our own age by seeing ourselves vis-a-vis others in different age
categories.

Our age consciousness is regularly reinforced and sustained by
the bureaucratic nature of the modern world. In advanced industrial
societies age is an ubiquitous and all pervasive concern. There is
hardly a form that one fills out — be it a job application, a credit inquiry, insurance form or lease, which does not ask for the age of the
applicant. Today's most basic identity card, the driver's license, is
often used as "proof" *par excellence* of one's real age. It is almost as if
society were saying: "If you don't have a driver's license, then you
don't have an age!"

Legal statutes make continual reference to behaviors permitted
adults but denied children. Certain legal violations, such as murder,
carry more serious penalties when committed by adults in contrast to
"youthful offenders." In short, persons in the modern world are daily
confronted with representatives of official agencies and institutions
who want to know their age in order to respond in "appropriate"
ways.

Persons in our society define themselves in terms of their
membership in particular age categories. Our self-concepts are intimately bound up with how old or young we view ourselves. Not all
age categories, however, have equal saliency for the individual. A

study by Manford Kuhn (1960) revealed that in response to the question "Who are you?" only slightly more than 25 percent of nine-year-olds identified themselves by age. The incidence of identification by age among his respondents increased regularly and steadily with 75 percent of the thirteen-year-olds mentioning their age in response to this question. These statistics certainly indicate that the age of thirteen, marking the beginning of the teenage years, is of great significance in the consciousness of American youngsters.

In our discussion so far we have used terms such as child, teenager, and adult. These terms pose no problem for contemporary readers since they are so much a part of our everyday reality. We see a world composed of babies with their parents, children playing in the park, teenagers at a school dance, and young adults in a "single's bar." The use of these terms to describe individuals of varying ages appears to us a natural and taken-for-granted reality. For that reason, to question their universal existence seems almost ludicrous. Surely there have always been, and indeed always will be, children and teenagers. But, is that really the case? As social psychologists studying the aging process, we do regard such age categories as problematic. That is to say, we must pose the seemingly absurd questions, "Where do children and teenagers come from? Have such age categories always existed throughout history? How do the definitions of what constitutes appropriate behavior for an age category vary from culture to culture?" These questions derive from the position that age categories are socially constructed phenomena. The behaviors underlying such categories ultimately derive their meanings from the social contexts in which they occur. Communications occurring among members of an age category and between members of different categories are symbolic in nature and reflect the larger society's definitions of reality. In sum, as we stressed in Chapter 1, one of the basic themes of this book is that persons are as old as *others* make them feel.

In this chapter we will focus on four contemporary age categories: childhood, adolescence, middle age, and old age. Our aim is to examine a part of our everyday reality. In doing so, we will be concerned with how certain changes in the organization of society have created the context in which persons' sense of aging—their experience of the passage of time—has undergone a change as well.

CHILDHOOD AS A SOCIAL INVENTION

In reflecting on our pasts, we recall prior experiences that routinely get labelled as belonging to certain periods in our life—childhood and adolescence, for example. Some of you may now be parents yourselves and involved in the continual daily care of children. Persons under the age of twelve have, of course, always existed. However, membership in that age category has not always carried the same meaning. The question of whether children have always existed is not, in fact, such a bizarre one. In what follows we will be concerned with how persons in that age category were viewed by others. What behaviors were expected of them? Even more important, were such expectations comparable to those held toward children today?

It comes as quite a jolt to our consciousness to realize that childhood as a distinct age grouping has a fairly recent history. Children did not exist during the Middle Ages (Aries, 1962).[1] During that historical epoch the life of the individual proceeded in terms of a passage from *infancy* to *little adulthood* and then to *adulthood*. There were no periods corresponding to our contemporary notions of childhood and adolescence. Those we label children today were then considered adults on a smaller scale. Aries ingeniously uses art history as the vehicle for illustrating this thesis.

In paintings done prior to the twelfth century there was no attempt to portray children. Their absence from paintings reflected the fact that, at the time, society had no place for childhood. Indeed, when children were presented in paintings, they were given the shape and form of adults, with highly developed muscles. While not focusing exclusively on the child, paintings that depicted children among the characters portrayed did begin to appear between the fifteenth and sixteenth centuries. This development suggests that "children mingled with adults in everyday life, and any gathering for the purpose of work, relaxation, or sport brought together both children and adults.... Painters were particularly fond of depicting childhood for its graceful or picturesque qualities...and they delighted in stressing the presence of a child in a group or crowd" (Aries, 1962:37).

---

[1]Aries' work, like all provocative and "mind-altering" achievements has stimulated a great deal of critical controversy among social scientists. The interested reader might consult Hunt (1970), Demos (1970), Stannard (1977), and van de Walle (1971).

With the emergence of the portrait of the *dead* child in the sixteenth century, we witness a "very important moment in the history of feeling." In this period the growing influence of Christianity created a new sensibility, namely "that the child's soul too was immortal." This sensibility is particularly interesting in view of the fact that infant mortality rates continued to remain quite high during this period. Previously, the likelihood of numerous offspring dying in birth had inhibited parents from investing a great deal of emotion in newborns for fear of their sudden deaths. Families during this period had many children in order to increase the survival odds of at least some making it past the early years.

Seventeenth century portraits for the first time depict children *apart* from their parents. The contemporary custom of having childhood portraits done has its origins in seventeenth century parents' wish to preserve the memory of what their offspring were like as children. The even more widespread practice of parents taking their children to discount stores, such as K-Mart and Zayre's, to be photographed is part of the same transformation in sentiment begun in the seventeenth century.

The nature of daily contact between adults and children was a crucial factor in the absence of a distinct age category such as childhood prior to the seventeenth century. There was no such thing as childhood because adults and what were then viewed as "little adults" participated in virtually all the same activities. They worked and played together. They were bound up in continual physical contact with each other. In our world of Little Leagues, Girl Scouts, Pop Warner football, and so on, it is extremely difficult for us to imagine a situation in which adults and children played exactly the same games with the same degree of involvement, enthusiasm, and, most importantly, seriousness. And yet, that is what life was like in earlier periods of Western history.

Earlier paintings portrayed children playing games of chance for money and soldiers alongside young boys in "taverns of ill fame." Adults played games such as leapfrog that nowadays are limited strictly to children. Interestingly, Aries quotes a twentieth century historian, Van Marle, who said of this period, "As for the games played by grown-ups, one cannot honestly say that they were any less childish than those played by children" (1962:72). To which Aries replies, "Of course not: they were the same!" (1962:72). And that is the point. One could just as well say that the children of the time played *adultishly* as that the adults played *childishly*. The games were the *same* for both because children, as viewed today, simply did not exist.

After the seventeenth century the increasing physical segregation of children into schools and the corresponding separation of the worlds of *work* and play created a situation in which work became the province of adults and play the domain of children. The emergence of childhood, then, as a distinct age category was associated with the increasing age segregation of social activities. In earlier periods, persons lived most of their lives outdoors in the community, continually intermingling with persons of different ages and statuses. With the rise to prominence of the middle classes (or the "triumph of the middle classes," as Moraze [1968] has noted) and the increasing emphasis accorded the capitalistic world of work, the nature of community life was fundamentally transformed. The middle class, as several observers (Sennett, 1970; Shorter, 1977; and Lofland, 1973) have noted, began to retreat into self-enclosed, spatially isolated enclaves in an effort to ward off the "polluting" nature of contacts with the "dangerous masses." The passage of such legal devices as zoning ordinances was an important part of the newly emerging middle-class concern with respectability and status.

The emergence of childhood was intimately associated with the development of the modern family as a particular type of social and emotional arrangement. The middle class was instrumental in cultivating a new sensibility requiring that those in their early years be protected from contact with various kinds of "dangerous" persons. Children were thrown together into schools that processed them bureaucratically into distinctly marked age groupings.

The successful "middle classification," if you will, of Western society ushered in a new set of moods and values about relations between parents and young children. It is difficult for contemporary readers to appreciate the recency and rather short history of this new sensibility since we are born into a world where those attitudes are now completely taken for granted. It goes without question, we would all readily agree, that parents should not physically abuse their children, nor should parents treat their offspring in cold, emotionally distant ways. Children, we believe, are to be protected from the ugly and often brutal realities of what life is "really like." It has not always been this way.

As Lloyd DeMause (1975:85) has argued, "the history of child-hood is a nightmare from which we have only recently begun to awake." While the middle-class response toward children gained impetus after the seventeenth century, its widespread dissemination throughout Western society did not occur until considerably later. Until recently children were routinely beaten. "The beatings described in most historical sources began at an early age, continued regularly throughout childhood, and were severe enough to cause bruising and bloodying" (1975:85). Two dramatic examples noted by DeMause will suffice to illustrate our point:

> As late as the 19th century in Eastern Europe, baptism was not a matter of simple sprinkling, but an ice-water ordeal that often lasted for hours and sometimes caused the death of the infant. The regular practice of the plunge bath involved nearly drowning the infant over and over again in ice-cold water "with its mouth open and gasping for breath" (1975:86).
>
> Another method that parents used to terrorize their children employed corpses. A common moral lesson involved taking children to visit the bigget, where they were forced to inspect rotting corpses hanging there as an example of what happens to bad children when they grow up. Whole classes were taken out of school to witness hangings, and parents would often whip their children afterwards to make them remember what they had seen (1975:86).

A far cry indeed from modern parental punishments such as suspending the child's TV privileges or allowance or "grounding" the child in the house for several days!

The Modern Family and the New Sensibility

As we have noted, the emergence of childhood as a specific age category, with new adult conceptions and expectations of children, is a concomitant of the emergence of the modern family. Here we see how changes in the structure of society, occasioned by the growing importance attached to the capitalistic world of work, set the stage for a new kind of consciousness concerning the subjective experience of aging.

The term *modern family* stands in marked contrast to the notion of *traditional family* (Shorter, 1977). They are distinguished in terms of the relationship between persons and the community. Critical here is the nature of the social bond.[2] Individuals in a traditionally oriented society gear their actions to the expectations of the community. Personal ambitions and individual desires are subordinated to the importance of community demands. As a result, persons in traditional families are—

> ...ready to postpone marriage until late in life, or indeed forego it entirely, so that the farm may prosper under the eldest; they're willing to overcome whatever strivings towards privacy slumber in their breasts...they resolve to fight off weariness in the evenings, to put the right lace on their bonnets for their neighbor's daughter's wedding. And they are willing to renounce the whole range of psychosexual satisfactions our social-work manuals guarantee us in order to keep the family's "honor" intact (Shorter, 1977:18).

Persons in the modern world, by contrast, are much more oriented toward "searching for the real self," toward the discovery of who one "really" is. Individual self-realization is a prominent concern in the modern world, and the community exerts a much weaker "pull" on individual allegiances and commitments. The family in the modern world, compared to its predecessor, the traditional family, exists like an island oasis within a communal desert. In earlier periods, community life flowed right into the household, and the boundary between household and community was quite porous, often making it difficult to determine where one began and the other ended. Persons in the traditional context spent much of their lives outdoors, outside the house. The notion of the home as a sanctuary, as a place to retreat from the pressures of society, was completely foreign to the traditional mentality.

According to Shorter, the modern family is characterized by the emergence of new sentiments in three different areas of social life: male–female courtship patterns, mother–child relations, and the connection between the family and the surrounding community. The most significant transformation in courtship concerned the emergence of "the couple" as a social unit emotionally divorced from the demands of family and community bonds. The ethos of "romantic love" propelled the two lovers to "follow their own stars" in the name of "love." Personal happiness and self-fulfillment now became

---

[2] A concern with the nature of the social bond has long been a central focus in sociological thought. Classical writers such as Sir Henry Sumner Maine, Ferdinand Tönnies, and Emile Durkheim devoted considerable attention to this issue. For analyses of their work *see* Nisbet (1966).

the dominant considerations in male–female relations. The traditional emphases on marriage for material considerations and family obligations was relegated to a secondary place.

Relations between mothers and children underwent a change in the transition to the modern family as a concern for the infant now became the main focus of the family whereas previously it had only been one among many concerns in the family's "desperate struggle for existence." With the "cult of domesticity," symbolized by the emergence of the couple and the "social invention" of the child, the family was increasingly cut off from an active communal involvement. Ties to the outside world were weakened and emotional ties between members of the family were correspondingly strengthened. The mother retreated to the privacy of the home to raise and care for her infant. ". . . (T)he modern nuclear family was born in the shelter of domesticity" (Shorter, 1977:5).

Our review of the historical literature causes us to question the timelessness and universality of contemporary family life. By examining the concept of childhood from an historically informed vantage point, we see our familiar, taken for granted, everyday social arrangements in a new and fresh way.

Cross-cultural studies conducted by social scientists in a wide variety of settings also offer a refreshing antidote to our assumptions about the behaviors thought to be natural and inevitable in childhood (*see* especially Mead and Wolfenstein, 1954; Whiting, 1963). Americans generally think of children as frail little creatures who must constantly be protected from dangerous situations and objects until they are "mature enough" to handle them. Similarly, we tend to think of freedom as something conferred on children by adults (witness the contemporary concern with "overpermissiveness"), rather than being intrinsic to the child's basic nature. Children do not take on important responsibilities and tasks until late in their development.

Various American Indian tribes, as the anthropologist Dorothy Lee (1959, 1976) has observed, have a conception of childhood that departs considerably from our own in their views of children's "innate" capabilities and basic "nature." For example, Navaho Indian children are allowed full participation in tribal affairs. Adults will not speak either for other adults *or* children.

. . . a father, asked to sell his child's bow and arrow, will refer the request to a five-year-old boy, and abide by the child's decision not to sell, even though he knows the child is badly in need of clothing that can be bought with the price of the toy. A woman, asked whether a certain baby could talk, said "Yes"; and when the ethnographer was puzzled by the "meaningless" sounds the baby was making, she explained that the baby could talk, but she could not understand what the baby said. All that she had the right to do was to speak for herself, to say that she could not understand. She would not presume to speak for the child and to say—as I think we would have said—that the child was making meaningless sounds (Lee, 1959:12).

When Navaho children start walking, adults do not run to put out the nearby fire nor do they anxiously remove any sharp and pointed objects from the child's path. They expect children to negotiate the situation on their own and, more importantly, to learn from their mistakes. Parents regard their children with a sense of trust and freedom that seems almost "crazy" to an outside observer. Yet, from the Navaho perspective this is the only way to ensure that the children will grow up to be persons who both trust themselves and others, who value their own autonomy as well as others'.

Another interesting comparison with American childhood may be seen in the lives of children raised in the traditional Jewish *shtetls*—or small settlements—of Eastern Europe. Such small towns existed until the 1930s and 1940s when the inhabitants fell victim to the horrors of the Nazi holocaust and an entire way of life was thus brutally eliminated. As in the case of American school children, children in the shtetl were expected to do well in school, although the schooling was largely limited to males. Unlike the American situation, however, where success in school is prized because of its linkage to later material and occupational success, the shtetl schoolboy was continually urged to learn for the sake of knowledge itself, to become a man of learning, a scholar. The intellectuality of shtetl life stands in marked contrast to the American historical tradition of antiintellectualism so convincingly described by the historian Richard Hofstadter (1966).

For the shtetl Jews an *amorets* (an ignoramus) was, as Mark Zborowski (1955:119) notes, "the most despised member of the community." The Jews in these settlements made an important linkage between learning and moral virtue. An amorets was not only ignorant but, more important, one whose ignorance prevented him from leading an ethical life and treating his wife and children in the proper way.

This concern with intellect manifested itself from the earliest months of the male child's life. "The whole family—mother, aunts, sisters, everyone who is in close contact with the baby—will watch for anything in his behavior that could be interpreted as a sign of intellectual precocity. A smile, an unexpected gesture, an imitation of an adult's expression, will be considered an indication of exceptional intelligence—and parents and neighbors will exclaim about the little prodigy" (1955:123).

Compared to our kindergartens and day school nursery situations, the expectations of shtetl elders for boys' academic performance seem incredibly demanding and even utterly unrealistic. Starting their formal education between the ages of three and five, young boys encounter "a curriculum that had a beginning but no end. Jewish learning never finishes because, as the proverb says, "The Torah has no bottom" (1955:124). There were no half-day sessions for these youngsters. Rather, they studied in a small room, with other children of other ages thrown together, from 8 AM until 6 PM, five days a week! No textbooks with pictures, no storytelling, no educational games were used. It was a very rigorous enterprise designed to produce scholars who would pursue learning as a lifelong activity. After an early period of training, based largely on memory and mechanical repetition, the students progressed to the study of the Talmud (a Jewish collection of historical commentaries). Now a real joy in learning and an exuberance about the play of the mind could operate in tandem with disciplined and serious intellectual work. Zborowski describes how the study of the Talmud could serve as a source of great emotional satisfaction and pleasure for the scholar-to-be:

> Penetration, scholarship, imagination, memory, logic, wit, subtlety—all are called into play for solving a Talmudic question. The ideal solution is a new, original synthesis, one that has never before been offered. This mental activity combines the pleasures and satisfaction of high scholarship and high sport. It is a delight both to the performer and his audience. Both enjoy the vigor of the exercise and adroitness of the accomplishment. And, at the same time, both relish demonstrating their ability to perform on such a lofty and esoteric level (1955:128).

Material wealth was important in the shtetl largely because it permitted the wealthy businessman to support the struggling scholar. Wealth, then, was valued in so far as it contributed to and made possible the production of shtetl scholars. In the shtetl community the wealthy merchant ranked considerably below the man of learning.

While young boys had the world of intellect in which to expand themselves, young girls in the shtetl faced a much more restrictive existence. As Zborowski and Herzog (1952:129) state in another study, "A woman's formal status is indirect. It relates not to herself as an individual, but to her position as wife and mother." Girls received much less formal schooling than boys and were not expected or encouraged to become scholars. Young shtetl girls were in a situation analogous to that of young girls in Western society during the last century.

We have chosen only two descriptions of childhood from among the many available in social science literature. Both should have sensitized you to the varied meanings of childhood by dramatically illustrating that many young persons' life experiences in other cultures differ greatly from our own.

What's a Mother to Do? Enter the Child Experts

Contemporary American childhood provides a striking contrast to the previous examples in view of the anxieties that American parents experience in their seemingly ceaseless quest to raise their children "properly." Indeed, a whole cadre of child "experts" has arisen to provide advice and guidance to perplexed and distraught parents on child-rearing matters. Barely a day goes by without some child-rearing authority appearing on a TV talk show dispensing the latest advice on how to raise healthy, productive, happy, self-actualizing, authentic, autonomous, normal children. A visit to any bookstore and a casual perusal of its holdings will quickly reveal the pervasiveness of the *how to* approach to both life and child rearing. Such advice cries out from the racks of supermarket newsstands via publications such as *The National Enquirer* and *The Star*, with nationwide circulations in the millions. In short, American parents are deeply concerned about their offspring and, as a response, seek the guidance of properly credentialed professional experts.

Our attentiveness to the outpourings of legions of child experts reflects a conception of children that is fundamentally different from that held by earlier generations of Americans, such as the colonial

Puritans, for example. The Puritans viewed the child as ". . . riddled with sin and corruption, a depraved being polluted with the residue of Adam's sin. If there was any chance of an individual child's salvation, it was not a very good chance—and in any case, ultimate knowledge of who was to be chosen for salvation and who was not was not a matter for earthly minds" (Stannard, 1977:49).

The child was seen as a creature dominated by powerful and lascivious impulses that could only be restrained, never totally purged, by incessant parental- and community-imposed punishments. The child was a depraved being and had to be taught quite early in life to recognize that inescapable fact. Read part of a sermon addressed to young children in 1711 by Increase Mather, an influential Puritan minister:

> What a dismal thing it will be when a Child shall see his Father at the right hand of Christ in the day of Judgment, but Himself at His Left hand: And when his Father shall joyn with Christ in passing a Sentence of Eternal Death upon him, saying Amen O Lord, thou art Righteous in thus *Judging*: And when after the Judgment, children shall see their Father going with Christ to Heaven, but themselves going away into Everlasting Punishment! (quoted in Stannard, 1977:62-63; italics in original).

No notion here of Mom and Dad being pals with their kids, or of the need for parental understanding and tolerance. For the Puritan, reality was a tapestry comprised of strands of sin and salvation.

Imagine how a Puritan parent would respond to a contemporary publication such as *Parental Effectiveness Training: The Tested New Way to Raise Responsible Children* by Doctor Thomas Gordon (1975), a clinical psychologist. A selection of titles from this book will make our point in a succinct way: Chapter 3: "How to Listen So Kids Will Talk to You: The Language of Acceptance"; Chapter 5: "How To Listen to Kids Too Young to Talk Much"; Chapter 8: "Changing Unacceptable Behavior by Changing the Environment"; and Chapter 10: "Parental Power: Necessary and Justified?" One of the main thrusts of Gordon's argument is that parents must protect their children from adults exercising arbitrary power and authority. Parents must, he states, "stand up and fight against those who advocate 'being tough with kids,' who sanction the use of power in dealing with kids under the banner of 'law and order,' who justify authoritarian methods on the grounds that *one cannot trust children to be responsible or self-disciplined*" (1975:301; italics added). For the Puritans, as we have just seen, Doctor Gordon's last sentence reflected their view. Under no circumstances could children be trusted to be responsible or self-disciplined.

It is not our aim in this discussion to comment on whether or not child-rearing experts' advice is beneficial or detrimental to the raising of children. That is a question best left to parents themselves. Rather, our intent is to see the emergence of these specialists from a sociological perspective. The proliferation of such experts indicates changes in our basic conceptions of children and our expectations of their capabilities.[3] Having briefly discussed some of the critical factors involved in the social construction of childhood, we now want to examine how the age category called adolescence became embedded in our consciousness as a distinct phase of our personal biographies.

TEEN WORLD

Many of you reading this book can probably recall a period in your life that has come to be called *adolescence*. We are all familiar with television commercials featuring a teenager anxiously coping with the latest acne attack while desperately preoccupied with landing a date for the weekend dance. Newspapers carry advice columns, such as "Ask Beth," specifically geared to the problems and needs of present-day adolescents. The emergence of child experts, as previously mentioned, has ushered in a host of experts for the adolescent set as well.

Having experienced the "agonies" and "ecstasies" of adolescence, we are quite prone to assume that this phase of life, like childhood, has a certain timelessness and universality to it, making it an inevitable passage in the lives of all human beings. As previously, we want to examine this age category from a sociologically and historically informed perspective. Such an approach, we believe, allows us to delineate that which may be unique in what we assume to be universal. Also, an historical approach lets us appreciate how our own lives may parallel or diverge from those of persons living in

---

[3]A good deal of the anthropological literature on child rearing reflects a strong commitment to a Freudian, psychoanalytic scheme of analysis. An unfortunate consequence of such a reliance, as the Stones (1976) note: ". . .(is that) we usually have less difficulty finding out how young people in remote places "play with themselves" than we do finding out how they play with others! (1976:46, Footnote 2).

different eras. A socio-historical perspective offers a much needed corrective lens to a present-oriented myopia.

In discussing childhood we showed that one of the major factors influencing its emergence was the increasing separation of work into an adult-defined arena and play into one limited to children. This led to the gradual abandonment of the continual intermixing of both adults and children in the same activities. Preindustrial society recognized no intermediate period between childhood and adulthood corresponding to our modern notions of adolescence and the teen years. Rather, there was a stage called *youth* (now called young adulthood) characterized by varying degrees of personal dependency on the family. Youth consisted of a very long transitional period between childhood and adulthood that had its beginning at about the age seven or eight when "the very young child first became somewhat independent of its family" (Gillis, 1974:2). The period of youth was terminated at the time of marriage, usually in the mid- or late twenties when the person achieved complete independence from the family.

Figures presented below nicely contrast the nature of age categories in three different historical periods: preindustrial Europe, European industrial society, and modern postindustrial society.

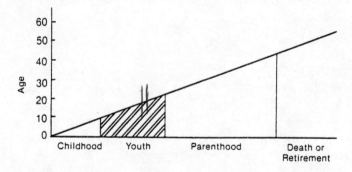

Figure 2-1. Phases of Life in Preindustrial Society. From John Gillis, *Youth and History*, 1974. Courtesy of Academic Press.

In preindustrial society *childhood* was, as Aries noted, viewed as *little adulthood,* and it was a period that normally lasted until the age of seven or eight. Then the person entered the stage of "youth," which encompassed both our contemporary notions of adolescence and young adulthood. During this stage persons lived in a situation of semidependency on the family since they were working as servants in someone else's household, as apprentices living with the master, or as students away from their families. The stage of youth lasted roughly until the mid-twenties when persons usually got married and assumed the role of parents. The period of parent-hood lasted until the late forties or early fifties. The point of our exposition is that no economically carefree period similar to modern adolescence existed during the preindustrial era.

Around 1900, because of the influence of middle-class ideology and increased life expectancy rates, childhood was extended until the age of eleven or twelve. In other words, the earlier preindustrial age category of youth was now broken down into two finer distinc-tions—*adolescence* and *young adulthood*. Adolescence lasted from roughly thirteen to nineteen. Young adulthood now occurred in the period from the early to late twenties, at which point persons were likely to become parents. These changes are reflected in Figure 2-2 below.

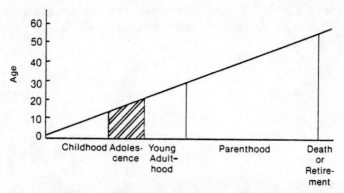

Figure 2-2. Life Cycle of the Middle Class, 1900. From John Gillis, *Youth and History*, 1974. Courtesy of Academic Press.

Now, if we examine age categories in contemporary society we see that the prior category of young adulthood has been replaced by an age category that might be termed *postmodern youth*, lasting from the early twenties until perhaps the early thirties. Kenneth Ken-niston (1968) has argued that the emergence of such an age category is mainly a phenomenon of upper middle-class youths who undergo increasingly extended forms of eduction via graduate and professional schools. As a result, their full-time status as students often lasts until their late twenties, or even early thirties, with the concomitant effect of prolonging the period in which they are not economically self-sufficient, and thus still reliant on financial support from their parents. In Chapter 4 we will consider the effects of this extended period of schooling on our age conceptions.

Figure 2-3 also indicates that life expectancy rates have climbed to the seventies and frequently the eighties. Most of us can now expect to live through a period of retirement after having completed the parenthood phase of our lives. As we shall see, these demographic changes have far-reaching implications for the emergence of the "middle-age" life category. At this point, however, let us focus on the specific case of adolescence in America.

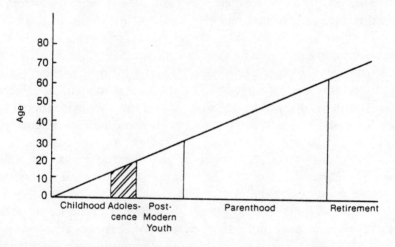

Figure 2-3. Phases of Life in Postindustrial Society. From John Gillis, *Youth and History*, 1974. Courtesy of Academic Press.

Where Do Teens Come From

The construction of adolescence as a specific age category in the United States was intimately linked with three late nineteenth to early twentieth century social movements: compulsory public education, child labor legislation, and specific legal procedures for the treatment of juveniles (Bakan, 1971). Just as the cult of domesticity became a focal concern of the modern family to protect the child from various "social dangers," social movements arose to protect children for increasingly longer periods of their lives. By establishing legislation in the areas of schooling, work, and criminal violations, social reformers succeeded in delineating precise chronological ages that "essentially removed the vagueness of all previous ideas of the time at which adolescence terminates. Thus adolescence became the period of time between pubescence, a concrete biological occurrence, and the *ages specified by law* for compulsory education, employment, and criminal procedure" (Bakan, 1971:981; italics added).

The emergence of these social movements was associated with the increasing urbanization and industrialization of the United States in the latter nineteenth century. The cities became viewed as places in which the young "fell prey" to all the debilitating vices of sexual immorality, crime, and alcohol. In short, urban life was increasingly seen as a "pathological" corruptor of innocent, defenseless youths urgently in need of the state's protection.

During the colonial period of American history, parents were largely responsible for their child's education, although, as Demos (1970) has described, there was some community involvement in the matter. In the late nineteenth century, however, public compulsory education for persons between six and sixteen became law in America. These laws were stimulated by reformers' desire to "bundle every child warmly in the garment of education, to make school a veritable asylum for the preservation and culture of childhood" (Kett, 1977:123). Where previously the rhythms of the school year were dictated by the nature of the agricultural seasons, with youths' school attendance linked to needs on the farm, now nonattendance became defined as a deviant act punishable by law. As a result, various states began instituting reform schools for the incarceration of truant youths (Platt, 1969).

The drive to *standardize* age categories in the various school grades significantly influenced the passage of compulsory education laws. In the school district of Acton, Massachusetts, in 1828, for example, about one-fourth of the boys were older than eighteen and one-fourth were nine or younger. For the girls the range was not as wide, but there were still seventeen- and eighteen-year-olds attending the same school as four- and five-year olds. At schools such as Exeter in 1812, the student ages ranged from ten to what seems a remarkable twenty-eight. By contrast, with the establishment of intermediate schools in the 1860s, the ages of students became more and more concentrated in the twelve to fourteen category, with only a few younger than ten or older than seventeen. The prolongation of education for youths in the twentieth century is dramatically illustrated by the fact that the proportion of seventeen-year-olds graduating from high school was 6.4 percent in 1900 and 62.3 percent in 1956 (Kett, 1977:245).

Child labor laws also had the consequence of removing teenagers from the work world, thus prolonging the period of their dependency on parents. In 1832, 40 percent of the factory workers in New England were children (Katz, 1968). Growing problems about a labor surplus in the post-Civil War period, however, led labor unions, such as the Knights of Labor, to campaign for child labor laws. The increasing technical sophistication of the economy put employers in a quandary. They wanted to avail themselves of the cheap labor pool provided by young persons and new immigrants, yet they also recognized the need for a more skilled and, most important, disciplined work force. Here we see an important interplay between the passage of child labor laws and compulsory schooling legislation. The historian Michael Katz (1968) has convincingly argued that numerous employers favored both kinds of legislation because it would prepare workers to live in the capitalistic, "industrial culture" that was taking shape in America. The lengthier process of schooling would produce disciplined and "manageable" workers who would unquestioningly follow a supervisor's orders. The relationship between the worlds of work and education during this period is nicely captured by Joel Spring (1976:88):

> In the early part of the twentieth century one of the most widely used textbooks in elementary teacher training stressed that the habits gained through marching to and from the playground and class, through drill and classroom routine, were all preparation for the world of industrial work. What should be recognized about these socialization arguments is that they were primarily directed toward *increasing industrial efficiency by increasing managerial control* (italics added).

The third thread in this tapestry of child concern involves the passage of legislation aimed at "juvenile delinquents." Gerald Platt's book *The Child Savers* (1969) makes the important argument that the "invention of adolescence" went hand in hand with the "invention of delinquency." With the passage of the first Juvenile Court Act by the Illinois legislature in 1899, a process was set in motion that aimed at grouping offenders by age categories and thereby separated youthful from older offenders. Consider the kinds of behaviors that were defined as constituting juvenile delinquency: "immoral conduct around schools, association with vicious or immoral persons, patronizing public poolrooms, wandering about railroad yards, truancy, incorrigibility, absenting self from home without consent, smoking cigarettes in public places, begging or receiving alms..." (Bakan, 1971:987).

These three social movements in the areas of schooling, work, and the law had important and far-reaching consequences on two related levels: social–structural and social–psychological. They succeeded in promoting the further bureaucratization of American society and the increased processing of youths in terms of membership in particular age categories that distinguished them from both children and adults. In terms of social–psychological issues, these movements had the profound consequence of shaping persons' consciousness of this newly emerging category called adolescence.

We should also acknowledge the significant influence of demographic factors on the construction of adolescence. From 1750 to 1900 the population of European society rose from 125 million to almost 300 million. By the 1840s the ratio of the age group fifteen to twenty-five to the age group thirty and older reached more than 79 percent (Gillis, 1974:39). The burgeoning of a youthful population throughout the nineteenth century in both Europe and the United States was also associated with medical and sanitary improvements leading to falling infant mortality rates. In preindustrial Europe it was rare for more than one-half of the children to reach the age of twenty-one. By 1871, however, the number of children of the English middle and upper classes surviving to the age of fifteen had risen to 83 percent (Musgrove, 1965:61). In the United States the years 1840–1900 witnessed almost a doubling of the number of people between forty-five and sixty-four. Thus, "more men and women survived to see their children become teenagers" (Kett, 1977: 216).

The sheer existence of growing numbers of persons between the ages of thirteen and nineteen has greatly shaped our consciousness of adolescence. While American teens, however, are busy saving for cars and getting ready for the upcoming high school dance, adolescents in other cultures are undergoing very different kinds of experience, experiences designed to groom them for tasks quite unlike our own. Among the Gusii tribe in Kenya, for example, young girls are exposed to a genital operation that symbolically represents their transition from childhood into a stage between childhood and adulthood. The completion of their passage into full adulthood will later be symbolized by their marriage, which usually occurs around the age of fifteen. By participating in such a ceremony the young girl receives the tribe's public acknowledgement that she has left the status of "little girl" and has entered the new status of "a circumcised thing," or an unmarried girl. The Le Vines (1963) argue that by participating in the circumcision ceremony the young girl is able to (1) leave behind the tasks and activities of childhood; (2) become eligible for the attentions of the older, circumcised boys; and (3) maintain a common bond with her similarly aged friends who have also undergone the circumcision ceremony. Those girls who do not participate in the ceremony in a particular year find that the ones who do will sever all their social ties with them.

Among the Gusii, the situation of an adolescent girl is a troublesome one. She is no longer a child, yet, still unmarried and living with her parents, neither is she fully an adult. The parents are greatly concerned that she will trade her sexual favors for the gifts of young men and maybe even elope. Should this happen they would be deprived of the traditional "bridewealth cattle," so important to the maintenance of their status within the tribal community. To be an adolescent girl, then, among the Gusii of Kenya would seem an anxiety-laden situation for both parents and offspring, although these anxieties differ considerably from those experienced by present day Americans.

Plainly adolescence among the Gusii thrusts one into a world permeated by events and rituals very different from those we encounter in our life courses. As earlier, we cite this case as only one among many that could be offered to illustrate how the meanings of being an adolescent are culturally produced. We now want to focus on a stage of life, middle age, that has only recently begun to command our attention.

MIDDLE AGE

Popular culture portrayals of middle age tend to emphasize the "crisis" or "trauma" aspects of this life period. It is a stage of life that is generally viewed as the period of forty to sixty years old (Neugarten, 1968).[4] One frequently hears stories about colleagues in their late thirties and forties who have suddenly dropped dead from heart attacks, of marriages gone awry, and careers that haven't turned out to be what they were once "cracked up to be." Daily newspapers are filled with similar items. Popular movies such as "An Unmarried Woman" and "Alice Doesn't Live Here Anymore" (now made into a weekly television series) portray the life traumas and also the possible rebirths of persons in the middle years. A bestselling country-Western song by John Connally tells the story of a man who starts drinking heavily when his wife and child leave him. It's called "On the Backside of Thirty." Books dealing with middle-life crises such as Gail Sheehy's (1977) *Passages: Predictable Crises of Adult Life*, now appear on the best-seller lists for months at a time. It's not all doom and gloom, however. The problems of middle age can be transformed into a blessing as Eda LeShan argues in *The Wonderful Crisis of Middle Age*—a book whose cover proclaims "Over 40? The best is yet to come." Clearly, something is in the air! By citing such popular mass media images of middle age we are not giving our assent to their portrayals of this age category. Indeed, the social science literature on this subject raises serious questions about the extent to which the middle-aged do, in fact, experience this stage of life as a trauma. We will discuss this issue in more detail in later chapters. At this point, we simply want to mention the great interest that this stage of life holds for contemporary Americans.

Most people in the Western world live their lives in the context of the family. We are born into what sociologists call a "family of origin," and later we marry and form a "family of procreation." While increasing numbers of persons are choosing to remain single, the overwhelming majority of Americans continue to marry, have children and, should divorce occur, remarry. The family involves us in a number of timing or transition problems (Modell et al., 1976; Chudacoff and Hareven, 1979). Issues such as when to leave home,

---

[4]A glance at newspapers and forms of the mass media suggests that increasingly the period of the mid- to late thirties is also being viewed as part of the mid-life period.

when to marry, when to have children, and how many children to have, for example, involve family members in a myriad of decisions that may prove difficult to resolve. Such decisions are heavily influenced by persons' perceptions of their own aging. The subjective experience of time and the sense of aging, we mean to say, are bound up with the nature of family life cycles.

Social demographers and historians have begun to produce a fascinating body of data on the historical transformations of American family life. These works are of great interest for anyone concerned with aging as a socially defined process. Let us examine some of this historical data with the aim of illustrating the recent emergence of middle age as a distinct age category.

Data presented by Paul Glick (1977), a demographer associated with the Census Bureau, reveals a number of changes that have occurred in American family life cycles from the 1880s through the 1970s. His data reveal that women marrying in the 1970s are having their last child about three years earlier than those marrying in the 1900s (median age of 29.6 years compared to 32.9 years). Contemporary women are also having fewer children than their counterparts in the 1900s (Glick, 1977:8).[5] In the 1970s the death of her spouse occurred when the wife's median age was 65.2 years compared to 57.0 in the 1900s. So today, couples are living together longer. Last, and most important for our purposes, the period called the *empty nest*—the time couples spend alone after the last child has left home— had been extended from 1.6 years in the 1900s to 12.9 years in the 1970s, an increase of over eleven years!

This means that where previously the death of a spouse usually occurred less than two years after the last child married, now married couples can plan on staying together for about thirteen years after their last child has left home. Tamara Hareven (1978) also notes that in the nineteenth century the major transition facing a woman concerned the decision to marry. In the contemporary period, however, the major transition facing persons concerns a "transition *out* of parental roles." This is largely a result of the recent extension in the length of time remaining in persons' lives after having "launched" the children.

---

[5]While Glick's data only refer to women, he does note that the changes for men at first marriage are "more substantial than those of women." He does not go into any detail, however, on the nature of those changes (1977:7).

What we are witnessing are some major demographic transformations having a considerable impact on both family structure and persons' sense of their own aging. Prior to the twentieth century persons normally lived only until their forties or fifties, if that, and spent their entire married lives raising children. When the last child was ready to leave home and establish his or her household, the parents usually died. Today, parents have their last child by their late twenties and when the child is ready to marry or leave home, they are themselves in their late forties or early fifties, leaving a considerable portion of their lives to be spent only in each other's company. With retirement coming at sixty-five or so for most workers, those in their forties still have another twenty years or more on the job. Consequently, the meanings attached to work earlier in the life cycle, such as supporting the family, take on a different hue. This situation is conducive to a great deal of inner "mind work" concerning the ultimate value and significance of one's occupational activities. Today one's sense of being middle-aged is associated with a new and distinctly bounded period of life — a period in between the completion of child rearing and retirement from work. Earlier generations in the nineteenth century experienced no such clearly demarcated life period.

We do not mean to imply here that demographic changes exert a mechanical one-to-one relationship with persons' psychologies. We must constantly stress the point that such demographic changes are themselves the product of countless interpretations of reality and "definitions of the situation" made by persons in the course of their daily lives. We do, however, want to note that such demographic transitions certainly affect the *context* in which persons make their ongoing interpretations of reality. If today's experience of middle age is one of introspection and existential examination, this is so because persons are confronted with new problematic situations. Having raised children and generally reached a peak or plateau at work, individuals find themselves in a situation requiring more insistent attention to questions about the "meaning" of life. These important themes will reappear and be further discussed in Chapters 3 and 4.

The Post-World War II Era and the Sense of Aging

We have already analyzed the significance of certain large-scale demographic changes for one's sense of aging, and now we want to examine the way in which events of the recent historical epoch have shaped our lives and our consciousness. The social critic Irving Kristol has suggested that the twentieth century began in 1945! How could that be? We all know, of course, that it began in 1900. Before we dismiss this remark as the outpouring of a lunatic, we would do well to ponder its significance. Kristol is implying that the events following World War II ushered in a period of such massive change in American values and social arrangements that a major discontinuity with earlier life occurred. Being born into or growing up in the post-World War II world was, in effect, like being thrust into a new century.

After World War II, new values concerning the management of one's personal affairs began to take root (Sarason, 1977). Foremost among these was the beginning of an intense concern with self in American life—with issues related to the individual's private life. A concern with such matters as personal authenticity, autonomy, self-growth, and development began to manifest itself. The organizational and structural accompaniments of such concerns is found in the establishment of the National Institute of Mental Health in 1946 by the federal government[6]; the emergence of psychotherapy as a standard feature of first upper middle-class and later middle-class life; the incorporation of Freudian notions such as "the unconscious" and "hidden sexual impulses" into the vocabulary of everyday parlance; and the proliferation of a wide range of encounter group movements emphasizing the need for persons to "get in touch with themselves."

The intensification of a concern with the inner life and intrapsychic affairs was related to the kinds of personal and familial readjustment problems that World War II veterans and their families were experiencing upon their return to civilian society. Seymour Sarason (1977:45) suggests, "One might as well characterize those postwar years as the Age of Mental Health because it became a national concern. It was not only the veteran who needed help, but, it was argued, so did millions of other people."

Changes in the psychological "climate of opinion" were also

---

[6]The actual establishment of the National Institute of Mental Health occurred in 1949. In 1946, however, Congress passed the National Mental Health Act authorizing the development of the NIMH.

created by the growing influence of psychoanalysts within university departments of psychiatry and psychology. The armed services' need for clinical therapists during the war had led to the increasing prominence of psychoanalysts who to that point had played a distinct second fiddle to university-trained Ph.D. psychologists. With psychoanalysis entrenched as a dominant paradigm of social thought in university departments, students were increasingly exposed to a view of "human nature" that stressed the themes of personal liberation, authenticity, and self-exploration. Many persons came to believe that personal liberation would be achieved through a deeper and deeper probing of their own "dis-ease." The popularity of existentialist writers such as Jean Paul Sartre and Albert Camus in the years immediately following the war also reinforced a focus on the individual while largely ignoring the social and structural context in which personal development unfolds.

When these legions of post-World War II college students entered managerial and professional occupations in the 1950s and 1960s, they were confronted with a set of work arrangements that they experienced as growth-inhibiting and autonomy-denying. Having had great expectations about their ability to control their own destinies and to experience continued self-growth in the work place, they now found themselves buffeted by a proliferating series of bureaucratic procedures and government regulations that made them accountable to others in ways they had not anticipated. As Sarason describes it, these professionals experienced a profound sense of being trapped, an outlook previously thought possessed only by blue collar workers and lower level white collar employees.

The creation of new values centering on personal growth and the increasing bureaucratization of the workplace, in tandem with twentieth century demographic changes, heightened individuals' subjective concern with aging. Thus, the stage was created for the present day, widespread concern with the "crisis" of middle age. In other chapters of this book we will elaborate on the nature of the situations confronting the middle-aged in the modern world. Our goal here has been to sketch some of the prominent factors involved in the emergence of a middle-age consciousness.

OLD AGE

Some popular images of the elderly in the mass media present them as frail and affectionate, but powerless and unable to care for themselves. They are often portrayed in scenes of playful involvement with grandchildren or pursuing one or another hobby. On the other hand, the words *old age* conjure up for many an image of gray-haired persons in poor health who are without sexual desire. A study commissioned by the National Council of Aging (1975) yielded some very illuminating results concerning public perceptions of the aged. Interviews with a national sample of 4,000 persons indicated that most people over sixty-five were viewed as (1) not any good at getting things done; (2) not very bright and alert; and (3) not very open-minded or adaptable. Large percentages of the public thought that people over sixty-five spend a lot of time sleeping, just doing nothing, watching television, and sitting around and thinking. These results were in marked contrast to the self-perceptions and self-reports of people sixty-five and over who saw themselves as very bright and alert, very open-minded and adaptable, and very good at getting things done.

The fact that the public at large views the elderly in much more negative terms than do the elderly themselves is itself a product of some historical processes that have transformed the situation of the elderly in the Western world. In this last section of the chapter, we examine some factors involved in the social construction of the category of old age.

Previously we argued that the age categories, childhood, adolescence, and middle age, were not "out there" in the natural world, but had to be understood as humanly created phenomena. We questioned the universality of their occurrence in all societies throughout history. In contrast to these other categories, however, there does appear to be some consensus among social scientists that members of *all* societies make some kind of distinction between the old and other age groups. Here again, though, we claim that the meanings of being old will vary depending on the historical period and the cultural setting involved. Let us look at this issue in more detail.

The Historical Context

The current definition of old age in Western industrialized nations is closely related to certain developments in the laws concerning pensions and retirement. The English situation affords an interesting example (Roebuck, 1979). In England and the United States the most frequent boundary points for the definitions of old age have been the ages of sixty and sixty-five. Since these ages have been linked to specific governmental actions, they seem to "naturally" define old age. As we shall see, however, the use of sixty and sixty-five to define the elderly is a fairly recent phenomenon.

Prior to the rise of official retirement and pension ages the meaning of old age was subject to much discretion and individual judgment. The Elizabethan Poor Laws of 1601 "set no specific age at which a person was to be automatically considered aged" (Roebuck, 1979:47). The authorities considered persons as old only when they were both getting on in years and unable to support themselves. Given the looseness of this definition, a wide range of ages could come under the label of *aged and infirm*. Results of a survey for an 1832 English government study indicated that the definition of old age could vary all the way from the late forties to the eighties.

Discussion of the state old age pension system in England in the 1880s and 1890s raised the question of "official" definitions of old age to a level of national significance. Efforts to adhere to the previous notions of old age — inability to work combined with advancing years — proved most difficult. Crucial here was the fact that "The ability of an individual to support himself at an advanced age varied according to the individual and his occupation" (Roebuck, 1979: 420). Ages that had been established in other countries did little to promote a consensus. Old age pensions began at seventy in Germany, over sixty in Copenhagen, Denmark, and ranged from fifty-five to seventy in France.

An interested investigator could point to evidence indicating almost any age above forty as the proper one for defining old age. Increasingly, questions of government finance dictated the "proper" point at which old age and thus pensions were to begin. In 1900 an official English Treasury Committee report indicated that a pension age of seventy rather than sixty-five would result in a national savings of more than three million pounds per year. Ultimately the pressures engendered by the widespread unemployment of The Great Depression in the 1930s pushed the pension age limit for women to sixty while remaining at sixty-five for men. What we learn from this example is that English definitions of old age may have had little to do with the inherent condition of the elderly themselves.

Rather, age definitions are a product of competing ideologies, political bartering, and particular economic conditions.

In the case of the United States, the Social Security Act of 1935 ushered in a distinct legal status for the elderly. Here, as in the English example, the choice of age sixty-five was heavily influenced by political and economic considerations. In this regard, Wilbur Cohen, former secretary of the Department of Health, Education, and Welfare and a pivotal figure in the original Social Security legislation, has said, "It was understood that a reduction in the age below 65 would substantially increase costs and, therefore, might impair the possibility of. . . acceptance of the plan by Congress. A higher retirement age, of say 68 or 70, was *never considered* because of the belief that public and congressional opposition would develop against such a provision in view of the wide-spread unemployment that existed" (italics added; quoted in Cain, 1974:169-170).

Our current attitudes toward the aged in America result from a "revolution" in the social relations between age groups (Fischer, 1978). Toward the end of the eighteenth century a series of radical changes in the fabric of everyday life occurred. Both the American and French Revolutions were part of this great upheaval. The ultimate culmination of this revolution was that the stage of life called youth increasingly usurped the veneration and respect that had generally been accorded the elderly in American life during the prior two centuries.

In the New England town meeting houses material possessions came to predominate as a criterion for obtaining seats. Previously age determined where persons sat. Then in the mid-eighteenth century seats were sold at auctions and those who could pay the most got the best bench. Toward the end of the eigtheenth century compulsory retirement laws were passed by a number of state legislatures. The phenomenon of *age heaping*, or the process by which persons systematically distort their ages in reporting them to the census interviewers reflects changes over time in the meanings given to age. Available data indicate a clear change in the patterns by which persons reported their ages:

> In early America, people did not try to make themselves out to be younger than they were; they tended to *represent themselves as older* instead. That tendency was weakest in early life, but existed at all age levels. . .In the nineteenth and twentieth centuries, on the other hand, people tended to

represent themselves as younger than they actually were. The bias toward youth grew steadily stronger with each succeeding census, from the late eighteenth century to the late twentieth (italics added; Fischer, 1978:84).

Linguistic usage reflects another change in the status and definition of the elderly. Terms such as *gaffer* and *fogy*, for example, which previously had been terms of respect, had by the mid-nineteenth century taken on all the negative connotations involved in the modern usage of "old gaffer" and "old fogy."

This revolution in age relations is also a product of both demographic and ideological factors. In terms of demography, a major change occurred after 1800. The proportion of people older than sixty rose from less than 2 percent of the population to more than 10 percent in 1970. Thus a significant increase in the number of persons living to the age of sixty helped to produce the setting for a change in age relations.

In the ideological arena, the notions of *equality* and *liberty* gained increasing ascendancy during the eighteenth century, culminating in the American and French revolutions. Both of these revolutions had the important consequence of changing persons' unquestioned, taken-for-granted respect for the traditional age hierarchy of society, as well as other hierarchical arrangements, such as those based on birth and wealth.

In America, despite the general movement toward greater equality, old age came to be viewed as a pathetic and undesirable state. David Hackett Fischer (1978:114) writes that "at the same time that old age came to be more common, it also came to be regarded with increasing contempt. Where the Puritans had made a cult of age, their posterity made a cult of youth instead."

A recent study by the historian Richard Calhoun (1978) documents an important contemporary change in the social expectations concerning old age. Calhoun's work shows how the image of old age is increasingly taking on more positive characteristics since the 1965–1970 period in the United States. New symbols of old age such as *senior citizen*, and the *new leisure class* call attention to significant revisions in the earlier attitudes described by Fischer. Thus, Calhoun notes—

...a term like "senior citizen" could not exist until older people were recognized as a potentially productive and useful segment of society. Twenty years before, most of the incentives given for mounting an effort on behalf of the aged had been generally negative, such as avoiding widespread economic dependency and political deviancy among the aged. By 1965 – 1970, however, there were new incentives to action as reflected in the new vocabulary being applied to the nation's aged (1978:24).

CONCLUSION

In this chapter we have examined the historical origins of contemporary age categories. In discussing childhood we illustrated how the emergence of the middle-class family and the developing segregation of work and play were associated with the "invention of the child." Our current experience of adolescence developed out of an historical context characterized by the increasing length of youth's dependency on their parents and the proliferation of bureaucratically organized agencies, such as schools, which "processed" persons as "batches" of similarly aged entities. In examining middle age as an age category we pointed to important demographic changes associated with family child-rearing patterns as well as the lengthening of the "empty nest" period. Finally, we discussed how various legal and economic issues affected current definitions of old age.

Throughout our discussion we stressed the necessity of viewing age categories as human "constructions." Age categories result from changing human interpretations of the meanings attached to specific phases of the biological life cycle. While demographic changes may be critical in producing certain numbers of persons between various ages, the behaviors expected of those numbers are products of an ongoing interpretive process in which persons are constantly trying to make sense of their life situations. Such a process, we argue in this book, is indeed a life-long one.

Having established the theoretical and historical dimensions of a social psychological view of aging, we now turn in Chapters 3 and 4 to an examination of the ways in which the specific life contexts of family and work affect our notions of aging and our views of self over the course of the *humanly* constructed life cycle.

REFERENCES

Aries, P.: *Centuries of Childhood*. New York, Vintage, 1962.
Bakan, D.: Adolescence in America: From idea to social fact. *Daedalus, 100 (Fall)*: 979:995, 1971.

Cain, L.: The growing importance of legal age in determining the status of the elderly. *The Gerontologist, 14*:167-74, 1974.

Calhoun, Richard B.: *In Search of the New Old*. New York, Elsevier, 1978.

Chudacoff, H., and Hareven, T.: From the empty nest to family dissolution: Life course transitions into old age. *Journal of Family History, Spring*:69-83, 1979.

Coleman, J.S.: *The Adolescent Society*. New York, The Free Press, 1961.

DeMause, L.: Our forbears made childhood a nightmare. *Psychology Today, April*: 85-88, 1975.

Demos, J.: *A Little Commonwealth*. New York, Oxford University Press, 1970.

Demos, J.: The American family in past time. *American Scholar, 43*:422-446, 1974.

Denzin, N.: *Childhood Socialization*. San Francisco, Jossey-Bass, 1977.

Fischer, D.: *Growing Old in America*. New York, Oxford University Press, 1978.

Gillis, J.: *Youth and History*. New York, Academic Press, 1974.

Glick, P.: Updating the life cycle of the family. *Journal of Marriage and the Family, 39*: 5-13, 1977.

Gordon, T.: *Parental Effectiveness Training: The Tested New Way to Raise Responsible Children*. New York, New American Library, 1975.

Hareven, T.: Family time and historical time. In A. Rossi, J. Kagan, and T. Hareven (Eds.): *The Family*. New York, W.W. Norton, 1978.

Harris, L., and associates: *The Myth and Reality of Aging in America*. Washington, D.C., National Council on Aging, 1975.

Hofstadter, R.: *Anti-intellectualism in American Life*. New York, Vintage Books, 1966.

Hostetler, J.: *Hutterite Society*. Baltimore, Johns Hopkins University Press, 1974.

Hunt, D.: *Parents and Children In History*. New York, Basic Books, 1970.

Katz, M.: *The Irony of Early School Reform*. Cambridge, Harvard University Press, 1968.

Kenniston, K.: *Young Radicals: Notes on Committed Youth*. New York, Harcourt, Brace, 1968.

Kett, J.: *Rites of Passage*. New York, Basic Books, 1977.

Kuhn, M.: Self-attitudes by age, sex, and professional training. *Sociological Quarterly, 1*:39-56, 1960.

Lee, D.: *Freedom and Culture*. Englewood Cliffs, NJ, Prentice-Hall, 1959.

Lee, D.: *Valuing the Self*. Englewood Cliffs, NJ, Prentice-Hall, 1976.

LeShan, R.E.: *The Wonderful Crisis of Middle Age*. New York, Warner Books, 1973.

LeVine, and LeVine, B.: Nyansonago: A Gusii community in Kenya. In B. Whiting (Ed.) *Six Cultures: Studies of Child Rearing*. New York, John Wiley, 1963.

Lofland, L.: *A World of Strangers*. New York, Basic Books, 1973.

Mead, M., and Wofenstein, M. (Eds.): *Childhood in Contemporary Cultures*. Chicago, University of Chicago Press, 1955.

Modell, J., Furstenberg, F., and Hershberg, T.: Social change and transitions to adulthood in historical perspective. *Journal of Family History, 1*:7-32, 1976.

Moraze, C.: *The Triumph of the Middle Classes*. New York, Anchor Books, 1968.

Musgrove, F.: *Youth and the Social Order*. Bloomington, Indiana University Press, 1965.

Neugarten, B.: The awareness of middle age. In B. Neugarten, (Ed.): *Middle Age and Aging*. Chicago, University of Chicago Press, 1968.

Nisbet, R.: *The Sociological Tradition*. New York, Basic Books, 1966.

Platt, G.: *The Child Savers*. Chicago, University of Chicago Press, 1969.

Roebuck, J.: When does "old age" begin: The evolution of the English definition. *Journal of Social History, 12*:416-428, 1979.

Sarason, S.: *Work, Aging, and Social Change*. New York, Free Press, 1977.

Sennett, R.: *Families Against the City*. New York, Free Press, 1977.

Sheehy, G.: *Passages*. New York, Bantam, 1977.

Shorter, E.: *The Making of the Modern Family*. New York, Basic Books, 1977.

Spring, J.: *The Sorting Machine: National Educational Policy Since 1945*. New York, David McKay, 1976.

Stannard, D.: *The Puritan Way of Death*. New York, Oxford University Press, 1977.

Stone, G.P., and Stone, G.: Ritual as game: Playing to become a Sanema. *Quest, 26*:28-47, 1976.

van de Walle, E.: Recent approaches to past childhoods. *Journal of Interdisciplinary History, 2*:359-365, 1971.

Whiting, B. (Ed.): *Six Cultures: Studies of Child Rearing*. New York, John Wiley and Sons, 1963.

Zborowski, M.: The place of book learning in traditional Jewish culture. In M. Mead and M. Wolfenstein (Eds.): *Childhood In Contemporary Culture*. Chicago, University of Chicago Press, 1955.

Zborowski, M. and Herzog, E.: *Life is With People: The Culture of the Shtetl*. New York, Schocken Books, 1952.

Chapter 3

INTIMACY, AGING,
AND THE FAMILY LIFE CYCLE

IN Chapter 1 we described various theories of aging and explored their implications for a social-psychological perspective on the life cycle. In Chapter 2 we analyzed how the age categories occupying our contemporary consciousness — childhood, adolescence, middle age, and old age — developed in response to particular historical events. In this chapter we will examine how our involvement in the family life cycle is associated with our conceptions of being young or old, of being "on time" or "off time." While increasing numbers of persons are choosing to remain single, data still indicate that well over 80 percent of the population will eventually spend a good part of their adult years married (Gagnon, 1977). We will discuss the different meanings persons confer on their lives during particular phases of the socially constructed family life cycle. Our concerns in this chapter are with some distinctive phases of the family life cycle: (1) the courtship, premarital period; (2) "constructing" the marriage; (3) raising children; (4) grandparenthood as a transition to old age; and (5) the later years.

COURTSHIP

In the late 1950s, a best-selling song, on the "top pop" charts for many months, was entitled "Teen Angel." The song told the tear-jerking, heartrending story of two teenage lovers whose earthly love ends after the girl, having been pulled by her lover from a car stalled on the railroad tracks, runs back and is killed by the oncoming train. She's found with her lover's high school ring "clutched in her fingers tight." Her lover sings "I'll never kiss your lips again, they buried you tonight." Other songs of the period, such as "A Teenager in Love," also echoed the intensity of adolescent romance. They uniformly describe persons' belief in their total inability to live without one another. All over American teenagers in the 1950s and today continue to "ask the stars up above: Why must I be a teenager in love?"

We have already described in Chapter 2 how the age category of adolescence emerged and was associated with a series of social processes having the consequence of throwing teens into a prolonged economic dependency upon their parents, in contrast with their earlier historical counterparts. At the same time, mass markets geared to teen tastes in music, food, and clothing developed to capture and cultivate this growing segment of the population. An important theme of today's popular music describes teenagers as caught between the demands of restrictive parents and their own desires. Teens today are physiologically "on time" but sociologically "off time" in terms of establishing permanent marital unions. The notion of timing here is an important one. As several social scientists have observed (Neugarten et al., 1965; Lyman and Scott, 1970; Roth, 1963), a critical aspect of the "normal" aging experience in any society is not just doing things in the *right sequence* but, more importantly, doing them at the *proper time*. The age at which we embark upon specific social encounters and obligations is a significant dimension of our self definition.

Just as we feel late upon arriving at a party long after everyone else is already settled in and early when we are the only ones to have arrived at the same party, we similarly experience certain points in our lives, such as getting married and having children, as being the "right" time for such actions. Studies by Neugarten (1965) and her colleagues nicely demonstrate that such time notions are not just a function of the person's unique psychological consciousness. Neugarten's work indicates that there is a general consensus in American society among various segments of the population as to the "proper" time for persons to enter into particular life cycle arrangements. Neugarten and her associates asked a representative sample of middle class men and women between forty and seventy such questions as: What do you think is the best age for a man to marry? What is the appropriate age to finish school? What age comes to your mind when you think of a young woman? At what age do you think a woman has the most responsibilities?

The same questions were also asked of other middle-class groups in the Midwest and New England, and the results were quite uniform. As the data in Table 3-I indicate, there is a high agreement concerning the expectations persons have about the "appropriate" ages during which we should move through each point in the life cycle. The early to mid-twenties are thought to be the best times for men and women to marry. By twenty-four to twenty-six men should be settled in careers. Most people should finish their schooling by their early twenties and then go to work. Men and women are considered middle-aged between forty and fifty. Women are thought old at sixty, while for a man old age begins around sixty-five. The respondents thought that between forty-five and fifty most people should become grandparents. We should note here that while Neugarten's work demonstrates the existence of age norms, the ways in which such norms are negotiated and enforced are areas urgently in need of further empirical study.

Table 3-1   CONSENSUS IN A MIDDLE-CLASS MIDDLE-AGED SAMPLE REGARDING AGE-RELATED CHARACTERISTICS

	Age Range Designated as Appropriate or Expected	Percent Who Concur	
		Men (N=50)	Women (N=43)
A young man	18-22	84	83
A young woman	18-22	89	88
Best age for a woman to marry	19-24	85	90
Best age for most people to finish school and go to work	20-22	86	82
Best age for a man to marry	20-25	80	90
A good-looking woman	20-35	92	82
When most men should be settled on a career	24-26	74	64
When a woman has the most responsibilities	25-40	93	91
When a woman accomplishes the most	30-45	94	92
The prime of life for a man	35-50	86	80
When a man has the most responsibilities	35-50	79	75
A middle-aged woman	40-50	87	77
A middle-aged man	40-50	86	75
When a man accomplishes the most	40-50	82	71
When most men hold their top jobs	45-50	71	58
When most people should become grandparents	45-50	84	79
An old woman	60-75	83	87
When most people should be ready to retire	60-65	83	86
An old man	65-75	75	57

Source: Adapted from Neugarten, Moore, and Lowe (1965).

If we compare this "prescriptive timetable for the ordering of major life events" (Neugarten et al., 1965) with the earlier material presented in Chapter 2 on Paul Glick's work on the demography of the family life cycle, we can see a reasonable fit between these age expectations and persons' *actual behavior*. Recall that Glick's work indicated the following: The median age at first marriage for women in the 1970s was 21.2; the median age at birth of first child was 22.2 and birth of last child was 29.6. Assuming that the children would continue to get married at about the same time as did their parents and have children at similar ages — the early twenties — they would generally become grandparents during their late forties to early fifties.

The fascinating thing about these demographic patterns lies in the fact that individuals' decisions to get married and have children, for example, appears to them solely a personal one. The two lovers caught up in the beauty of the lakeshore moonlight and uttering "I love you" cannot possibly imagine anyone else experiencing a moment similar to theirs. Yet, all over the country numerous couples in their late teens and early twenties are making the same proclamations and plans for upcoming weddings. From a more impersonal, objective point of view, we might think of persons as on a societal-wide escalator that is taking them, along with countless others, onto ever higher levels of commitment to the larger society. The escalator makes a stop at a point marked *Marriage* and particular age groups get off and go through the expected rituals. Our newlyweds then get back on the escalator and within two years or so disembark at the stop labelled *Time to Have Children*. By their late twenties they are expected to stop and *Make Career Commitments*. By the time they are between forty-five and fifty they will have gotten off at the *Empty Nest* stop since their children will have been "launched." The final escalator stop of *Retirement* awaits them in their journey through the family life cycle. At each of these escalator stops our couple will encounter millions of others whose family life cycles will have taken them to the same destinations. Do not take our somewhat humorous treatment as implying an automatic, mechanical process with persons moving along escalators like electroshocked rats in a B.F. Skinner experiment. Rather, we want to dramatize the *patterned* and *widely shared* features of what people experience as the innermost part of their personal lives.

For American men and women in their early to mid-twenties there are, as the data indicate, age norms constraining them to marry and settle down. Such a decision is usually preceded by a period of courtship and dating in which the partners present favorable impressions of themselves to each other. In the initial stages of this process there is likely to be very little self-disclosure of a negative sort. Both participants are inclined to play up their strengths and play down their less appealing characteristics.

Many writers (*see* Hobart, 1960; Kephart, 1967; Murstein, 1971; Fengler, 1974; and Schulman, 1974) view early courtship and premarital dating as a period of *idealization*. The youthful age of the participants, their lack of previous experiences with other long-term intimate relationships, and their work inexperience all contribute to a situation causing them to fall in love with *what they want the other to be* as against what the other *may actually be*. The combination of "all" their friends getting married and their parents' concerns about their single status plunge the partners into the on-rushing waters of the marriage stream.

Pressures on young women in particular to "save themselves" for marriage are poignantly described in an essay by Alix Kate Shulman (1977) entitled "The War in the Back Seat." Growing up in a suburban middle class community in Ohio during the 1940s, the author tells of the "battle" waged by boys trying to prove their manhood by "scoring" sexually on the date while the girls are trying to protect their reputations by not appearing "easy" or "fast." Certainly boys, then as well as today, are not worried by others referring to them as fast or easy! Speaking of her high school experiences Ms. Shulman writes the following (1977:152-153):

> We did sometimes go out for drama, for glee club, for art, for debating, piano, class politics, or even cheerleading (to this day I have yet to hear of a cheerleader scholarship to college); *but the life they prepared us for was marriage, for that is the sum of what, for most of us, life consisted*. As in later years when men may have positions and families while women have only families, so in high school boys had football and love while we had only love. When we cheered, we cheered the boys; whatever hobby we cultivated, it too ultimately led down the aisle.
>
> By the end of the decade we were openly and frankly discussing the subject, with all its pitfalls and implications. What kind of husband did one want? What kind of wedding? How many children? How many bridesmaids? And trickiest of all — how in the world to snare one? For it

was common knowledge that boys (who, with snowballs in winter and dunkings in summer, gave daily evidence of despising us) sought to avoid, or at least postpone, marriage as eagerly as we sought to achieve it. . . .

Wakefield succinctly captures the predominant male attitude toward marriage, at least as it was expressed by Middle-American boys: "With the talk of marriage his prick had gone soft" (the very talk that held some promise of arousing us). Or, again: "Shit, he wouldn't get married. He was getting laid all over Chi." Such an attitude was simply impossible for a girl. In other places and other years a girl might manage to use sex to *get* a spouse (in The Last Picture Show, for example), but never to escape from one.

While studies indicate a change in premarital sexual behaviors, with female views moving more closely to traditional male attitudes (*see* Eshleman, 1978:188-189), data still indicate that males and females seek very different qualities in potential marriage partners. Judith Richman's (1977) study of applicants to a dating service organization is quite revealing in this regard. The women applying to this service sought men who had achieved financial and occupational success, who were "well-established" in other words. Qualities pertaining to male physical attractiveness were mentioned but took a secondary place to status in the work world.

Of the women applicants, 44 percent referred to themselves in terms of their physical attractiveness. Only two of the twelve mentioned their intelligence. The women in the sample generally wanted to meet men older than themselves, with the desired age range going as high as fifteen years older. Of the male applicants, 66 percent mentioned physical attractiveness as an important quality in the women they desired to meet. In terms of their own self-conceptions, the men were more likely than the women to emphasize their own occupational and educational successes. These findings are in keeping with numerous studies reported in other works such as Zick Rubin's (1973) *Liking and Loving*.

A focus on such desired characteristics by the partners during the courtship period is an important ingredient in an "idealization" process that appears to be inherent in a marriage pattern based on notions of romantic love. In Chapter 2 we dealt with some of the historical factors involved in the emergence and construction of the modern family: the ethos of romantic love, the cult of domesticity, and the discovery of the child. The interplay of these factors along with the increasing *age segregation* of adolescents have the added effect of putting people on the marriage escalator in their early to mid-twenties.

CONSTRUCTING THE MARRIAGE

The courtship period, as we have seen, is a situation in which the two persons become progressively more emotionally involved and begin making various sorts of commitments to each other. As "proof" of such commitments, for example, they may date only the other or have sex only with each other. Equally significant in the duo's emergence as a couple is the fact that their significant audiences, friends and families, for example, come to define the two as being really "serious" about each other. Others come to expect a certain kind of behavior of the couple once their relationship has reached such a point. They will be expected to appear together at various social functions, such as friends' weddings or parties. Should either appear alone, he or she will likely be questioned about the reasons for the other's absence. Parents may start asking about their future plans with the implication that marriage is now expected and proper. The couple, in short, does not live its life solely in the reflected glimmer of each other's eyes, but is constantly performing in front of audiences of various sorts. We see here an important ingredient in the symbolic interactionist view of human life: persons are role players in the ongoing drama of daily existence. Everyone is constantly shuttling back and forth from being an audience member in one moment to a performer in the next. We speak and others listen. They talk and we hear.

Once the couple has made a commitment to engage in a long-term relationship they may symbolically proclaim this commitment in the public forum via engagement rings, newspaper announcements, bridal showers, and general discussion with friends and associates. As a result of marrying, the couple's view of themselves begins to change. They begin to differentiate themselves from their similarly aged counterparts who have not yet made such a decision. The decision to get married makes the couple feel more "mature," more "adultish" than their friends who don't have to cope with the responsibilities of marriage itself, including the legal and emotional ramifications of having children. Persons' sense of aging, then, is affected by the structural arrangements into which they enter. The transition to the marital state in Western society, with its new legal and social responsibilities, marks an important turning point in the "status passage" (Glaser and Strauss, 1971) from adolescence to adulthood.

From the interactionist perspective marriage is created, or "constructed," by the partners themselves. Marriage is not "out there" in nature like some glacial formation or heavenly body awaiting the astronomer's gaze. The "structure" of the marriage, such as whether the couple lives by itself or with relatives, and the division of labor between husband and wife, are, to be sure, defined by the culture. But the day-to-day reality of the marriage must be mutually reaffirmed by the participants in their ongoing daily communications. In the broadest sense, as Peter Berger, Thomas Luckman, and Hans Kellner (1967, 1977) have argued, social reality itself is something that must be created and maintained through human activity. Social statuses such as mother, father, friend, and cousin are not biological constructs. They are products of particular cultures and historical contexts (Brain, 1976). If it were simply a matter of biology, the meaning of being a mother, father, or friend would be the same for all peoples throughout human history. There is little evidence to support such a position.

A crucial element in the social production of the marital relationship, as we have just noted, is the nature of the daily conversations that the couple has with each other. In previous periods of history the family was deeply embedded in the life of the larger community, with only a porous membrane separating the two. With the emergence of the modern family as a "private sphere," cut off from communal involvement, "the marriage partners are now embarked on the often difficult task of constructing for themselves the little world in which they will live" (Berger and Kellner, 1977:182). In today's world each partner to the marriage becomes the most "significant other" for the other. This situation calls forth a style of action in which "all other significant relationships have to be almost automatically reperceived and regrouped in accordance with this drastic shift" (1977:183).

Prior relationships that the couple individually maintained with single friends are now transformed by a process that Berger and Kellner (1977) aptly describe as "conversational liquidation." In regard to former friends, for example—

...the husband's image of his friend is transformed as he keeps talking about this friend with his wife. Even if no actual talking goes on, the mere presence of the wife forces him to see his friend differently. This need not mean that he adopts a negative image held by the wife. Regardless of what image she holds or is believed by him to hold, it will be different from that held by the husband. The difference will enter into the joint image that now needs to be fabricated in the course of the ongoing conversation between the marriage partners. . . The old friend is more likely to fade out of the picture by slow degrees, as new kinds of friends take his place (Berger and Kellner, 1977:183).

Having conversationally liquidated their former acquaintances over the course of time, the couple now lives in a new reality—the world of the marrieds—and its preferences for friends and associates will increasingly tend toward linkages with other couples in a similar stage of the family life cycle. Certain nights might still be reserved for "the boys" or the "girls at the office," but the nature of conversation about the intimate details of the couple's life will be increasingly restricted to the marital partners themselves.

Taking on the new identities, then, of wife and husband, involves the partners in carving out a new, joint niche for themselves in the larger social order. While persons may feel "on time" about their marriages at the time of the marriage, years later they may come to believe that they married "too soon" and thus missed out on life's adventures. The psychologist, James Marcia (1966), has referred to a process of "identity foreclosure" operating among persons who get married before they have had a chance to explore various avenues of personal growth and development. The term is a fitting one. Just as a bank forecloses on a mortgage by bringing one's home ownership to an abrupt halt so, too, Marcia suggests, can personal development be forestalled by entrance into arrangements that too hastily limit one's option.

A sense of feeling "old" at a rather young age, chronologically speaking, is beautifully captured in Lillian Rubin's (1976) sensitive study of life in working class families. The typical woman interviewed in her study married shortly after high school, had children early in marriage, and by the late twenties or early thirties feels old. For many of these women getting married and escaping their parents' homes was a way to establish their own independent status as an adult. A thirty-year-old housewife and mother of three, married nine years, says the following:

I was only seventeen when I got married the first time. I met him just after I graduated from high school, and we were married six weeks later. I guess that was kind of fast. I don't know, maybe it was rebound. I had been going with a boy in high school for a couple of years, and we had just broken up. Actually, I guess the biggest thing was that there was no other way if I wanted to get away from the house and to be a person in myself instead of just a kid in that family. All three of us girls married when we were very young, and I guess we all did it for the same reason. All three of us got divorced, too, only for my sisters it didn't work out as lucky as for me. They've both had a lot of trouble (Rubin, 1976:57).

In another revealing statement a thirty-one-year-old husband and father of three tells Rubin, "I used to think I was already in the same place as my father, and here I was only twenty. I felt like I was old, and I couldn't stand it. I just *had* to do something to get away from that feeling. When I cut out on work, it was sort of like I could be a kid again, just hanging around, doing what I wanted to do, like cutting school and just hanging out on the street" (Rubin, 1976: 81-82).

As Rubin's work makes very clear, the sense that persons have of themselves as being youthful or old is associated with their feeling either of being trapped or in control of their destinies. There is real irony in the fact that for many working class youths an institution such as marriage, which exercises its lure because of its *adult-conferring status*, a few years later comes to be experienced as a "prison" that has robbed the participants of their "youthfulness." We see here what Vern Bengston and Patricia Kasschau (1977:337) refer to as the "quickened timing of the life cycle among those of lower class standing." Additional studies by Kenneth Olsen (1969) and Bernice Neugarten and Joan Moore (1966) also reveal a relationship between time tracks and social class. As Neugarten and Hagestad (1976:49) note, "For both men and women, the higher the social class, the higher the median age for each of the following events: completion of formal education, leaving the parental home, first full-time job for men, marriage, birth of first child, birth of last child, first child leaving the parental home, first child married, and first grandchild born."

Having briefly examined how marriage can be seen as a joint social production of the partners and their significant audiences, let us examine how the arrival and presence of children relate to the parents' sense of aging.

HAVING AND RAISING CHILDREN

As we have seen, persons make assessments about their progress or lack of it on the "time tracks" provided by society. Some may feel that they had children too soon and others may feel that they waited too long to have them. Either response involves persons in a subjective evaluation of themselves as young or old, as being at a certain stage in their life. We should note, however, that these personal evaluations are not made in a social vacuum. Our views of ourselves as on or off time are always comparative ones, based on an interpretation of the situation vis-a-vis relevant reference groups.

The decision to have a child nicely reveals how comparing ourselves with others influences our views about where we are in the life cycle. A recent study by Ralph Larossa (1977) of persons expecting their first child provides some illuminating qualitative data on this subject. LaRossa interviewed the couples in his study four times during approximately the twelfth, twentieth, twenty-eighth, and thirty-sixth week of the pregnancy. The comments of his respondents suggest that a concern with being on the "right" time track played an important role in the timing of the pregnancy. Debbie, a former elementary school teacher married to Daryl, an engineer, says the following regarding their decision to have a child:

> It is probably because so many of our friends have adorable babies. . .that had something to do with it I'm sure. Plus our relationship had something to do with it. When you're 22 or 23 and you're very independent and someone says, "Well don't you want to get married, settle down, and have kids," your first reaction is to tell them what they can do with it—"Go take a flying leap out the next highest window!" But I think after settling down and getting married it just seemed the logical thing to do! (1977:34).

Another couple, Jennifer and Joe, see the decision to have children or not as related to whether people become more selfish or caring as they get older. Witness this interchange:

> Joe: I think people having children is a fulfillment. . . . People that are married and don't have children tend to get more selfish as they get older. And I think there's a lot of truth in that.
>
> Jennifer: If you see people without children, they tend to be very selfish, very self-centered.

Joe: I think people who have children tend to be more outgoing,
and have a healthier attitude toward life (1977:74-75).

As one final example we can see how the notion of timetables is
closely related to the significant audiences in one's life. In this instance, the wife's parents have strong expectations about the proper
time to have children. In what follows the couple's dog jokingly gets
defined as a "grandchild." We might suggest here, lightly of course,
that the "baby vacuum" creates pressures on the couple to symbolically produce objects that might serve as surrogate children. It
would be interesting to explore the extent to which such a
phenomenon occurs in the wider population.

Norman (the husband): He's the only grandchild right now, the dog.
Nancy (the wife): We tease him (my father) about that, tell the
dog, "Go see Grampy," You know, tease him
about it. My sisters don't have any kids.
Norman: When we go visit somewhere he'll say "Yes, I got
a grandchild," and he'll tell them all about the
dog and they'll look at him, you know. It's really
funny.
Gloria (another wife): My mother is the European mother, and I'm the
oldest child, and I'm the first one married. And I
think after the first year goes by, they start to
worry about you. She's tried to be cool about it,
but she's hinted that she'd like to be a grandmother. I called her up and said "This is the
phone call you've been waiting for for three
years" (1977, 110-111).

A theme that comes through very dramatically in LaRossa's informative study is how the process of deciding to have a child reveals
the fundamental significance of *power relations* in the marital context.
His work suggests that the effort of each partner to maintain control
over his or her destiny is a continual and ongoing source of problems
in the life course of a marriage. Some issues may be resolved to the
partner's mutual satisfaction only to reemerge later as a problem.
Or, perhaps, new issues may emerge that were totally unexpected
and unanticipated by the couple. The birth of the first child creates
the necessity to decide who is responsible for which tasks. The couple is now faced with very different daily activities than those confronting them prior to the child's arrival.

LaRossa's work presents both the *crisis* aspects of the first birth as
well as the *transitional* nature of the changes such an occurrence

brings forth in the family's activities. In this regard, Ross Eshleman (1975:510) notes the following:

> Whether it should be termed crisis or not, there is little doubt that when a dyad (husband and wife) becomes a triad (parents and child) a major reorganizaton of statuses, roles, and relationships takes place. The effect of the birth of a child and the preschool years of the children on the adjustment of the parents seems fairly well established... general marital satisfaction of couples tend to decrease after the birth of their children through the preschool and school years until the children are getting ready to leave home. The experiences of childbearing and child rearing appear to have a rather profound and negative effect on marital satisfaction, particularly for wives, even in their basic feelings of self-worth in relation to their marriage.

Parenting: Children at Home

While gerontologists and family sociologists have each developed an enormous literature in their respective fields of specialization, it is surprising that virtually no systematic studies exist on the effects of child rearing on the parents' sense of aging. Indeed, in a wide-ranging review of the literature on adult socialization, Orville Brim Jr. (1968:214) notes:

> Apparently no one has even asked in a systematic way of a sample of parents whether they perceive their children to have had any influence on their own values, life plans, personal desires, work orientation, or marital relationships. It is a commonly, if informally, reported experience by most not overly defensive parents that one or more of their children influenced them in profound ways and at deep levels on occasion and that they are different persons because of their continued intense interaction with children.

A later survey review by John Clausen (1972) of the literature on the life course of individuals contains a section on "Children in the Home." Clausen's article, however, fails to cite any studies of how children influence their parents' social–psychological sense of aging. Given the absence, then, of data on this important topic, we will draw upon all available sources, including our own personal experiences. We will also pose some issues here that are certainly worthy of future investigation by students of the life cycle.

Having children in the household, as Clausen suggests, affects the kind of car and housing choices that a family makes. The quality of the school and the proximity of residence to the school all become important parental considerations. The presence in the neighborhood of the same-aged children also enters into the parents' decision about where to live. We are assuming here, of course, that the parents are in a financial position to make the decision whether or not to move.

As we saw in our earlier discussion of the "social construction of marriage," the decision to marry involves the newly minted couple in a process of conversationally liquidating their former single friends. We might suggest here that the presence of children in the home similarly influences the parents' choice of friends and tends to propel them toward increasing associations with other parents who are in a similar family life cycle stage. The idea referred to in Chapter 1, *experiential age*, is salient here. A woman in her early thirties with young children, for example, might find it easier to become friendly with a similarly placed woman in her early twenties than with a similarly aged woman who does not have young children. We use the example of a woman here rather than a man since it is still the case, although things are changing, that women handle the bulk of child-rearing tasks in American society.

Children at home also force the parents to acknowledge their own *mortality* in a very direct way. Wills may now be drawn up and life insurance taken out on one's dependents. The will serves as a social objectification of the person's subjective sense of time's passage. As a legal and public document it serves as society's reminder of parental responsibilities, while also functioning as a temporal benchmark in the person's self-placement in the rhythm of the life cycle. Since modifications in the will and life insurance coverage accompany changes in the parents' life situation, it would be informative to interview people in detail concerning the manner in which such changes influence their sense of aging.

Important events in the life cycle of the child — such as starting to talk and walk, entering school, being confirmed or bar mitzvahed, and starting to date — also become significant transition points in the parents' awareness of their own journey through the life cycle. The writer Nancy Friday (1977) has touched upon this issue in her book *My Mother/My Self*. She points out how the onset of menstruation in the daughter, for example, arouses various fears and anxieties in the mother. Friday (1977:116) quotes the psychiatrist Lily Engler who says, "Mothers don't want to face their daughters' menstruation because it means the girl is now sexual. If there's another woman in the house, it makes her the 'older' woman. I've known mothers who really want to prepare a daughter and even think they *have* done it. . .but have not. We don't like to admit this, but it often has to do with jealousy."

Consider the words of another woman interviewed by Friday (1977:116): "I get such mixed emotions about her growing up, going to high school, says a mother of a premenstrual twelve-year-old. I'm proud of her, but I know that she's going to be leaving me. It's very ambivalent, these feelings when your daughter begins to menstruate and goes into a new, grown-up phase of life. I see my own life changing." It would be fascinating to know the significance of their daughter's menstruation to the father as well. As the case of menstruation suggests, the emergence of the child as a *sexual* being appears to be an important indicator of aging for the parent.

Parenting: The Middle Years

How do you know when you are middle-aged? Do you get a letter in the mail from the government or some official organization of middle agers welcoming you into this new life stage? What are some of the social cues that persons are sensitive to during this period? In short, how does one develop a consciousness of being a member of a particular age category? While gerontologists have conducted a number of empirical studies on the age consciousness of the elderly (*see* Bengston and Kasschau, 1977 for a review of this literature), there have been surprisingly few studies of this problem in connection with other life stages. In this regard, the work of Bernice Neugarten and her colleagues at the University of Chicago's Committee on Human Development provides some suggestive data on how persons in America come to see themselves as middle-aged.

Neugarten (1968) interviewed 100 middle– and upper-middle class persons at length concerning their conceptions of what it means to be middle-aged. Her data reveal that persons do subjectively experience this period of life as having special characteristics that distinguishes it from other periods. Her study testifies to the fact that the chronological passage of time is not crucial per se; rather, the *social meanings* that are conferred on that passage serve as the primary cues for the person's sense of aging.

Personal concerns such as the condition of one's body, the state of one's career, and changes in family structure serve as the cues in our developing awareness of age. We see here again the importance of focusing on the situation and how persons define it if we are to understand the nature of the life process. Located between two different generations — children and parents — middle agers increasingly become aware of their position as a bridge between the generations. This awareness leads Neugarten's respondents to feel increasingly less involved with their children while becoming more identified with their parents. Quotes from two of her respondents nicely reveal this point. One man remarked, "When I see a pretty girl on the stage or in the movies we used to say a 'cute chick' — and when I realize, 'My God, she's about the age of my son.' It's a real shock. It makes me realize that I'm middle-aged" (1968:94-95). And a woman notes, "I was shopping with mother. She left something on the counter and the clerk called out to tell me that the old lady had forgotten her package. I was amazed. Of course the clerk was a young man, and she must have seemed old to him. But the interesting thing is that I myself don't think of her as old.... She doesn't seem old to me" (1968:95).

Probably the most significant change occurring with the acquisition of a middle-aged identity concerns a reorientation to time, a changing time perspective. Persons now become much more conscious of *time left to live* rather than *time since birth*. The deaths of one's friends and associates serve as "mortality markers," as constant reminders of one's own limited time to earth. Middle age as experienced today is a concomitant of certain historical changes in the organization of Western society. Our sense of being middle-aged is significantly a product of the emergence of a new and distinctly bounded period — a period in between the completion of child rearing and retirement from work. Earlier generatons in the nineteenth century experienced no such clearly demarcated period in their lives as the work of social historians illustrates (*see* Chudacoff and Hareven, 1979).

The middle-age category, then, is inextricably bound up with a host of social–psychological "in-betweens." They are placed between their children and their parents. Earlier they worked to support a family and to get ahead. Now, they must start thinking about the future retirement years. It is this "bridging" situation, this feeling of being suspended between two worlds, that lends a special poignancy to the interiorization of life that now occurs. This turning inward is a frequently noted aspect of middle-age existence (*see* especially, Gould, 1972 and Levinson, 1978). The psychological interiorization of this period bears a resemblance to the life problems often described as belonging to adolescence. Even more interesting, perhaps, is the fact that given the demographic situation described earlier, middle-age parents are also likely to have children who, depending on their specific ages, are progressing through various stages of adolescence. Teenage sons and daughters are struggling to form their own identities and to establish independence from their families at the same time their parents are confronted with their own anxieties about physical health and career lines. For many women there is the additional concern brought about by their transition out of the mother role into that of working wife. The grandparents, who are either retired or close to it, are also making demands on their middle-aged children. In contrast to their teenage grandchildren, the grandparents, as Chilman (1977:319) notes, are "apt to be struggling for a sense of connectedness to rather than separation from the pivotal parental family...each generation is likely to have a different perspective on the familial situation."

It would be a mistake for us to view the middle-age situation as a *crisis* in the usual negative sense of that term. Indeed, it might be helpful for us to recall that "The Japanese word-symbol for crisis is composed of the combined characters of challenge and opportunity" (Cath, 1976:3). Such challenges, we might suggest, relate to the kinds of opportunities provided by the social structure to members of particular age groups. While persons are confronted with the need to reevaluate the larger meaning of their accomplishments and goals, they are also presented the opportunity to grow and develop in new directions. As Neugarten and Datan (1974) argue in a wide-ranging review of studies on the middle years, the *anticipated* or *unanticipated* character of the events that confront persons are critical:

> It is an inaccurate view that middle age constitutes a crisis period in the life cycle any more than any other period of life. For most persons middle age brings with it the anticipated changes in family and work and health. Some of these changes are not necessarily interpreted as losses by the people who experience them. Whether perceived as losses or gains, the life events of middle age may produce new stresses for the invididual, but they

also bring occasions to demonstrate an enriched sense of self and new capacities for coping with complexity (1974:606).

GRANDPARENTHOOD AS A TRANSITION TO OLD AGE

Grandparenthood is an interesting case of a role in contemporary American society that can be viewed, in contrast to earlier historical periods, as ushering in the transition to old age. While the popular mass media continue to portray grandparents as having all the characteristics and physical attributes stereotypically associated with the elderly, the significant fact is that grandparenthood is occurring increasingly among *middle-aged* segments of the population. Results from some recent empirical studies illustrate this point. Neugarten and Weinstein's (1973) study reported an age range from the early fifties to the mid-sixties for the grandmothers. In another sample of grandparents studied by Wood and Robertson (1974), 31 percent of the grandfathers were between forty and fifty-nine, with a corresponding figure of 35 percent of the grandmothers. Additional data provided in this study indicate that 20 percent of their sample became grandparents during the ages of thirty-one to forty-six with another 44 percent having become grandparents during the ages of forty-seven to fifty-four.

The onset of grandparenthood is something that appears to be increasingly associated with the middle years of the middle-age period. In earlier periods of history, reported in Chapter 2, persons married later and continued having children right up until the last years of their life. As Lillian Troll and her associates (1979) note, "Earlier marriage, earlier childbirth, and longer life expectancy are producing grandparents in their forties. These grandparents, because they themselves have only a few children, are truly grandparents in identity, and not at the same time parents of young children." As more parents come to *anticipate* becoming grandparents, seeing it as a natural part of the life cycle, they find themselves in a social role bridging middle and old age. Men find that they are grandparents while still in the work force, and women increasingly become grandmothers during the period when they have reentered the work force after a long absence due to child-rearing activities.

How do persons prepare for the period when their children have become adults and are living with families of their own? How do the parents' conceptions of themselves change as a result of this transition? Data gathered in interviews with urban middle-class respondents by Irwin Deutscher (1962) illustrate some of the factors involved. His findings indicate that contemporary Americans are provided with a number of "socializing opportunities" that prepare parents for the transition to postparental life. He argues that acceptance of "change for its own sake" appears to be one of the dominant cultural themes in American society and helps persons deal with the changes in the family life cycle. When one of Deutscher's respondents was asked how it felt to become a grandfather, he remarked —

> Of course you hate to give up your daughter, but I think we all understand that it is the way of life; you can't stand still; you can't be the same forever. Life moves on and it is the most natural thing. You see them grow. You see them graduate from high school. Then you see them graduate from college — you follow along. It is changing all the time. First it is childhood. You hold them on your lap and then you go walking with them. Then you see them through high school. I was her chauffeur, all the time taking her to social functions. She went through music school, then she got a bachelor of arts, then we sent her for four years to Julliard and she got her bachelor's and master's there. Then she comes out and teaches in college for one year and then she gets married and settles down (1962:511).

Middle-class parents' receptivity to change in later periods of their lives is enhanced by frequent opportunities to anticipate the onset of the "empty nest" period via their children leaving home for extended periods of time, such as college attendance. In this regard, a female respondent notes, "The breaking point is when your children go away to college. After that you grow used to it. By the time they get married you're used to the idea of their being away and adjust to it" (1962:511-512).

Military service provides yet another basis for parents to adjust to the idea that their children are achieving a high degree of independence from them. Although Deutscher does not mention it, we might suggest that for working-class and lower-class parents their childrens' military service rather than college attendance may be the prime means by which they are socialized for the postparental stage. Just how the child's military service might lead to changes in parent–child relations is aptly revealed in a mother's statement:

> After he came out of the service he had aged a lot. He used to confide in us about life and to tell us about everything that was happening in school. But after he went into service he changed. We always spent our after-

noons together—both the children. We'd go out for drives or picnics or something like that. But after he came home from service he didn't do that anymore. He wasn't contented (sic) to be at home (1962:513).

For middle-class males the work role may help to prepare the father for his childrens' departures. Work is a source of continuity in the father's life since he works while the children are growing up. He is also likely to be working upon becoming a grandparent. Deutscher suggests that the "cultural myth of the mother-in-law" prepares middle-class women to accept their childrens' departures. His female respondents were very reluctant to get caught up in the kind of mother-in-law role that would have them "meddling" in their childrens' marriages. As a result, they prided themselves on their acceptance of the reality of their offsprings' independence.

The current meanings of grandparenting in American society also illustrate how persons redefine themselves and their social circles during the family life cycle. Interviews conducted by Neugarten and Weinstein (1973) with a sample of grandmothers and grandfathers in seventy middle-class families let us see the varied meanings associated with this role. Comments of these respondents suggest five different responses to grandparenthood: (1) biological renewal and/or biological continuity; (2) emotional self-fulfillment; (3) activity as resource persons; (4) vicarious accomplishment; and (5) feelings of remoteness.

Those who saw themselve in terms of biological renewal emphasized the fact that their grandchildren provided them with the opportunity to "feel young again." The sense of biological continuity with the future was also expressed in statements such as "It's through these children that I see my life going on into the future" (1973:507). A second group of grandparents saw their role as providing a chance to be an even better grandparent than one was a parent. One respondent said, "I can be, and I can do for my grandchildren things I could never do for my own kids. I was too busy with my business to enjoy my kids, but my grandchildren are different. Now I have time to be with them" (1973:507).

Grandparents who saw themselves as resource persons tended to stress the ways in which they were able to help the child with financial aid and the wisdom gained from a lifetime of human experience. Here one respondent remarked, "I take my grandson down to the factory and show him how the business operates—and then, too, I set aside money especially for him. That's something his father can't do yet, although he'll do it for *his* grandchildren" (1973:507).

Some respondents relive, through their grandchildren, many of their own frustrated ambitions, hoping the grandchildren will achieve something that neither they nor their own children were able to accomplish. This opportunity to "aggrandize the ego" is suggested by one grandmother's comment about her grandaughter: "She's a beautiful child, and she'll grow up to be a beautiful woman. Maybe I shouldn't, but I can't help feeling proud of that" (1973:507). A final group of grandparents were categorized as feeling remote from their grandchildren. These persons felt little involvement in their grand-childrens' lives and saw little relationship between their own lives and those of the grandchildren.

Based on their findings Neugarten and Weinstein argued that two new styles of grandparenting are emerging in the United States: the "Fun Seekers" and the "Distant Figures." The Fun Seekers function as the child's playmates and the emphasis here is on *mutuality of satisfaction*. Both the child and the grandparent are expected to have fun and amuse each other. By contrast, the Distant Figures make their presence felt only on holidays and family celebrations, such as birthdays. They are kindly toward their grandchildren but do not play much of a role in their lives.

When the grandparental styles were analyzed according to the age of the respondent, both the Fun Seekers and the Distant Figures tended to be found frequently among the younger group, those under sixty-five, while a style called "The Formal" was associated with the older group, those over sixty-five. Also significant is the finding that many of the persons interviewed in this study describe themselves as "more youthful than my parents were at my age." This is true for a large majority of both the middle-aged and older interviewees. Given the increasing youthfulness of the grandparent generation, our attention is called to some of the changes that may be occurring in the meanings conferred on a role increasingly held by middle-aged rather than elderly persons strictly.

A later study by Wood and Robertson (1974) examined the significance of grandparenthood for middle-aged and older adults in a Midwestern working-class community. These researchers found "the more involved grandparents did tend to have slightly higher levels of life satisfaction" (1974:299). Wood and Robertson argue that "it is not possible to dismiss the importance of the grandparent role for most older adults. Grandchildren appear to be significant to older individuals because they provide primary group reference. . . Over-all, grandparents do not seem to expect tangible commitments from their grandchildren; they appear to be content if their grandchildren give them a modicum of interest and concern, however ritualistic or superficial this may be" (1974:302).

The significant issue here is not whether the grandparent role evokes a great deal of satisfaction from all its participants. Rather, we have suggested that its increasing occurrence among middle-aged segments of the population provides such persons with an important temporal benchmark by which they can gauge their own movement through the life cycle, while simultaneously ushering them into the transition to old age. Grandparenthood, we want to communicate, is not a fixed status. It is best viewed as a *process*. Thus the interrelations between grandparents and their children will be affected by the aging process, which *both* parties are undergoing during their lives. Works by Eva Kahana and Boaz Kahana (1970, 1971) illustrate the changing meanings of grandparenthood for children of varying ages. These researchers found that "Young children (ages 4-5) valued grandparents mainly for their indulgent qualities, the middle groups (ages 8-9) preferred the fun-sharing active grandparent, and the oldest group (ages 11-12) reflected distance from their grandparents" (1970:266).

In sum, then, we must constantly bear in mind that the meanings of aging, as seen in the grandparental role, must be viewed in terms of the larger context, or network of relations, in which such roles are embedded. As childrens' needs and cognitive abilities change, so do their relations with grandparents.

THE LATER YEARS

While grandparenthood may be viewed as providing a possible status passage into old age, gerontologists are currently divided on the issue of whether or not persons are successfully "socialized to old age" in America. Irving Rosow (1974) has been perhaps the foremost advocate of the position that there are few clear-cut normative ex-pectations concerning the behavior of elderly Americans. The aged inhabit a kind of limbo status in which they are unsure of what others expect of them as well as what they should expect from each other.

According to Rosow, status changes that occur in earlier phases of the life cycle have several salient characteristics. First, they usually involve some form of public ritual, or rite of passage, in which there is a *social* confirmation of the person's assumption of the new status. Baptism and high school graduations would be examples of such rites of passage in American society. Second, in earlier status transitions persons usually move into positions of greater independence and responsibility, such as promotions in the work world. As Rosow (1974:17) notes, "These gains are specifically *age-related*. They are independent of any other rewards, such as those underlying social mobility. The sheer transition from one stage of the life cycle to the next systematically increases the person's prerogatives in accordance with greater social maturity and competence." Finally, earlier status transitions provide sources of *role continuity* for the person. Rosow is talking about the ease of movement from one life stage to another. Such movement will be easier when earlier expectations can be incorporated into those associated with the later stages.

For Rosow the characteristics of earlier status transitions are not applicable to the process of growing old. Rather, he argues, growing old is best viewed as an instance of what Glaser and Strauss (1965) refer to as a "non-scheduled status passage" in the sense that it is not marked by any one specific event in the person's life. Instead, growing old is a "vague and unregulated process." Unlike earlier periods of life in which there is some upward movement in terms of *social gains*, aging in America involves *social decline*. Removed forcibly from the world of work via mandatory retirement, the elderly are thrust into a world where they take on the character of devalued objects. To use a metaphor, the situation of the elderly might be compared to that of a railroad line that has suddenly gone bankrupt. Prior to the bankruptcy the line may have been worth a certain amount of money. After the bankruptcy the railroad's *physical condition* may not have changed at all, yet now that same physical condition has been symbolically redefined to mean *valueless*. Similarly, after retirement a worker who might have had some value in society's eyes while working is now symbolically redefined as less worthy.

Additionally, Rosow claims much role discontinuity in the transition to old age since earlier periods of life do not prepare people to confront adequately the situation facing them in later life. Preretirement programs are sporadic and ineffectual. Little is done to prepare men and women for living as widows and widowers, a common lot of many elderly persons. "In general, old people must learn from their own experiences and adapt by themselves" (1974:27). The *looseness*, if you will, in the life situations of the elderly has led one researcher, Russell Ward, to note that "While a lack of socialization for old age may create problems, the very vagueness of old age roles allows older people to negotiate and 'make' their own roles" (1979:133).

The picture of old age painted by Rosow in the course of his argument is challenged by the works of other gerontologists who find much less alienation and demoralization among the elderly. Vivian Wood's (1971) review of studies dealing with behaviors expected of the elderly indicates that we may be witnessing "emergent norms in varying degrees of crystallization about appropriate behaviors for older persons enacting specific roles" (1971:77). According to Wood, age norms may be developing in the following areas: being an older husband or wife, widowhood, parenting adult children, and grandparenting.

Lillian Troll's and her colleagues' (1979) review of studies dealing with older couples indicates that while the literature on marital satisfaction during the family life cycle is often very contradictory, still "most older couples are happily married" (1979:53). In an earlier work, Troll and Smith (1976) argue that the marital life cycle leads to an inverse relationship between attraction and attachment. People are initially drawn into involvement with each other through their mutual *attraction*. As the marriage progresses over time, however, the sense of attraction wanes, as novelty wanes, but *attachment* increases (1979:60). Other data (Reedy, 1977) support this notion by showing the importance accorded love in the early years of marriage, while those married considerably longer viewed their relationship more in terms of loyalty. Such studies are significant in illustrating how one's sense of aging is embedded in an ongoing process of symbolically redefining and renegotiating (Strauss, 1978; Marshall, 1978) one's sense of self as life situations change. Forms of relationships that were significant or meaningful at certain stages of life become redefined as we move through the life cycle.

Troll and her colleagues (1979) conclude their review of parent–adult relations by citing the frequency of contacts between older Americans and their children, as well as the mutual assistance patterns existing between them. These findings call into question the alienation often presumed to exist between the elderly and their offspring. "The older person prefers to maintain his independence as long as he can, but. . . when he can no longer manage for himself, he expects his children to assume that responsibility; his children in turn expect to, and do, undertake it, particularly in terms of personal and protective services" (Troll et al., 1979:98).

Images of an alienated elderly population result from the limited nature of the contacts between professionals and their elderly clients. Here we have a self-selection phenomenon since the elderly who seek out professional helpers (social workers, mental health counselors, and the like) tend to be in much worse shape than those in the elderly population at large, otherwise they would not seek such help in the first place.

Given the available literature in gerontology, the issue of the elderly's "socialization to old age" is still a question requiring further investigation. In the case of the general family situation of older Americans, however, there does appear to be some agreement concerning the existence of an interactional dilemma faced by the elderly and their offspring. Several reviewers have referred to this issue in terms of the concept "intimacy at a distance" (*see* Rosenmayr and Kockeis, 1963; Streib, 1973). "Again and again in surveys, case studies, and from clinical observations, one learns that old people wish to have continuous meaningful contact with their children and their kin, but they do not wish to reside in the same household. This is what is meant by 'intimacy at a distance'" (Streib, 1973:536).

The intimacy-at-a-distance concept reflects a definition of the situation put forth by the aged themselves in awareness of and in response to their life condition. They may need help from their adult children but at the same time do not want to become a burden or to meddle in their childrens' families. In earlier periods of the family life cycle, when they were parents of younger children, the now elderly generation wanted intimacy *without* distance vis-a-vis their children. Being solely responsible for their offspring's welfare, the fear of being a burden or becoming dependent on their children was not a salient concern. Now, however, the elderly find themselves placed in a situation whereby they may well end up being parented by their now middle-aged children (Vincent, 1972).

A crucial issue in this whole "dilemma" concerns the conceptions that members of various age categories have of each other. How accurately, we might ask, do the young, the middle-aged, and the elderly see each other? In one investigation (Ahammer and Baltes, 1972), the researchers studied the perceptions that members of three age categories — adolescents (15-18), adults (34-40), and older people (67-74) — had toward each other in four areas of behavior: affiliation, achievement, autonomy, and nurturance. They were concerned with the extent to which members of these age groups misperceived each other.

Findings from this study indicated that the adult group had the most inaccurate perceptions of the other two age groups. More specifically, adults perceived adolescents "as valuing autonomy more than they actually do" and older people as "valuing nurturance more and autonomy less than they actually do" (1972:50). The adult generations' situation is captured in these perceptions. They are "caught" between the demands of their own children and their elderly parents. Their view that the elderly want more help than they in fact actually desire can lead the middle-aged into problem situations with their parents. The latter, in turn, may resent the helpful efforts of their children, only to be viewed as ungrateful or childish by them.

Findings reported above lend further support to a wide range of studies in sociology and social psychology arguing that power and the ability to take the role of the other vary inversely (*see*, for example, the review in Karp and Yoels, 1979). Thus, persons in lesser positions of power will have more accurate perceptions of their superiors' behaviors than vice versa. Insensitivity, then, is a *socially distributed* phenomenon. Studies show, for example, that women are better able to take the role of men than vice versa; blacks are better able to take the role of whites than vice versa; and, as we have seen, the young and the elderly are better able to predict the behavior of the middle-aged than vice versa. The realities of the powerful and the powerless, then, are quite different with the latter having to be far more perceptive about the reality of the former.

We do not mean to imply by the foregoing discussion that the elderly and their middle-aged offspring are inevitably propelled toward interactional collisions. As the studies previously cited indicate, relations between older persons and their children are generally marked by feelings of satisfaction and respect. The point of our discussion here has been to highlight the interactionist position that the meanings of aging are very much products of persons' particular situations in society. As we move through the various status passages associated with the family life cycle, we are involved in changing patterns of relationships with our parents and our children. Such changing patterns indicate that relations between members of various age groups are always products of ongoing negotiations.

CONCLUSION

This chapter has examined how various aspects of the family life cycle affect persons' sense of aging and the meanings we attribute to particular phases in our own lives. As we date, "get serious," and decide to marry we find ourselves on time tracks provided by the larger society. Our experiences of "falling in love," deciding to have children, and so on, while deeply personal in nature, are also influenced by the organization of society and the character of the social circles in which we move.

Social relations, we argued, are not out there in nature. Rather, they are constructed through the daily communications between persons. In constructing a marriage the partners find themselves travelling in different social circles than those they participated in while single. The couple's sense of aging is shaped by their communications with both offspring and other couples in similar life cycle situations.

Transformations that people undergo in their view of themselves as young or old powerfully affirm the processual nature of human life. As parents move into the middle years of family life, their attention and interests increasingly turn away from an involvement with their children to one with their now elderly parents. As parents move into the later years of family life, they find themselves desiring relations with their children best described as intimacy with a distance, in contrast to their earlier relations with their offspring based on notions of intimacy without distance.

Having discussed the significance of family life cycles for our sense of aging, we now turn to another critical context of human development. In Chapter 4 we describe how careers and the work world shape our sense of aging.

REFERENCES

Ahammer, I.M., and Baltes, P.: Objective versus perceived age differences in personality. *Journal of Gerontology, 27*:46-51, 1972.

Aldous, J.: Intergenerational visiting patterns. *Family Process, 6*:235-51, 1967.

Bengston, V.: Inter-age perceptions and the generation gap. *The Gerontologist, Winter:*85-89, 1971.

Bengston, V., Olander, E., and Haddad, A. The "generation gap" and aging family members: Toward a conceptual model. In Jaber F. Gubrium (Ed.): *Time, Roles, and Self in Old Age.* New York, Human Sciences Press, 1974.

Bengston, V., and Kasschau, P.: The impact of social structure on aging individuals. In J. Birren and W. Schaie (Eds.): *The Handbook of the Psychology of Aging.* New York, Van Nostrand Rheinhold, 1977.

Berger, P., and Kellner, H.: Marriage and the construction of reality. In P. Stein, J. Richman, and N. Hannon (Eds.): *The Family.* MA, Addison-Wesley, 1977.

Berger, P., and Luckmann, T.: *The Social Construction of Reality.* New York, Doubleday, 1967.

Blau, Z.: *Old Age in a Changing Society.* New York, New Viewpoints, 1973.

Blenkner, M.: Social work and family relationships with some thoughts on filial maturity. In E. Shanas and G. Streib (Eds.) *Social Structure and the Family.* Englewood Cliffs, Prentice-Hall, 1965.

Bolton, C.: Mate selection in the development of a relationship. *Marriage and Family Living, August:*234-240, 1961.

Brain, R.: *Friends and Lovers.* New York, Basic Books, 1976.

Brim, O.: Adult Socialization. In J. Clausen (Ed.): *Socialization and Society.* Boston, Little Brown and Co., 1968.

Cath, S.: Individual adaptation in the middle years. *Journal of Geriatric Psychiatry, 9:*19-40, 19__.

Chilman, C.: Families in development at mid-stage of the family life cycle. In J. Wiseman (Ed.): *People as Partners.* San Francisco, Canfield Press, 1972.

Chudacoff, H., and Hareven, T.: From the empty nest to family dissolution: Life course transitions into old age. *Journal of Family History, Spring:*69-83, 19__.

Clausen, J.: The life course of individuals. In M. Riley, M. Johnson, and A. Foner (Eds.): *Aging and Society,* Volume 3. New York, Russell Sage, 1972.

Deutscher, I.: Socialization for postparental life. In Arnold Rose (Ed.): *Human Behavior and Social Processes.* Boston, Houghton Mifflin, 1962.

Dundes, A., and Pagter, C.: *Work Hard And You Shall Be Rewarded.* Indiana, Indiana University Press, 1975.

Elder, G.: Age differentiation and the life course. In J. Coleman and N. Smelser (Eds.): *Annual Review of Sociology.* Palo Alto, Annual Reviews, 1975.

Eshleman, J.: *The Family.* Boston, Allyn and Bacon, 1978.

Eslinger, K., Clarke, A., and Dyne, R. The principle of least interest, dating behavior, and family integration setting. *Journal of Marriage and Family, May:* 269-272, 1972.

Fengler, A.: Romantic love in courtship: Divergent paths of male and female students. *Journal of Comparative Family Study, Spring:* 134-139, 1974.

Friday, N.: *My Mother/My Self.* New York, Delacorte Press, 1977.

Gagnon, J.: *Human Sexualities.* Glenview, IL, Scott-Foresman, 1977.

Glaser, B., and Strauss, A.: *Status Passage.* Chicago, Aldine, 1971.

Glick, P.: Updating the life cycle of the family. *Journal of Marriage and the Family, 39 (February):*5-13, 1977.

Gould, R.: The phases of adult life. *American Journal of Psychiatry, 129:*523-531, 1972.

Hobart, C.: Attitude changes during courtship and marriage. *Marriage and Family Living, November:*352-359, 1960.

Kahana, E., and Kahana, B.: Grandparenthood from the perspective of the developing grandchild. *Development Psychology, 3:*98-105, 1970.

Kahana, E., and Kahana, B.: Theoretical and research perspectives on grandparenthood. *Aging and Human Development, 2:*261-268, 1971.

Karp, D., and Yoels, W.: *Symbols, Selves, and Society: Understanding Interaction.* New York, Harper and Row, 1979.

Kephart, W.: Some correlates of romantic love. *Journal of Marriage and the Family, August:*470-474, 1967.

Kogan, N., and Shelton, F.: Beliefs about "old people." *The Journal of Genetic Psychology, 100:*93-111, 1962.

LaRossa, R.: *Conflict and Power in Marriage: Expecting the First Child.* Beverly Hills, Sage Publications, 1977.

Levinson, D.: *The Season's of a Man's Life.* New York, Knopf, 1978.

Lowenthal, M., and Havens, C.: Interaction and adaptation: Intimacy as a crucial variable. *American Sociological Review, 33:*20-31, 1968.

Lyman, S., and Scott, M.: *A Sociology of the Absurd.* Pacific Palisades, Goodyear, 1970.

Marcia, J.: Development and validation of ego identity status. *Journal Personality and Social Psychology, 3:*551-558, 1966.

Marshall, V.: No Exit. *Aging and Human Development, 9 (4):*345-57, 1978-79.

Miller, D., and Swanson, G.: *The Changing American Parent.* New York, Wiley, 1958.

Murstein, B.: Self-ideal — Self discrepancy in the choice of marital partners. *Journal of Consulting and Clinical Psychology, 27:*47-52, 1971.

Neugarten, B., Moore, J., and Lowe, J.: Age norms, age constraints, and adult socialization. *American Journal of Sociology, 70:*710-717, 1965.

Neugarten, B., and Moore, J.: The changing age status system. In B. Neugarten (Ed.): *Middle Age and Aging.* Chicago, University of Chicago Press, 1968.

Neugarten, B.: The awareness of middle age. In B. Neugarten (Ed.): *Middle Age and Aging.* Chicago, University of Chicago Press, 1968.

Neugarten, B., and Weinstein, K.: The changing American grandparent. In M. Lasswell and T. Lasswell (Eds.): *Love, Marriage, Family.* Glenview, IL, Scott-

Foresman, 1973.

Neugarten, B., and Datan, N.: The middle years. In Silvano Arieti (Ed.): *American Handbook of Psychiatry*. New York, Basic Books, 1974.

Neugarten, B., and Hagestad, G.: Age and the life course. In R. Binstock and E. Shanas (Eds.): *Handbook of Aging and the Social Sciences*. New York, Van Nostrand Reinhold, 1976.

Olsen, K.: *Social Class and Age Group Differences in the Timing of Family Status Changes*. Ph.D. dissertation, University of Chicago, 1969.

Reedy, M.: *Age and Sex Differences in Personal Needs and the Nature of Love*. Ph.D. dissertation, University of Southern California, 1977.

Richman, J.: Bargaining for sex and status: The dating service and sex-role change. In P. Stein, J. Richman, and N. Hannon (Eds.): *The Family*. MA, Addison-Wesley, 1977.

Rosenmayr, L., and Kockeis, E.: Propositions for a sociological theory of aging and the family. *International Social Science Journal, 15*:410-426, 1963.

Rosow, I.: *Socialization to Old Age*. Berkeley, University of California Press, 1974.

Roth, J.: *Timetables*. Indianapolis, Bobbs-Merrill, 1963.

Rubin, L.: *Worlds of Pain*. New York, Harper and Row, 1976.

Rubin, Z.: *Liking and Loving*. New York, Holt, Rhinehart, and Winston, 1973.

Schulman, M.: Idealization in engaged couples. *Journal of Marriage and Family*, February:138-147, 1974.

Sheehy, G.: *Passages*. New York, E.P. Dutton, 1976.

Shulman, A.: The war in the back seat. In P. Stein, J. Richman, and N. Hanson (Eds.): *The Family*. MA, Addison-Wesley, 1977.

Strauss, A.: *Negotiations*. San Francisco, Jossey-Bass, 1978.

Streib, G.: Older families and their troubles: Familial and social responses. In M. Laswell and T. Laswell (Eds.): *Love, Marriage, Family*. Glenview, IL, Scott-Foresman, 1973.

Troll, L., Miller, S., and Atchley, R.: *Families in Later Life*. Belmont, CA, Wadsworth, 1979.

Troll, L., and Smith, J.: Attachment through the life span. *Human Development, 3*:156-171, 1976.

Vincent, C.: An open letter to the "caught" generations. *The Family Coordinator, 21*:143-150, 1972.

Waller, W.: *The Family: A Dynamic Interpretation*. New York, Gordon, 1938.

Ward, R.: *The Aging Experience*. New York, Harper and Row, 1979.

Wood, V.: Age-appropriate behavior for older people. *The Gerontologist, Winter*: 74-78, 1971.

Wood, V., and Robertson, J.: The significance of grandparenthood. In J. Gubrium (Ed.): *Time, Roles, and Self in Old Age*. New York, Human Sciences Press, 1974.

Chapter 4

WORK, CAREERS, AND AGING

SIGMUND FREUD, the father of psychoanalysis, was once asked what was required for human happiness. The questioner no doubt expected a long, abstractly complicated answer that would reflect Freud's years of thinking on the matter. His immediate and simple response was that we need to love and to work. In the previous chapter we explored how our intimate relationships, especially within the context of family life, shape the aging process. Recall our argument in that chapter. The way we feel about our age and the meaning given to age is significantly influenced by the particular stage in the family life cycle we happen to be experiencing. In this chapter, we shall turn to the second central life sphere named by Freud as defining and circumscribing the quality of our lives. Consistent with the overall perspective of this book, a central goal of this chapter will be to look at how chronological age is differently interpreted and subjectively understood depending upon the kind of work we do and the stage of the work life cycle we are experiencing at a given point in time.

The central thesis of this chapter is that our involvement with work is a prime determinant of the way we experience the passage of time. Work structures the way that we think about the present and how we anticipate the future. In short, persons' work is a primary source for their "sense of aging" (Sarason, 1977). Those who pursue quite different work lives or work careers will hear different messages about the meaning of age. One's viability as a worker is in some instances vitally affected by age, and in others it is not. In most societies the work career and the aging career overlap. Different career patterns involve varying conceptions of what it means to be on time, ahead of time, or late. The way individuals measure and evaluate their own life progress, and so their experiences of growing older, is significantly a function of where they are "supposed to be" occupationally at any given point in time. Since different work career curves exist, we postulate, as in previous chapters, a variety of aging patterns. In the pages to follow we will especially want to consider how the character of professional work, white collar work,

96

and blue collar work orders persons' conceptions of the past, present, and future.

WORK AND IDENTITY

A whole tradition of sociological literature (*see* Hughes, 1958: Becker, 1970) illustrates the centrality of work to personal identity. To use Everett Hughes' phrase, work is one of our "master" attributes or statuses. Although all of us occupy many statuses, some are more critical than others for the way others define us and how we define ourselves. From a very early age persons are expected to begin considering, however broadly and loosely, what kind of work they will eventually do. Especially in the higher segments of the social stratification system, children are frequently asked what they wish to be when they grow up. These children are provided a picture of an occupational world that is thoroughly open to them. They are taught to believe that they can "become" virtually anything they want to become. We do well to consider that for most of us, the kind of work we eventually do is literally equated with what we will have become. Our eventual occupational status may become the source of such diverse feelings as pride, shame, guilt, power, and authority. Occupational status is a central yardstick against which our "social value" is determined.

Work is a powerful force in shaping our sense of identity. Once we have chosen our work, we have pretty much determined how we will fill out much of our adult lives. Although the total amount of time spent at work by the average worker has sharply decreased over the last century, it is still quite considerable today. In 1870, the average worker entered the work force at age fourteen and worked until his death at age sixty-one. It has been estimated that during the forty-seven years of his working life the 1870 worker would put in a total of 146,640 hours on the job. A century later in 1970, the average worker who retired at age sixty-five would have spent 90,000 hours at work (Miernyk, 1975). The reader must, of course, recognize that the statistics provided here are averages. Many in today's society work hours that exceed the time spent by their counterparts a century earlier. It is not especially surprising, therefore, that we tend to define ourselves in terms of the occupations or work organizations to which we belong. The question "Who are you?", asked directly or indirectly, often elicits an organizational response: "I am a professor at Boston College." "I am an engineer at IBM." If not an organizational response persons normally name at least their occupation. "I'm a steel worker." "I am a policeman." In large measure, then, one *is* what one *does* for work.

Work is not just a peg for self-identity. Our sense of self-esteem and personal well-being is wrapped up with the work we do (Coles, 1978). Studies of prolonged unemployment illustrate that persons in that situation are denied much more than a weekly or monthly pay check. They are denied the ability to view themselves with respect. Loss of work is accompanied by chronic depression (Cohn, 1978; Tiffany et al., 1970). Our mental health, in other words, depends on the ability to provide a satisfactory answer to the ubiquitous question, "What kind of work do you do?" Without work persons feel lifeless, rootless, and marginal. Elliot Jacques comments on the connection between work and self-esteem this way:

> ... working for a living is one of the basic activities in a man's life. By forcing him to come to grips with his environment, with his livelihood at stake, it confronts him with the actuality of his personal capacity—to exercise judgement, to achieve concrete and specific results. It gives him a continuous account of his correspondence between outside reality and the inner perception of that reality, as well as an account of the accuracy of his appraisal of himself. ... In short, a man's work does not satisfy his material needs alone. In a very deep sense, it gives him a measure of his sanity (Jacques, 1973:6).

Readers should note that Jacques' comment refers exclusively to the meaning of work for men. Social scientists have only recently turned their attention to the work lives of women. We might expect that as women increasingly pursue traditional male career paths, many of the work situations dealt with in the following pages will be experienced by them as well.

SOCIAL CLASS AND THE MEANING OF WORK

Several years ago Joseph Kahl (1957) noted that *career* constitutes a major value orientation for upper middle class persons. Especially for upper middle-class males, personal status and prestige are directly linked with occupational status and prestige. For upper middle-class men, the structure of family life, patterns of consumption, and leisure time activity revolve about their climbing the career ladder.

As we shall see, work life is inseparable from other aspects of persons' existences. Work and family life interpenetrate and determine each other's shapes. In this respect, Kahl notes, "The central value orientation of the upper middle class is 'career.' Their whole way of life—their consumption behavior, their sense of accomplishment and respectability, the source of much of their prestige with others—depends upon success in a career. The husband's career becomes the central social fact for all the family" (Kahl, 1957:194).

Typically, the upper middle-class men we have been discussing, those who are near the top of the American work world as leaders in business and the professions, have spent years gaining the educational credentials necessary to attain their occupational positions. The choice is a fateful one in the sense that with few exceptions these persons will spend most of their lives involved in an occupation chosen during their twenties, and in some cases even earlier. So important is work and career development that other life choices are often dictated by the demands of occupation. Consider for a moment the way organization men construct and define their friendships.

In his well-known book, *The Organization Man* (1956), William H. Whyte describes the friendships of career-oriented business executives as short-lived and largely utilitarian. Friends were frequently cultivated for their potential value in hastening one's career rise. Such friendships were often dissolved or forgotten when the aspiring executive moved up the corporate ladder or left the area. Today, the transitory character of friendships among corporate executives is partly a function of their geographical mobility. Vance Packard (1972) has estimated that the average corporate manager moves every two-and-a-half years. Such a transient life-style militates against the development of lasting friendships and impacts on the executive's whole family. The kind of tension between the demands of work and family is caught in this statement made by one manager's wife:

> I think sooner or later every family has to decide what is more important—money and position or roots. For me, family and friends—old friends—mean a great deal. I am sorry that my children will never know the same kind of family closeness that I did. Travel and new experiences are good for children. All the ladies' magazines keep telling us that the good outweighs the inconvenience. I don't buy this any more. I think that the security of having a real home with family and friends I don't have to

say good-bye to again means more to me than the security of a bigger pay check (1972:146).

We might suppose that the tension between the demands of work and family are increased still further as more women come to define their identities in terms of careers previously reserved nearly exclusively for men. The emergence of the "two-career family" (Holmstrom, 1972) has already strongly influenced such demographic patterns as the age at which persons choose to have children, and if they choose to have them at all, the number of children they have.

Following the literature, we have maintained that work is central to the identities of those following professional and managerial career routes. Studies of working-class people suggest that occupation is also critical to their identities and family lives, although in ways different from white-collar and professional workers. An early study contrasting the function and meaning of work for middle- and working-class men takes issue with the image that work has no meaning for blue-collar persons other than to provide money. Morse and Weiss (1955) report that working serves functions other than an economic one for those in both middle-class and working-class occupations. The nonmonetary functions served by working, however, are somewhat different in these two broad occupational classifications. Eighty percent of the 401 men they surveyed indicated that they would continue to work even if they inherited enough money to live comfortably without working. Such a statistic confirms the importance of work to life satisfaction for persons at all occupational levels. The authors, however, go on to indicate the differences between their middle-class and working-class respondents in the reasons they would want to continue working in the absence of economic need. Many of the individuals in middle-class occupations emphasize the intrinsic interest their jobs hold for them and their sense of accomplishment in completing their work. "On the other hand, the typical individual in a working class occupation emphasizes the necessity for some directed activity which will occupy his time, his mind, and his hands" (Morse and Weiss, 1955). Additional data based on national surveys conducted by the National Opinion Research Center reveal that 70 percent of persons interviewed in 1977 and 79 percent of those interviewed in 1980 replied that they would continue to work even if they had enough money to live comfortably the rest of their lives (Davis, 1980:135).

While Morse's and Weiss' study dispels the idea that working-class individuals work only for the money, we should not minimize the measure of disillusionment and alienation experienced by many blue-collar workers whose jobs often provide them little discretion in pace and schedule and also extremely limit their career paths. The depth of alienation, no doubt felt by many, is captured in the words of one blue-collar worker interviewed by Lillian Rubin: "God, I hated that assembly line. I hated it. I used to fall asleep on the job standing up and still keep doing my work. There's nothing more boring and more repetitious in the world. On top of it, you don't feel human. The machine's running you, you're not running it" (Rubin, 1976:155).

We might hypothesize that the foreshortened career paths contributing to the so-called blue-collar blues precipitate an early sense of growing old among these workers. In more general terms, lack of movement, change, mobility, and novelty, at any level of the work structure, influences aging conceptions. A *sense of change* at work is intimately bound up with *a sense of aging*. Although we are discussing the issue of stagnation here with respect to blue-collar workers, Sarason (1977) has pointed out that disillusionment among professionals has been greatly underemphasized. Later, we will explore this point more thoroughly.

As a last direction for illustrating the centrality of work to personal identity and consequently to all other aspects of our lives, we should consider the kinds of adaptations required of those whose work fails to provide them with feelings of self-worth, respect, and honor. In one well-known study, Eliot Liebow (1967) contends that the behaviors of the black street-corner men he studied in Washington, D.C., can be understood in terms of a class position that renders them powerless and virtually ensures their failure to succeed by middle-class standards.

To protect themselves from the assaults on the self created by work failure, these men construct what Liebow terms a "shadow system of values." He maintains that the street-corner men actually subscribe to middle-class achievement values, but unable to realize these values because of the constraints of their class position, they develop an alternative value system. Unable to sustain the bread-winner role, for example, the men respond by deprecating the value family life. Rather than face a demeaning work world each day, it is easier to demean the value of work itself.

In another book with much the same theme, Richard Sennett and Jonathon Cobb (1973) describe how the working-class men they interviewed, like Liebow's corner men, create their own interpretation of dominant American social values. According to these writers, working-class men who stand near the bottom of the occupational system must somehow adapt to a society that measures their value in terms of occupational achievement. How do these working-class men come to grips with their occupational powerlessness? How do they regain control over lives that seem controlled by others? One dominant response, according to these authors, is to define work as a sacrifice one must make for his family. In return for their sacrifice, working-class men demand complete power within their families. Denied a power role within the larger occupational system, working-class men exercise their role in their day-to-day relations with children and wives.

In the last few pages we have meant to convey the central place of work to persons' identities and sense of self-esteem. This is especially true in American society, which places a very high emphasis on work achievement, a theme continually reaffirmed in the several mass media and in school. We are taught to measure a person's worth, honor, and respect in terms of his or her work achievements. Moreover, we have reported on studies that suggest directly or indirectly the range of meanings given to work at different occupational levels. Now we shall consider how this master attribute influences our experience of aging.

CAREER PATHS AND AGING: SOME GENERAL CONSIDERATIONS[1]

In the past few pages we have made reference several times to the general notion of *career*. There are, of course, an extraordinary array of careers that persons may follow. No two careers will be identical. However, there are clear regularities in the way that particular organizations structure the careers of their members. In a more general sense, there are broad uniformities in the way that careers are

---

[1]The following pages in this chapter elaborate on the ideas found in David A. Karp and William C. Yoels, Work, careers, and aging. *Qualitative Sociology*, 4 (2):145-166, 1981.

structured within particular occupations. As an example, there will be a generally uniform career pattern experienced by all those who enter medicine (*see* Hall, 1948). Moreover, there are broad career patterns shared by those whose occupations cluster together into such larger categories as professional, white-collar, and blue-collar work.

The notion of career is central to our analysis since it is the nature of careers that, by definition, they are *age graded*. Career is a most useful concept for helping us to understand the linkage between the varieties of work in any society and the age meanings those work situations produce. Individuals whose adult lives from age twenty or so to retirement are built around particular career contingencies will experience aging at least partly in terms of the age-related dictates of their careers.

In his voluminous and influential writings on work, Everett Hughes (1958) has shown the value of conceptualizing career as "the moving perspective in which the person sees his life as a whole and interprets the meanings of his various attitudes, actions, and the things which happen to him." This definition of career accords well with the interactionist position we have adopted throughout this volume. Hughes certainly recognizes, as we mentioned earlier, that there is an objective aspect of occupational careers. There are, in other words, formally prescribed stages to careers that are often established within particular work organizations. Should one pursue an academic career, for example, he or she will inevitably pass through a prescribed series of stages: acceptance to graduate school, completing course work, passing comprehensive examinations in the discipline, writing a doctoral dissertation, being sponsored for an academic appointment, gaining first employment, and being an assistant professor, then an associate professor, a full professor, and eventually a professor emeritus. We have cited only major benchmarks in the career of an academic, and the reader should appreciate that we could describe many more "informal" stages within each of those named.

Hughes' definition directs attention to a second aspect of the career process. Based on communication with others in their work situation, persons attach subjective and evaluative responses to the typical sequence of movement constituting the objective career pattern they pursue. The notion of career is not just a conceptual tool employed by social scientists to look at the nature of work. Career is a notion used by all of us as a frame for interpreting where we are in the life course and how the things happening to us at any point in our lives make sense. Once again we are caused to recognize the close correspondence between career regularities and personal identity. We make sense of who we are in terms of our appropriate location along an occupational career route. Whatever the specific occupational path we embark upon, the regularized career pattern associated with it helps us to evaluate our life performance to that point and also helps us to preview our likely futures. Persons feel uneasy if there is a discrepancy between where they stand in their careers and where persons their age are generally expected to be. In other words, success in a career, as judged by the individuals themselves and their colleagues, is closely connected with age. When we say that careers are age graded, we think, as in other chapters, of persons being on an escalator of sorts. Here as that escalator travels up the career ladder, we are expected to be at certain points by certain ages. "One's career is 'working out' if one has 'made the grade' at the appropriate age. Getting there earlier gives grounds for special pleasure and a reputation as a 'comer' or 'flier.' Getting there late brings first anxiety then relief" (Sofer, 1970:53).

Career Contingencies and Subjective Aging

If the members of several personnel departments were asked to describe the typical career pattern in their organization, they would likely tell pretty much the same story. They would tell a story indicating that the youngest members of the organization are at the most bottom ranks and possess the least status, power, responsibility, and income. As they grow older and acquire greater skills and expertise, they rise in the organization at regular and predictable intervals. With each step up the organizational ladder they acquire more income, prestige, and power. Part of this happy picture is an image of organizations as meritocratic systems that reward the most able workers by placing them eventually at the top of the career ladder. In fact, however, as anyone who has worked in an organization knows, the process is rarely so neat. A number of factors, other than merit, may be responsible for one's movement within an occupational hierarchy to occur more slowly or more quickly than is suggested by the ideal pattern. Informal factors having little to do with merit may be seen as most responsible for mobility within an organization. Some years ago, the sociologist Melville Dalton (1951), in a study of the careers of 226 managers, was able to show the importance of such "informal factors" as religion, ethnicity, political beliefs, and organizational affiliations in determining their selection and promotion through the ranks of the organization.

Other factors may account for irregular career routes. Some may find themselves in organizational settings where their mobility is blocked because there are fewer places above them than persons seeking those spots. In such cases, individuals will feel stifled by the feeling that there is nowhere to go and that their future is limited. Alternatively, older members of the organization may die suddenly, opening up spaces and making possible mobility at a faster rate than might otherwise be expected. Some persons will be sponsored by someone above them and singled out for quick advancement. Others may deem it reasonable to transfer to units within an organization where they believe their chances for movement will be increased. At some point during their careers workers may come to recognize that they have achieved the highest position they will. As Howard Becker said, "Even when paths in a career are regular and smooth, there always arise problems of pacing and timing. While, ideally, successors and predecessors should move in and out of offices at equal speeds, they do not and cannot" (1970:253).

In an interesting article on the subject, Robert Faulkner (1974) argues that age may be the fundamental variable along which career lines are established. Age defines the roles available and unavailable to persons within certain work organizations and consequently affects the construction and meaning of their work commitments. In his piece, Faulkner is concerned with how individuals acquire career outlooks as part of the process of "coming to terms" with organizational structures that are "youth intensive" and that produce very rigid career lines. To illustrate the interconnection between the career demands within certain occupations and our personal sense of aging, Faulkner draws data from two occupations: from the worlds of professional hockey players and orchestra musicians. Careers within these occupations raise special contingencies for those involved and force onto their participants an especially direct age consciousness. Listen to the words, first, of a hockey player who recognizes the decreased probability of making it to the "majors" beyond a certain age:

> ...This is a business and they go with youth. I'd say that after 28, the odds are against you....You take a look at what others are doing and you see where you are and with guys who have had as much experience as you've had, the guys in the same position as you are. My wife and I say we'll give it till 26 or 27 maybe, then I'll know if I'll be in the NHL. After that they give up on you (Faulkner, 1974:156).

In the second occupation studied by Faulkner, there are also concerns about making it to the majors. In the case of orchestra musicians, making it to the majors means getting a job with one of only a select few city orchestras. As in any occupation, many who reach a certain age and take stock of their occupational position must adapt to the fact that they will not make it to the big leagues: "Look, let's not kid ourselves. I'm nearly forty years old. I make a good living here. I do some recording work on the side, I'm not going to be first in the New York Philharmonic anyway, not at my age...(but) things could be worse, like being stuck in some bush league place with little money and no musical satisfaction."

These data suggest that every occupation generates its own distinctive career path and consequently its own set of symbols and meanings of age. In most occupations persons are required to engage in a continual process of interpretation and reinterpretation about their current occupational position and its meaning. Periodically persons must assess the degree of their success, whether they are currently "making it" and their chances for eventually making it. These questions about career success and failure constantly call attention to age. Age consciousness, then, is "an aspect of occupational and organizational life whose centrality...has a paramount reality in experience" (Faulkner, 1974:167).

We see from the examples we have offered that to a very significant degree it is the structure of occupational life that injects meaning into the phrase "growing older." Additional sociological studies of such specific and diverse occupations as fashion models (Becker and Strauss, 1956), boxers (Weinberg and Arond, 1952), lawyers (Smigel, 1964), scientists (Reif and Strauss, 1965) and strippers (Skipper, 1970) affirm the relationship between the way one experiences the world of work and aging self-conceptions. Being off the time track refocuses attention on the relationship between occupational and other life sectors. Cain (1964) calls attention to the imbalances that may exist when an individual's age status position in one organization or institution does not fit well with his or her position and obligations in other institutions. Consider, as an example, the lawyer who begins his legal career in his late forties. This same person may have followed a very conventional family life cycle. We could imagine that, at forty-five or so, he has children about to enter college. In this case we have an example of what Cain terms "age-status a-synchronization." Normally workers approach the peak of their earning capacity in mid-life years. Here there would be a discrepancy, a contradiction, or imbalance between the relatively low wages the lawyer was earning at work and the demands imposed on him by his family life cycle status. Cyril Sofer (1970) sums up some of the points we have been making. "A man is in a socially 'appropriate' and personally reassuring situation when he is in the 'right' career phase for his age. He is in an embarrassing and discomforting situation when he is 'too old' for his current career phase or where the career phase is discordant with his status elsewhere" (Sofer, 1970:55).

The general line of analysis in the last few paragraphs carries special interest for analyzing the career paths of women. Let us note again that social scientists have only recently begun to pay attention to women's careers. We might consider the fact that many women have delayed entry into the labor market until after their children have become at least school age. This has meant entering school and then an occupation anywhere from their mid-thirties to their early forties or beyond. Given the rigidity of both age and sex role expectations, the woman who violates both career/age and related gender role expectations may find herself defined as deviant and stigmatized. "Mid-life women are limited by what is perceived to be appropriate behavior for their age and sex; they are expected to be in step with the 'social clocks.' To be off time is to be 'age deviant.' For a fifty-five year old woman to start work on a graduate degree or a forty-two year old woman to have a first child is considered to be 'age deviant.'" (Troll, 1978:16) For the woman who has invested her energies until mid-life in the rearing of a family and who discovers at that point just how limited her career options are, the response is often bewilderment and anger. We might suppose that the following woman speaks for many others in a similar position when she says,

"It's unbelievable when I think of it now. I never really saw past about age forty-two, where I am now. I mean I never thought about what happens to the rest of life. Pretty much the whole adult life was supposed to be around your husband and raising children. Dammit, what a betrayal! Nobody ever tells you that there's many years of life after children are raised. Now what?" (Rubin, 1979:123).

Recently, the wife of one of the authors decided to attend graduate school for professional training. Aside from the dramatic fashion in which the age distribution of her student colleagues forced recognition of her own aging process ("God, it was such a surprise. I don't think of myself as old at all, but when I learned that I was the oldest in the class, it really did make me feel old at that moment."), the example calls attention to the larger cultural expectation that careers are things to begin at a young age.

An age profile of the 1979 entering class at the Harvard business school is interesting to look at:

Age Profile of the Harvard MBA Class of 1979

under 23	17%
23–24	37%
25–26	20%
27–28	13%
29 and over	13%

Note that the data are presented in five age categories referring to an age span of only six years. The age of entering students is so uniformly between twenty-three and twenty-nine that very fine distinctions are made between those who are twenty-three to twenty-four (not a very wide category) and those aged twenty-five to twenty-six. By inference, the age distribution described above reflects the statistically "deviant" character of beginning careers "late."

There are many questions to be raised about the increasing numbers of women in the age-career position we have been describing. What kinds of age-graded career expectations can these women have? What kinds of status inconsistencies do they experience when they relate to younger male colleagues higher up on the status hierarchy? Do women think about careers and evaluate job success differently than do men? To what extent do different career patterns of men and women contribute to the different aging experiences they have? These are among the questions for which we have little current data. Stimulated by changing career options for women, we are only now beginning to understand how women are reshaping the work world and how they will themselves be reshaped in turn.

Our effort thus far in the chapter has been to affirm the idea that work careers force persons to think about and confront their aging process. There is one further and related point to make here. Although our focus has been on the variable of career, we should stress that careers do not simply exist in the world as "thing-like" entities, mechanistically "causing" particular aging conceptions. A more accurate description of the connection between careers and aging requires a dialectical view of things. By causing us to focus on the aging process, careers become part of that process. Once occupation enters into our consciousness as a cue for interpeting our movement through the life course, it alters our conception and experience of the life course itself.

While we can name "objective," structural arrangements associated with particular careers, we best conceptualize career as a process that is constantly being "negotiated" (Strauss, 1978) by persons in their day-to-day working lives. As Gubrium and Buckholdt (1977) suggest, through the commonplace daily events and work-situated conversations that often pass as trivial by those involved in them, career structures may either be sustained or modified. Each time that workers in an organization talk about how one or another event affects their careers, they produce a new, plausible conception of those careers. A social–psychological approach to aging will attend to how career structures give rise to work-situated, age-related dialogues that consequently change the very structures that stimulated such talk. Among the objective aspects of career that constitute the frame for persons' discussions and interpretations of chronological age are the following:

1. The length of the career ladder.
2. The extent to which the capacity to do the work is intrinsically related to physical attributes that decline with age.
3. The relationship between age and earning in the career.
4. The degree of personal autonomy in the occupation generally and at each career point.
5. The relationship between age and career mobility.
6. The nature and degree of intersection between work life and family life.

7. The age distribution of colleagues.
8. Whether the career requires the continual acquisition of new talents, skills, or information.
9. The extent to which one's career movement is influenced by changes, e.g. technological changes, in the larger society.

Although the variables we named probably cluster together in predictable ways, there are many possible combinations of them that can be produced in different career settings. We think that the variables named above can constitute the basis for more detailed empirical research into the work/aging relationship. However, it cannot be our goal in this chapter to detail how each separate occupational career structures persons' sense of time. Each occupation does pose different career contingencies and, therefore, confronts persons with somewhat unique messages about age. Put concretely, the meaning of being thirty-five, let's say, is going to vary for college professors, baseball players, musicians, steel workers, dancers, salesmen, coal miners, librarians, and so on. Beyond this, the meaning of being thirty-five will vary within each of those occupations depending upon where one stands on that occupation's general career ladder, and more explicitly still, on the career ladder unique to the particular organization with which one is affiliated. In short, the number of permutations and combinations of occupational, cultural milieus that define aging expectations and contribute to individuals' subjective sense of age is staggeringly large. There are as many specific senses of age as there are specific career positions in specific organizations.

To say, as we just have, that the number of subjective responses to work settings can be enormously large need not paralyze our analysis of the connection between work, careers, and aging. We need not resort to a kind of individual reductionism that requires the description of each individual's special case. Here, as elsewhere, it is not our goal to document each individual's aging experience as a unique phenomenon. In other words, we should not lose sight of the fact that there are general cultural regularities that cut across and transcend the unique experience of persons. We argue that social life would be impossible were there not general agreement concerning the meanings we give to objects, events, and situations (career situations being a major one) in our lives. There are collective careers that derive from the general expectations of the society. In the following pages we will analyze broad stages of working life that are normally experienced by everyone regardless of their particular occupation. Whether one eventually does professional, white-collar, or blue-collar work, he or she will go through a process that involves at least these stages:

1. Preparation and Exploration
2. Learning the Ropes
3. Coming to Grips
4. Settling In
5. Exiting

In naming these stages we recognize that they simplify the nature of work lives. We also recognize that each of the stages we have named might be further subdivided into additional stages. We consider the stages named as a tool for guiding and organizing our thinking about the relationship between work and aging over the course of the life cycle. These stages will also provide a useful framework for pulling together, ordering, and showing the plausible connections between what are now two discrete bodies of literature—that on work and that on aging.

WORK, AGING, AND THE LIFE CYCLE

In naming stages to the work career we should acknowledge the interrelationship between work experience and the life cycle as a whole. We have already claimed that it would be a false separation to discuss the work cycle as though it were independent of other spheres of persons' lives. We introduced this chapter with Freud's comment that happiness required satisfying work and interpersonal relationships. You should appreciate that Freud did not mean for these two spheres to be viewed separately or discretely. They very much interlap and blend into one another so that the state of one's personal life outside of work is significantly affected by one's experience at work and vice versa. In other words, the stages of work life are central to, correspond to, and mirror key benchmarks in one's progress through the life course in all its aspects. With this idea in mind, let us briefly consider how age consciousness corresponds to the stages named earlier.

Preparation and Exploration

Human beings, in contrast to other animals, require enormously long periods of nurturing before they are able to set out on their own. Parents are obligated to care for their children's physiological needs for an exceptionally long time compared with other animals. Children can do very little for themselves for a couple of years, and beyond that must be monitored very carefully by their parents for several years. It is not just with regard to physiological development that we are relatively slow in progressing. Our society, like other modern industrial societies, expects persons to seek work as a full-time activity only after they have completed a very long period of schooling. Although many leave before graduating from high school, such "dropping out" is defined as a "problem." Americans consider it desirable to achieve at least a high school education, and in most quarters a college degree. The ante, however, keeps increasing and many occupational positions previously filled by college graduates now require graduate degrees.

The long period of education requisite for many occupational positions creates a situation where a large proportion of the population does not enter the work world in a full-time fashion until their middle twenties and sometimes later. In the case of certain professional careers that demand especially long training processes, persons may not enter the occupational world on a full-time basis until their early to mid-thirties. On average, then, a considerable number of contemporary Americans spend about a third of their life *preparing* for the remaining two-thirds.

The long period of training prior to entering an occupation has a signifiant implication for persons' developing sense of self, including their subjective view of their own age status (White, 1966). Until we have entered an occupation we are not considered as fully occupying an adult status. We might say that the long period of schooling in American society keeps persons in a kind of protracted adolescent "holding pattern." After all, it is through occupational involvement that we acquire the things normally associated with being an adult. Adults have control over their personal lives, and this control is chiefly accomplished by having the economic resources that only a job provides. Those without work do not have the money to shape a life-style and acquire the goods (an automobile, and one's own apartment) that symbolize one's adultness to the world. Certainly part of our conception of being an adult also involves taking on responsibilities. In our society that means the responsibilities of work and family. In the previous chapter we indicated that entering into marriage constitutes an important "rite of passage" into adulthood. This is equally true, we think, of entrance into the work world.

> A set of generalized cultural expectations about the relations of an adult male to the work world operates in our society. . . . At a given age (which varies in different parts of the society) a man is expected to have assumed a particular occupational role. Such adult responsibilities as marriage require him to have made arrangements guaranteeing the financial independence necessary for adulthood by making such an occupational commitment. With increasing age he is expected to behave "sensibly" and stick with such a choice once made, thus demonstrating his maturity. . . (Becker, 1957:207).

The equation between work and one's identity as an adult is learned from a very early age. Can you remember how you felt when you were hired for your first part-time job? The feeling of "growing up" or being treated as a "grown-up" is intimately connected with having a job. Each of the jobs we have held throughout our adolescence and on into college constitutes part of a general socialization process leading eventually to a more enduring occupational choice. Each job we hold becomes a tentative exploration of some aspect of the occupational world. These jobs gradually introduce persons to the world of work and imbue them with the belief that a work identity is one of the most important social identities they must eventually acquire.

Social scientists have always recognized that the transition from adolescence to adulthood is a critical one in any society. Anthropologists, for example, document how a variety of societies mark off this transition. In preliterate societies the transition to adult status, with its new roles, obligations, and rights, may be marked off by such dramatic ceremonies as facial scarring and ritual circumcision. Although certainly less dramatic, one might see the acquisition of a driver's license or graduation from high school as being ritual markers of approaching adulthood. Observers of American culture, however, suggest that, in contrast to "simpler" societies, our definitions of adulthood are often especially confusing and complicated precisely because of the long wait required before one can enter fully into the occupational world. Indeed, our treatment of persons in the society is often deeply contradictory. At certain ages we call persons adults while at the same time withholding many of the concrete rewards of adulthood. Because of the structuring of work in the society, persons are forced to postpone participation in the roles of husband or wife and parent despite their biological and emotional readiness to discharge these roles. Thus "adolescents are cut off from adult roles and relegated to a prolonged preparatory status in which they are no longer children but are not yet adults" (Cloward and Ohlin, 1960:55).

Cloward and Ohlin (1960:55) elaborate further on the dilemmas and contradictions of status created around adulthood in America:

> Although the adolescent is barred from immediate access to adult roles, every effort is made to ensure that he does not relinquish his aspirations for eventual adult status. Even though he is formally deprived of the major rewards of adult status—money, personal autonomy, sexual relations, and the like—he is at the same time imbued with the belief that these are rewards worth having. He is thus led to orient himself toward ends which are not immediately available to him by socially approved means. Despite his aspirations and his physical and emotional readiness, he is forced to remain in a state of social, economic, and legal dependency.

As reported by Cloward and Ohlin, several theories are based on the idea that the frustrations built up under these social conditions may cause deviant behavior among adolescents. The underlying idea of these theories is that the curious half-child, half-adult role experienced by American youth leads them to protest against the adult world. This protest often takes the form of delinquent acitivities, such as boisterous ganging and attacks on property. One might speculate whether the widespread and costly destruction of university property by some students can be at least partially explained in terms of society's denial to students of a full adult role and the consequent frustration they experience.

Many of you reading these lines are in the process of spending at least two years beyond high school, studying in a college. If your current experience is like the authors' past experience, there are probably many times when you *feel* less than an adult. In discussing this issue, your authors discovered that they had the mutual experience of periodically feeling somewhat "childish" during their very long period of schooling. After all, even as we approached thirty years old, we still had never held a "real" job. Perhaps you too have moments when this feeling begins to grow in you and you consider leaving school for the "real world." During those times you might be thinking about getting a job and becoming financially independent of your parents. From the sociological point of view, your feelings of frustration stem from the impatience generated by occupying something less than an adult status for what seems too long.

Social scientists have constructed several models that attempt to describe the process through which individuals come to occupy a particular occupational niche. For example, in an early study based on biographical data from a group of middle-income children, Eli Ginsberg describes a progressive narrowing of their aspirations from a fantasy stage extending between ages six to eleven, to a tentative stage of adolescent vacillation, and then to a stage of realistic choice beyond this point (Ginsberg, 1951). Other sociologists have examined the influence of such specific factors as social class (Blau and Duncan, 1967; Sears, Maccoby and Levine, 1957), peer group influence (Coleman, 1961), and the college experience itself (Jenks and Riesman, 1969) on occupational choice. Whatever the specific processes described in this literature or the variables stressed, the studies describe or imply a process through which the individual achieves adult status. Socially confirmed adulthood, we might say, is the end product of the lengthy process leading up to full entrance into the occupational world.

Learning the Ropes

The process of socialization does not stop in childhood. We are continually learning how to perform correctly the variety of roles that are part of being an adult. Especially in complex and changing societies, ". . .One cannot be socialized in childhood to handle successfully all of the roles he will confront in the future" (Brim and Wheeler, 1966:19). Socialization continues on throughout the life cycle. However, it seems apparent that the socialization we undergo in adulthood is more intense at certain junctures, one of these periods being the early years within the occupation we choose. Whatever work organization persons enter as fresh recruits, they must learn the ropes of that organization. Those who enter certain careers engage in a high measure of "anticipatory socialization" (Merton, 1957), as in the case of medical students who learn throughout medical school how to act as a doctor. Still, once the medical student becomes a doctor, he or she has a great deal to learn about just how to interact with patients, their families, nurses, colleagues, and administrators. They must also learn the specific behavioral demands of the organization (here, the hospital) employing them.

The period of learning the ropes is especially intense for new workers since they are being evaluated by superiors who may have a significant say regarding the course that their careers will take within the organization. One's whole career fate can be influenced by the relationships that one builds or fails to build with superiors. Plainly the question of power comes to the forefront when discussing the early career-building years of workers. New entrants are the least powerful members in the work setting, and they must learn how to manage their subordinate status. As Daniel Levinson (1978) points out, the early career years are likely to be the time during which young workers, particularly in professional occupations, look to older workers as their role models. As Levinson describes it, these older workers, who already know the ropes and are in the positions of power often become mentors who take an interest in, sponsor, and provide advice to the young worker:

> In the usual course, a young man initially experiences himself as a novice or apprentice to a more advanced expert and authoritative adult. As the relationship evolves, he gains a fuller sense of his own authority and his capability for autonomous, responsible action. The balance of giving/receiving becomes more equal. The younger man increasingly has the experience of "I am" as an adult, and their relationship becomes more mutual. This shift serves a crucial development function for the young man: it is part of the process by which he transcends the father–son, man–boy division of his childhood. Although he is officially defined as an adult at 18 or 21, and desperately wants to be one, it may take years to overcome the sense of being a son or a boy in relation to "real" adults (Levinson, 1978:99-100).

Much is going on for the individual during these early years of his or her work life. Most primarily, the effect of the work socialization at this career point is to increase the young worker's *identification* with and *commitment* to the occupational choice made. Gradually, the "junior" member of the work organization identifies more strongly with his or her work. This increased identification results from growing pride in the acquisition of new occupational skills, the progressive development of an occupational ideology, the sponsorship of older members of the occupation, and, through interaction with others on the job, the internalization of specific motives for engaging in the occupation's work (Becker, 1956). Young workers also acquire occupational titles that secure their place in the larger society and provide them a concrete way of defining their work identity to themselves and to others. Now, for the first time, the new entrants into the occupational world, equipped with the title bestowed upon them by the work organization, are able easily to provide an answer to queries about their occupational identity. Through commitment to a line of work persons simultaneously become committed to particular identities.

As Howard Becker (1956, 1960) describes it, initial entry into a particular occupation or organizational structure sets an "investment" mechanism going. Once persons "cue themselves into" and embark upon the career ladder provided by their work organization, they become progressively more committed to the route they have taken. The further along the career route they travel, the more difficult will they find it to "start over." Becker points out, however, that commitment to a line of work and to an associated occupational identity is not necessarily made in a conscious and deliberate way. Although some commitments are based on quite rational decisions, others are built up more slowly and unself-consciously. To use Becker's term, we often become committed through a series of "side bets"; that is, through a series of behaviors that seem peripheral to the main line of our activity, e.g. putting money into a pension fund is a side bet. According to this theory, commitment "arises through a series of acts no one of which is crucial but which, taken together, constitute for the actor a series of side bets of such magnitude that he finds himself unwilling to lose them. Each of the trivial acts in such a series is, so to speak, a small brick in a wall which eventually grows to such a height the person can no longer climb it" (Becker; 1960:270).

The complexity of the socialization process occurring during the early years of the career process is a substantial topic by itself. Suffice it to say that early career years constitute a period of intense involvement during which the young worker is actively building a life structure. In terms of our interest in this chapter, it is a period during which one is made to feel "youthful." Having acquired an occupational identity the person is accorded the deference associated with adult status in the larger society. Still, within the work context, being only on the first rungs of the career ladder, one is "the young man or woman" from the point of view of the older workers in the organization. An analogy here might be to the way children perceive their age status in school. The sixth grader who is the oldest in his school is responded to that way by younger children in the school. However, once the student enters junior high school and steps onto the first rung of this new ladder, he or she is pushed back, as it were, into the age status of the "youngest." During the years in which workers are learning the ropes, establishing a work identity and becoming committed, they are considered by others and by themselves as novices, apprentices, junior members of the organization, and so on. Such definitions contribute to an age consciousness of oneself as "young."

In a social–psychological sense, age consciousness is significantly related to one's image of both the past and the future. The consciousness of the young worker we are describing at this point in the career route is exclusively on the *future*. These people are busy building their lives. They sense themselves at the beginning of a journey, the work journey, and are in the process of making and exercising their opportunities. They are still very much creating themselves, still "becoming" something. Theirs is a life trajectory that seems very much at its beginning and which they view as extending far into the future. The sense of change, movement, vitality, growth, and the emphasis on building for the future contributes to a sense of just "starting out," to a youthful self-perception.

A turning point or transition in one's aging consciousness, the point at which one begins to "feel older," corresponds to that juncture in the work career when the basic structure of one's life has been established. It is the point when one has an occupational past to look back upon and when the general parameters of one's future work growth have been determined. Toward the middle of their career, persons develop a clearer sense of what they have, in fact, become. Now they are no longer the youngest members of their respective work organizations. They are no longer learning the ropes. Instead, they are probably teaching the ropes to the new recruits. They are no longer advice seekers, but advice givers. At this point workers must assess, interpret, and evaluate their career successes and failures. We are not suggesting here that persons stop experiencing work growth and change in their middle years (although some do), but that in their mid-life years workers acquire a clearer vision of the occupational identity they have created and must come to grips with that vision.

Coming to Grips

Every five years the members of each graduating class at Harvard College are asked to describe briefly what their lives have been like during the preceeding five years. The responses of the class members are then collated into a book that makes fascinating reading and is a potentially valuable data source for examining changes in self-perception over the life course. In a recent issue reporting on a class that had been out of college for twenty years, one alumnus elegantly summed up what a number of his classmates intimated in their comments when he said that "the *anticipation* of his life had been superseded by its *actuality*." By this he meant that he had substantially built his life and now had to face that fact. By the age of forty or so, workers have reached an occupational plateau. Whatever might have been their private dreams, aspirations, or fantasies, they must now acknowledge the realities of their occupational positions.

By mid-life the lawyers who are partners in a small law firm know that they will never be supreme court justices; doctors in private practice know that they will not be renowned surgeons; academics with a few publications know that their names will not be recognized by the vast proportion of colleagues in their field; factory workers on the line know that they will not become supervisors; supervisors of several years know that they will never wear a business suit to work. However far persons have advanced in their occupations, they pretty well know, by mid-life, how much change they can realistically expect throughout the remainder of their work careers. Certainly some new opportunities will arise, some alterations in work tasks can be anticipated, and there will still be regular increments in salary and status. However, the central parameters and basic form of one's occupational life will have been established. As a result, many are, for the first time, sharply awakened to their own aging:

> When I hit 40, it was really a traumatic experience. As long as I was in my thirties, I visualized myself as a kid. When I hit 40, I really felt that. I'd

always viewed myself as a young guy who is doing pretty well, a young
guy on his way up, and all of a sudden, I am not a young guy anymore. I
cannot do things I once did. It's kind of scary (Levinson, 1978:170).

In much of the developmental literature on aging it is currently
fashionable to describe the so-called mid-life crisis. In fact, the idea
of a mid-life crisis, as popularized in books such as Gail Sheehy's
Passages, has now become part of the public's everyday image of the
mid-life period. It is hard to attend a party composed of persons approaching or experiencing their mid-life years without hearing some
reference, often in a joking fashion, to the mid-life crisis. We suspect
that the existence of the mid-life crisis idea, newly minted in the
psychological literature, provides those in their early forties a way of
interpreting any bad feelings they may be having. The notion of a
mid-life crisis may provide others with *ex post facto* justifications and
explanations for such behaviors as extramarital affairs and excessive
drinking. Of course, many persons in their mid-years do experience
severe psychological crises in their lives. However, as we indicated
in Chapters 1 and 3, our interactionist perspective makes us wary of
any view of human behavior postulating rigidly uniform human experiences. While we question the *inevitability* of crisis in mid-life, we
would imagine that, at mid-life, all but the most unreflective persons
must think about the congruence between what they hoped their
lives would be like and the reality of their lives.

Earlier in this chapter we provided data from Faulkner's study of
hockey players and musicians who were forced to recognize their
limited chances for career mobility. Data from other occupational
contexts indicate that workers at all occupational levels must
redefine their goals during the mid-life period. A classic sociological
study describing how blue-collar workers create and are forced to
redefine their occupational ambitions is Ely Chinoy's (1955) study
entitled "The Automobile Worker and the American Dream." The
automobile workers investigated by Chinoy deeply believed in the
American dream of occupational advancement and success. For
them, success was defined as eventually leaving the factory and
becoming independent entrepreneurs. However, Chinoy's story is
one describing how the workers come eventually to abandon hope in
the dream. Over and over, he heard the words of those who, by age
thirty-five, had relinquished plans for leaving the auto plant and had
surrendered the dream. Their psychology is summed up by the

worker who told Chinoy, "I've got a family and I can't take chances."

As they get older and pass into their forties, most of the men accept the fact that they will remain in the plant for the rest of their working lives. At this point, the focus of the workers turns to the steady pay that the job provides and their growing seniority. Ambitions to leave the plant are replaced by security goals. The central life satisfactions of the worker now come from outside the factory. Their families, their homes, their vacations, and their hopes for their children become the focus of their emotional investments.

One of the most poignant statements in American literature on the connection between work and aging is found in Arthur Miller's play entitled *Death of a Salesman*. The main character, Willy Loman, has tried his whole life to "make the grade" as a salesman and, at age sixty, finds himself a relative failure, about to be "let go" by his former boss' son. At one point the son, Howard, is impatiently trying to get Willy to leave his office, and they have these words: "Howard, *starting to go off*: I've got to see some people, kid. Willy, *stopping him*: I'm talking about your father! There were promises made across this desk! You mustn't tell me you've got people to see. I put thirty-four years into this firm, Howard, and now I can't pay my insurance! You can't eat the orange and throw the peel away — a man is not a piece of fruit!" (Miller, 1949:82). *Death of a Salesman* is not, though, just about Willy's pain. Part of Willy's response to his own occupational condition is to expect great accomplishments from his son, Biff. The problem is that Biff is not living up to Willy's expectations. At one point, Biff has a conversation with his brother Happy who, although two years younger, has succeeded at carving out a career. The following dialogue between the two brothers describes the confusion and psychic difficulty that can arise around attempts to come to grips with definitions of work success and failure. The conversation begins as Biff openly acknowledges personal confusion about his chaotic work career:

> **Biff:** I tell ya, Hap, I don't know what the future is. I don't know what I'm supposed to want.
> **Happy:** What do you mean?
> **Biff:** Well, I spent six or seven years after high school trying to work myself up. Shipping clerk, salesman, business of one kind or another. And it's a measly manner of existence. To get on that subway on the hot mornings in summer. To devote your whole life to keeping stock, or making phone calls, or selling or buying. To suffer fifty weeks of the year for the

sake of a two-week vacation, when all you really desire is to be outdoors, with your shirt off. And always to have to get ahead of the next fella. And still—that's how you build a future.

Happy: Well, you really enjoy it on a farm? Are you content out there?

Biff, *with rising agitation*: Hap, I've had twenty or thirty different kinds of jobs since I left home before the war, and it always turns out the same. I just realized it lately. In Nebraska when I herded cattle, and the Dakotas, and Arizona, and now in Texas. It's why I came home now, I guess, because I realize it. This farm I work on, it's spring there now, see? And they've got about fifteen new colts. There's nothing more inspiring or—beautiful than the sight of a mare and a new colt. And it's cool there now, see? Texas is cool now, and it's spring. And whenever spring comes to where I am, I suddenly get the feeling, my God, I'm not gettin' anywhere! What the hell am I doing, playing around with horses, twenty-eight dollars a week! I'm thirty-four years old, I oughta be makin' my future. That's when I come running home. And now, I get here, and I don't know what to do with myself. *After a pause*: I've always made a point of not wasting my life, and everytime I come back here I know that all I've done is to waste my life.

Happy: You're a poet, you know that Biff? You're a—you're an idealist!

Biff: No, I'm mixed up very bad. Maybe I oughta get married. Maybe I oughta get stuck into something. Maybe that's my trouble. I'm like a boy. I'm not married, I'm not in business, I just—I'm like a boy. Are you content, Hap? You're a success, aren't you? Are you content?

Happy: Hell, no!

Biff: Why? You're making money, aren't you?

Happy, *moving about with energy, expressiveness*: All I can do now is wait for the merchandise manager to die. And suppose I get to be merchandise manager? He's a good friend of mine, and he just built a terrific estate on Long Island. And he lived there about two months and sold it, and now he's building another one. He can't enjoy it once it's finished. And I know that's just what I would do. I don't know what the hell I'm workin' for. Sometimes I sit in my apartment—all alone. And I think of the rent I'm paying. And it's crazy. But then, it's what I always wanted. My own apartment, a car and plenty of women. And still, goddammit, I'm lonely (Miller, 1949:22-23).

The conversation between Biff and Happy is particularly instructive because it calls our attention to the fact that even those who are defined as successful by others at mid-life are not immune from mental stress. We might think, by common sense standards, that the Biffs of our world or Chinoy's factory workers, who are near the bottom of the American work structure, will experience greatest mid-life distress. In his provocative book entitled *Work, Aging, and Social Change*, Seymour Sarason (1977) compellingly argues that the mid-life "crash," when it occurs, is likely to be most dramatically felt precisely among those defined as most occupationally successful in the society. Sarason points out that while surveys of work satisfaction have always reported professionals as most satisfied with their work, these statistics may be misleading. It is difficult to square such claims of high satisfaction with relatively high rates of suicide, drug addiction, alcoholism, and divorce among professional persons. Professionals who are defined by others as involved in an endlessly fascinating and rewarding line of endeavor find it hard to admit, even to themselves, anything other than high satisfaction.

We should note that data on work satisfaction are normally collected via survey research techniques which rely on fixed-choice questions. There is good reason to believe that this methodology may not elicit frank, candid answers about work, especially from professionals. As interactionists, we prefer methodologies such as *in-depth* interviewing. Such interviews, we should note here, do present the researcher with problems of representativeness and generalizability to other settings, issues that are less problematic for survey researchers. Nevertheless, intensive interviewing does offer the opportunity to probe respondents on sensitive matters such as the meanings they attach to their work and thus maximizes the likelihood of hearing honest self reports. Talking in-depth with a number of doctors, Sarason uncovered a deep well of disillusionment; disillusionment that remains hidden in attitude surveys.

We have been describing the mid-life period as one in which persons are forced to evaluate the disparity between the expectations they have at the outset of their work life and the actual state of their occupational experience at age forty or so. Let's consider for a moment the kind of consciousness with which the physicians interviewed, approached their middle years. First, we must realize that those who become doctors have typically begun anticipating and preparing for that career at a very early age (Hall, 1948). Throughout all of their schooling prospective doctors hear cultural messages telling them that all their extensive training is worth it because once they are doctors they will daily be doing work that is enormously self-satisfying, important, challenging, and always novel and interesting. Theirs will be the very best work that the society has to offer. This is a theme that is constantly reinforced and reaffirmed throughout college, premed programs, and medical school. Through communication with faculty members and fellow students, the belief is sustained that medicine is the best of all professions, that after leaving medical school one's personal and occupational growth would be unending. As reported in a landmark study of the medical school experience entitled *Boys in White* (1961), this belief is evident in the words of students themselves: "I think all of life is a stairway and I hope there will never be anytime when you come out on any platform at the top. I like to think that we could always look upward and never have to look down" (Becker et al., 1961:73). In short, doctors, like other highly trained professionals, begin their work lives with great expectations.

Once Sarason got mid-life physicians to talk candidly with him about their jobs, he learned that many physicians are puzzled by the fact that their lives simply are not working out as they planned. They find much of their work routine and even boring; they feel hemmed in by government regulations, and face a public that is ever more frequently questioning the autonomy of physicians. Many feel that something has gone awry and that they are on a treadmill that, albeit a well-paid treadmill, is nevertheless a treadmill. Precisely because of the very high aspirations with which these doctors began their careers, these professionals experience a particularly intense sense of disenchantment. It is a sense of disenchantment that requires them to give special and extensive attention to the question, "Is it all worthwhile?"

Certainly it is not our intention to picture all mid-life professionals as unhappily grappling with questions of work meaning and satisfaction. However, we agree with Sarason that we need more data on how "successful" people *really* experience their work. Studies of lawyers, professors, and other professionals might reveal similar patterns of disenchantment. More broadly, data presented on the last few pages indicate that workers at all levels of the occupational structure, from factory workers to physicians, must come to grips with the life structure they have built by mid-life.

...Mid-life is a confrontation between myth and reality. It is more like a war in which many battles or skirmishes are being fought. Death starts to take away parents, colleagues, friends, and loved ones. Marriage may become imprisonment. Children may not "turn out well" or they will leave for distant places, leaving emotional vacuums. And, of course, one begins to reevaluate whether one wants the future of one's career to be a continuation of its past, and in that battle is the question: What are my alternatives? (Sarason, 1977:105).

Settling in

Most of the available literature on work describes career experience through the mid-life period. There is, however, a paucity of research on the experience of work during the decade or so following the mid-life period. We know very little about the way workers aged forty-five to fifty-five define themselves and their occupational lives up to the point when they begin to think of retirement. For some these might be the "glory years" when they are at the height of their personal power and influence. Following Levinson (1978), this may be a period during which workers become mentors for younger workers. For still others, these years may vary little from the experience of work in preceding years. Existent data suggest contrary lines of argument. One body of data reviewed by Glenn (1980) in a recent article suggests that work satisfaction increases with age, "that workers tend to become more satisfied with work as they grow older, probably because job changes eventually result in a better fit between workers and jobs" (1980:628). Glenn concludes his view of the work satisfaction literature, however, with the caveat that the relationship between work satisfaction and aging may not be a function of aging per se, but rather a result of "composite effects' that "may result from movements of different kinds of persons into and out of the labor force within birth cohorts as aging occurs" (1980:629). Given the uncertain state of research on the relationship between work satisfaction and aging, we will develop an alternative argument based on available data that during the ages of forty-five to fifty-five many workers reevaluate how they will distribute their energies among work, leisure, and other spheres of their lives.

As we might expect, much of the research on the meaning and use of leisure time activity is concerned with questions of work alienation. This literature presumes that the things persons choose to do in their free time relate to their work experience. One theory, for example, holds that leisure activities have the function of *compensating* for what persons find absent in their work lives. Thus people whose work is undemanding, repetitive, and unrewarding build up a reservoir of dissatisfaction that often results in violent reactions during nonwork time: excessive drinking, aggressive behavior on the roads, and the like. A second theory holds that persons who find their work lives empty will compensate for this degradation by an obsessive leisure time preoccupation with *consumption*. Still another theory has it that leisure activity is a carry over from work activity. So, workers who have little autonomy, interest, and control at work retreat into passive leisure time activities such as television viewing. While there is much debate about the relative validity of the three theories we have briefly described (*see* Bacon, 1976; Kelley, 1976), they are all based on the assumed connection between work satisfaction and the nature of persons' nonwork involvements.

Now, consider the logic that persuades us that workers rearrange their commitments to work and other life spheres during middle to late adulthood? We begin with the assumption that decreases in work satisfaction will lead to the search for satisfactions outside of work. While we must be wary of variations that remain hidden in any aggregate data, such as social class, ethnic, and occupational level differences, there is evidence that work satisfaction does regularly decrease with age. In a recent article, Richard Cohn (1979) demonstrates a decline in intrinsic work satisfaction during the later stages of work force participation. As part of his own analysis, Cohn presents data on work satisfaction from two earlier studies, one done in 1953 and the other in 1971. The comparison provided in Table 4-I below shows (1) a general decline in work satisfaction between 1953 and 1971 and (2) a systematic decline in each successive age group.

At the same time that work satisfaction decreases, as shown in Table 4-I, there is a corresponding increase in rates of participation in social and political activities (Smith, 1980). Persons in the middle-age range have higher rates of voluntary action participation than younger or older persons (Verba and Nie, 1972; Curtis, 1971; Hallenstveldt, 1974). In his book *Participation in Social and Political Activity* David Smith (1981) also shows that with age there is a gradual increase in virtually all spheres of leisure activity. Even when researchers control for gender and social class, there is a regular and uninterrupted increase in such leisure time activities as participation in cultural activities, movie going, and reading. Not surprising, the only leisure activities for which there is a decrease with age are those involving rigorous physical activity. Most important for us is the finding that the increased leisure activity we have been describing *peaks* during the decade following mid-life (45-55).

Table 4-I Percent Who Would Continue to Work if There
Were No Financial Necessity, by Age of Worker
(Currently Employed Males)

	Study	
	Morse & Weiss[a]	Campbell, Converse & Rodgers[b]
	1953 (N = 354)	1971 (N = 652)
Age Group	%	%
21-34	90	82
35-44	83	81
45-54	72	68
55-64	61	57
Total	80	75

[a]"If by some chance you inherited enough money to live comfortably
without working, do you think you would work anyway or not?"

[b]"If you were to get enough money to live as comfortably as you'd
like for the rest of your life, would you continue to work?"

We should repeat the caveat that the argument we are presently offering needs refinement. We should like to know more about the relative degree to which members of different occupational groups rearrange their priorities during the forty-five to fifty-five life cycle period. It should follow from the general perspective outlined above that the greatest redistribution of activity from work to nonwork settings will occur in those sectors of the occupational world where dissatisfaction is highest. Chinoy's research on auto workers, reported earlier, indicates that after mid-life these blue-collar workers begin a rather extensive disengagement from work. At the other end of the occupational continuum, we might predict that professional workers on the whole will also invest less energy in work than previously, but that the change will be relatively slight. In other words, it would be instructive to see precisely the associations between work level, work satisfaction, and the nature of changed commitments to different life sectors.

Before we leave this topic we should make mention of a body of literature that may help to explain the nature of the interaction between work and family life during the decade following mid-life. In recent years a number of observers, e.g. Oppenheimer, 1978; Estes and Wilensky, 1978, have described the effects of what they term the "life cycle squeeze." The "squeeze" arises from the situation where a man's resources are inadequate to meet the needs engendered by the number and ages of his children. Studies of how economic needs vary by family life cycle state indicate that an exceptional high point of need occurs when men are in their forties and early fifties. Further, the squeeze, as you might expect, is greatest for blue-collar and lower level white-collar jobs. At these occupational levels, median earnings are highest for younger men. Their income during the later years when their children may be entering college, for instance, does not correspond to their needs. Alternatively, those with relatively high paying professional, managerial, or sales occupations are more insulated from this life cycle squeeze. Based on a sample of 230 professional workers, Estes and Wilensky (1978) describe the interrelationships between family life cycle, one's financial condition, and personal morale. You should note in the figure below that the decline in morale begins in the late forties and typically reaches its low point in the mid-fifties.

In the last few pages we have tried to piece together existing data that reflect the nature of the work/family/leisure experience of workers during the ten to fifteen years after they come to grips with their occupational position. Although we report that curiously little is known about this period in the life cycle, the data persuade us that much is happening; that it is a period posing its own unique problems and struggles for individuals. Perhaps the notion of the life cycle squeeze is an important connecting link between family life, work satisfaction at different occupational levels, and the way persons redistribute interests and energies during their middle forties to late fifties.

Exiting

When the work world has been discussed in the gerontology literature, the focus has been most primarily on the nature and consequences of retirement. Social scientists have compiled an enormous amount of data on such topics as the relationship between demographic changes and mandatory retirement policies (Cowgill, 1974; Riley, Johnson, and Foner, 1972), the extent to which persons view retirement favorably or unfavorably (Katona, 1965; Riley and

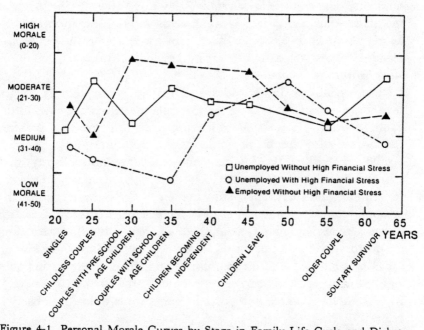

Figure 4-1. Personal Morale Curves by Stage in Family Life Cycle and Dichotomous Level of Financial Stress. From Richard Estes and Harold Wilensky, Life cycle squeeze and moral curve, *Social Problems*, 25:286, February, 1978. Reprinted by permission.

Foner, 1968; Atchley, 1971), how retirement decisions are made (Barfield and Morgan, 1969; Palmore, 1964), the nature of the retirement process itself (Atchley, 1976), whether or not a retirement role exists (Rosow, 1974), and the effects of retirement on personal adaptation (Thompson, Streib, and Kosa, 1960; Streib and Schneider, 1971). As you might expect by now, the literature shows substantial variability in the meanings persons attach to leaving the work world.

As indicated in the first chapter of this book, we should not be dismayed by differences in the way that individuals approach the end of their work lives. Some workers, apparently increasing in numbers, look forward to early retirement, while others wish to maintain their occupational positions as long as possible. Not surprisingly, individuals' attitudes toward retirement are closely linked to their economic situations. The greatest proportion of persons with favorable attitudes toward retirement is in those groups assured adequate incomes in their later years (Riley and Foner, 1968). Also, as might be expected, there is an inverse relationship between the degree to which persons find their jobs intrinsically rewarding and meaningful and the extent to which they look forward to leaving the work world.

The variability in attitudes and responses of workers to approaching retirement reflects the multiple meanings attached to the value of work. The process of leaving work will carry quite different meanings to persons depending upon the values, attitudes, and symbol systems of those with whom they are normally in communication. There can be little doubt that the attitudes held toward retirement, and the preparations made for it, are influenced by the symbolic contents and cultures in which retirements take place. Early retirement among physicians, for example, is quite rare, and for doctors to do so may well be viewed as "deviant." As Harold Orbach (1969) reports, on the other hand, there is increasing subcultural support for early retirement among auto workers. Robert Atchley shares our point of view in his following observation:

> Attitudes of friends and family also probably play an important role in the retirement decision. One man's children want him to retire, another's do not. One woman's husband wants her to retire, another's does not. One man lives in a neighborhood where retirement is sneered at, another lives in a leisure community where retirement is the rule rather than the exception. If we retire, then the characteristics that our friends and family impute to retired people will be imputed to us. All of these factors may encourage or discourage retirement, but they are almost sure to have an influence (Atchley, 1976:45).

Despite the wide range of studies we have cited dealing with numerous features of the retirement process, we still "know very little about the complexity of the retirement transition *as it is experienced by individuals*" (Ward, 1979:203, italics added). More precisely, researchers have not studied how the anticipation of leaving work and the actual event of retirement, as a rite of passage, influences persons' sense of age. As interactionists, we wish to know how leaving the work force makes one *feel* about his or her aging. Although this is a matter for empirical research, we speculate that, like becoming grandparents, leaving the work force constitutes a significant transition to old age.

Whether workers have enjoyed their jobs or found them alienating, they mutually face a range of cultural definitions associating work, retirement, and age. First, since persons are often required to retire at a particular age (usually 65 years old), their attention is dramatically called to age by that concrete fact alone. Probably more critical to older persons' sense of age, however, is the recognition that, regardless of their physical and mental conditions, they must leave their jobs to make room for *younger* workers. In short, during the years immediately preceding retirement, workers hear a chorus of associates defining them as approaching too old an age to continue working. In addition, older workers face the stereotyped images of many younger workers that they suffer from declining performance because of poor health and intellectual failings. Although evidence does not at all support such stereotypes (Meier and Kerr, 1976), their existence nevertheless constitutes a social fact that influences interaction between older and younger workers, and so the aging conceptions of both.

In his frequently cited model of the retirement process, Robert Atchley describes a *preretirement period* that includes "a *remote* phase in which retirement is seen by the individual as a vaguely positive something that will happen someday, and a *near* phase, in which individuals orient themselves toward a specific retirement date" (Atchley, 1977:154). As he describes it, the far phase may begin at the outset of the work career since even then there is the realization that one will someday leave the work force. We would, however, be most interested in learning just when the near phase begins for persons in different occupations and at different occupational levels. Many workers probably develop an "exiting consciousness" several years prior to actual retirement. It is, we presume, a consciousness forged by subtle changes in the way they are viewed by younger workers as they enter the later years of their working lives. In response, they may adopt a "short timer's attitude" that includes fantasies about and preparation for their approaching retirement. The specific manner in which an exiting consciousness is constructed and impacts on workers' subjective aging conceptions should be a concern of future inquiry.

CONCLUSION

This chapter began with the somewhat obvious assertion that the work we do is central to our developing identities, including our aging identities. From that base, our effort has been to elaborate more precisely on the way work shapes our sense of age. Central to our analysis has been the concept of *career*. Because careers are typically age-graded in a highly structured way, they serve as constant reminders of where we stand in the life course more broadly. Careers frame our expectations about what we should be doing at different points in our lives and become, for that reason, a yardstick against which we measure our life progress, interpet the past, and anticipate the future. Aside from showing the overall significance of work to the way we experience the passage of time, the reader should now appreciate the mutually transformative character of our work and nonwork lives.

Since we have repeatedly claimed the importance of an ongoing, processual view of aging that relates our age perceptions at any given point to earlier constructed meanings, we examined the work-aging relationship over the whole life cycle. Thus, we proposed five generic career stages that help us to understand regularities across occupational levels in the way individuals subjectively respond to the work experience. We have tried to demonstrate how each of the work-life periods named corresponds to and fashions a distinctive aging consciousness.

Our entrance into the occupational world makes us feel like adults. During the early years of our work lives we are made to feel youthful in comparison to older workers from whom we learn the ropes of our respective jobs. During the middle years of our lives we must come to grips with the discrepancies between our earlier dreams, aspirations, and fantasies and the reality of what we have "become" occupationally. Many of the problems and "crises" of middle age relate to confrontations between myth and reality. We proposed that the decade roughly following mid-life is a period during which workers reevaluate how they will distribute their energies between work and nonwork aspects of their lives. Last, we reviewed literature suggesting how the anticipation and experience of retirement may constitute an important transition to old age.

Along the way, we acknowledged an important limitation of the available literature on work. It describes nearly exclusively the experience of men. We expect that social researchers will have a great deal to say in coming years about the work experiences of women who are increasingly following work careers previously restricted to men. Based on our discussion in this chapter, we imagine that women's expanded participation in the work force will greatly alter their experience of aging. In the following chapter we will draw on the body of literature in the social sciences that has been most thoroughly attentive to the life worlds of women. Using research on sex roles, Chapter 5 will consider similarities and differences in the ways that men and women age.

REFERENCES

Atchley, R.: *The Sociology of Retirement.* New York, John Wiley, 1976.

Atchley, R.: *The Social Forces In Later Life*, CA, Wadsworth Publishing Co., 1977.

Bacon, A.: Research perspectives on work and leisure. *Journal of Leisure Research, 8*: 131-134, 1976.

Barfield, R., and Morgan, J.: *Early Retirement: The Decision and the Experience.* MI, University of Michigan, Institute of Social Research, 1969.

Becker, H., and Carper, J.: The elements of identification with an occupation. *American Journal of Sociology, 21*:341-348, 1956.

Becker, H., and Strauss, A.: Careers, personality, and adult socialization. *American Journal of Sociology, 62*:253-263, 1956.

Becker H., and Carper, J.: Adjusting of conflicting expectation in the development of identification with an occupation. *Social Forces, 36*:51-56, 1957.

Becker, H.: Notes on the concept of commitment. *American Journal of Sociology, 66*: 32-40, 1960.

Becker, H., et al.: *Boys In White.* Chicago, University of Chicago Press, 1961.

Becker, H.: Personal change in adult life. *Sociometry, 27*:40-53, 1964.

Becker, H.: *Sociological Work: Method and Substance.* Chicago, Aldine, 1970.

Blau, P., and O. Duncan: *The American Occupational Structure.* New York, John Wiley, 1967.

Brim, O., and Wheeler, S.: *Socialization After Childhood.* New York, John Wiley, 1966.

Cain, L.: Life course and social structure. In R. Farris (Ed.): *Handbook of Modern Sociology.* Chicago, Rand McNally, 1964.

Chinoy, E.: *The Automobile Worker and The American Dream.* New York, Random House, 1955.

Cloward, R., and Ohlin, L.: *Delinquency and Opportunity.* New York, The Free Press, 1960.

Cohn, R.: The effect of employment status change on self-attitudes. *Social Psychology, 41*:81-93, 1978.

Cohn, R.: Age and the satisfaction from work. *Journal of Gerontology, 34*:264-272, 1979.

Coleman, J.: *Adolescent Society.* New York, The Free Press, 1961.

Coles, R.: Work and self respect. In E. Erikson (Ed.): *Adulthood.* New York, W.W.

Norton and Co., 1978.

Cowgill, D.: Aging and modernization: A revision of the theory. In J. Gubrium (Ed.) *Late Life: Communities and Policies*. Springfield, IL, Charles C Thomas, 1974.

Curtis, J.: Voluntary association joining: A cross-national comparative note. *American Sociological Review*, 36:872-880, 1971.

Dalton, M.: Informal factors in career achievement. *The American Journal of Sociology*, March:407-415, 1951.

Davis, J.: *General Social Surveys, 1972-1980; Cumulative Codebook*. Chicago, National Opinion Research Center, 1980.

Estes, R., and Wilensky, H.: Life cycle squeeze and the morale curve. *Social Problems*, 25:278-292, 1978.

Faulkner, R.: Coming of age in organizations. *Sociology of Work and Occupations, 1*: 131-174, 1974.

Ginsberg, E., et al.: *Occupational Choice: An Approach to a General Theory*. New York, Columbia University Press, 1951.

Glenn, N.: Values, attitudes, and beliefs. In O. Brim and J. Kagan (Eds.): *Constancy and Change in Human Development*. Cambridge, MA, Harvard University Press, 1980.

Gross, E.: *Work and Society*. New York, Crowell, 1958.

Gubrium, J., and Buckholdt, D.: *Toward Maturity*. San Francisco, Jossey-Bass, 1977.

Hall, O.: The stages of a medical career. *American Journal of Sociology, 53*:327-336, 1948.

Hallenstveldt, A.: Formal voluntary associations in Norway. In D. Smith (Ed.): *Voluntary Action Research, 1974*. MA, Lexington Books, 1974.

Holmstrom, L.: *The Two-Career Family*. MA, Schenkman, 1972.

Hughes, E.: *Men and Their Work*. New York, Free Press, 1958.

Jacques, E.: Equitable payment. Quoted in *Work In America*. Cambridge, MA, The MIT Press, 1973.

Jenks, C., and Riesman, D.: *Equality of Educational Opportunity*, 1969.

Kahl, J.: *The American Class Structure*. New York, Holt, Rinehart and Winston, 1957.

Katona, G.: *Private Pensions and Individual Savings*. MI, University of Michigan, Survey Research Center, 1965.

Kelley, J: Research perspectives on work and leisure: A reply to a critique of leisure and the alienated worker. *Journal of Leisure Research, 8*:129-131, 1976.

Levinson, D.: *The Seasons of A Man's Life*. New York, Knopf, 1978.

Liebow, E.: *Tally's Corner*. Boston, Little, Brown and Co., 1967.

Meier, E., and Kerr, E.: Capabilities of middle-aged and older workers: A survey of the literature. *Industrial Gerontology, 3*:147-156, 1976.

Merton, R.: *Social Theory and Social Structure*. New York, The Free Press, 1957.

Miller, A.: *Death of a Salesman*. New York, Viking Press, 1949.

Morse, N. and Weiss, R.: The function and meaning of work and the job. *American Sociological Review*, April:191-198, 1955.

Oppenheimer, V.: The life-cycle squeeze: The interaction of men's occupational and family life cycles. *Demography, 11*:227-245, 1974.

Orbach, H.: Social and institutional aspects of industrial workers' retirement patterns. In *Occasional Papers In Gerontology, No. 4*. MI, University of Michigan—Wayne State University Institute of Gerontology, 1969.

Packard, V.: *A Nation of Strangers*. New York, David McKay Co., 1972.

Palmore, E.: Retirement patterns among aged men. *Social Security Bulletin, 27*:3-10, 1964.

Reif, F., and Strauss, A.: The impact of rapid discovery upon the scientist's career. *Social Problems, 9*:213-221, 1965.

Riley, M., and Foner, A.: *Aging and Society. Volume I. An Inventory of Research Findings*. New York, Russell Sage, 1968.

Riley, M., Johnson, M., and Foner, A. *Aging and Society. Volume 3. A Sociology of Age Stratification*. New York, Russell Sage, 1972.

Rosow, I.: *Socialization to Old Age*. Berkeley, University of California Press, 1974.

Rubin, L.: *Worlds of Pain*. New York, Harper and Row, 1976.

Rubin, L.: *Women of a Certain Age*. New York, Harper and Row, 1979.

Sarason, S.: *Work, Aging, and Social Change*. New York, The Free Press, 1977.

Sennett, R., and Cobb, J.: *The Hidden Injuries of Class*. New York, Random House, 1973.

Slocum, W.: *Occupational Careers*. Chicago, Aldine, 1966.

Smigel, E.: *The Wall Street Lawyer*. New York, The Free Press, 1964.

Smith, D.: *Participation in Social and Political Activity*. San Francisco, Jossey-Bass, 1981.

Sofer, C.: *Men in Mid-Career: A Study of British Managers and Technical Specialists*. Cambridge, England, The Cambridge University Press, 1970.

Strauss, A.: *Negotiations*. San Francisco, Jossey-Bass, 1978.

Streib, G., and Schneider, C.: *Retirement In American Society*. New York, Cornell University Press, 1971.

Thompson, W., Streib, G., and Kosa, J.: The effect of retirement on personal adjustment: A panel analysis. *Journal of Gerontology, 15*:165-169, 1960.

Tiffany, D., et al.: *The Unemployed: A Social Psychological Portrait*. New Jersey, Prentice-Hall, 1970.

Troll, L., and Turner, J.: Overcoming age-sex discrimination. In *Women in Midlife—Security and Fulfillment*. U.S. Government Printing Office, 1978.

Verba, S., and Nie, N.: *Participation In America: Political Democracy and Social Equality*. New York, Harper and Row, 1972.

Ward, R.: *The Aging Experience*. New York, Harper and Row, 1979.

Weinberg, S., and Arond, H.: The occupational culture of the boxer. *American Journal of Sociology, 57*:460-469, 1952.

White, R.: *Lives in Progress*. New York, Holt, Rinehart and Winston, 1966.

Whyte, W.H.: *The Organization Man*. New York, Simon and Schuster, 1956.

Chapter 5

MEN, WOMEN, AND LIFE CYCLES

A JOKE currently making the rounds asks "What's 10, 9, 8, 7, 6, 5, 4, 3, 2, 1?" The answer is: "Bo Derek aging." Bo Derek, for those who may not recognize the name, is the instant female star of a recent movie, "10." It is the story of a middle-aged man who, seeing the dream woman of his fantasies, a perfect 10 on a rating scale from 1 to 10, stops at nothing in his efforts to win her. This joke, we sadly note, illustrates what Susan Sontag (1972) has called the "double standard of aging." That is to say, women lose "value" as they age because of the declining "worth" of their physical appearance, whereas men, through their success at work, can gain in status as they age. She argues that women in the Western world are victimized by being evaluated in terms of only *one* standard of beauty — that of a young woman. Standards of appearance for men, on the other hand, change as they get older, with the term *distinguished looking* used to describe successful older men.

In this chapter we will discuss the different life curves of men and women. We examine how early childhood socialization experiences create a world of male and female identities, beginning literally at birth. The early shaping of the self as a social object continues throughout the life cycle, and the ways in which men and women experience their passages through various age categories significantly affects their subjective senses of aging.

SEX ROLES AS SOCIAL CONSTRUCTIONS

A social–psychological approach to aging and sex roles leads us to stress one point at the outset: the terms *male* and *female* have very little to do with biology and a great deal to do with history and culture. As James Spradley and Brenda Mann (1975) state —

> Every society takes the biological differences between male and female to create a special kind of reality: *feminine and masculine identities*. Cultural definitions are imposed on nature, creating a vast array of different identities from one culture to another. Male and female become linked to specific roles, attitudes, feelings, aspirations, and behavior patterns. What

it means to be a woman, what it means to be a man — these are intimately linked in every culture. Femininity often becomes the antithesis of masculine virtues and vice versa (1975:144; italics in original).

Numerous studies by social scientists also call our attention to the ways in which the notions of masculinity and femininity are socially constructed by various peoples around the world (*see*, for example, Chodorow, 1971; Leavitt, 1971). While all cultures make distinctions between persons based on sex and age, the content, or meanings, of these distinctions vary considerably, thereby calling into question any "universal" male versus female human nature. Just as we have seen in our previous discussion of the social construction of age categories, sexual gender is a socially invented category, a product of the social meanings conferred on selected physical differences between persons. Consider the following: A tribe known as the Manus insist that only men enjoy playing with babies; therefore this activity is restricted to males; the Arapesh people of New Guinea believe that women's heads are stronger than men's; another tribe, the Mundugumor, living in close proximity to the Arapesh of New Guinea, view fishing as a "naturally" feminine activity and restrict it to women; the tribe known as the Todas believe that *all* domestic work is too "sacred" to be handled by women (Mead, 1950). In the broadest sense, Margaret Mead pointed out the following many years ago:

> In the division of labour, in dress, in manners, in social and religious functioning—sometimes in all—men and women are socially differentiated, and each sex, as a sex, is forced to conform to the role assigned to it. In some societies, these socially defined roles are mainly expressed in dress or occupation...Women wear long hair and men wear short hair, or men wear curls and women shave their heads; women wear skirts and men wear trousers, or women wear trousers and men wear skirts. Women weave and men do not, or men weave and women do not. Such simple tie-ups as these between dress or occupation and sex are easily taught to every child and make no assumptions to which a given child cannot easily conform (1950:XIV-XV).

Cultural distinctions made between the sexes have a very important self-fulfilling quality. Having decided that those called men are "naturally" different than those called women, all cultures proceed to restrict the activities available to each sex in such a way as to continually reproduce those characteristics selected as "natural" for each sex. Thus among the Mundugumor people, only those boys born with a strangulating umbilical cord around their neck are allowed to be painters. Only these boys are trained by older men to paint intricate designs upon pieces of tree bark. They, in turn, become the teachers for the next generation of similarly born boys. Since no one else is allowed to paint and compete with these boys, their painting is taken as the ultimate "proof" of innate, artistic talents (Mead, 1950).

As our previous examples suggest, relations between men and women are products of social arrangements, with the nature of the arrangement varying across societies. More specifically, men and women interact in terms of the specific situations in which they encounter one another. As we saw earlier in our discussion of aging and family life cycles, the behaviors expected of persons change as they move from the situation of courtship into the later years of married life.

From a common-sense point of view we often think of the environment as something "out there," as something that clearly reflects basic underlying differences between men and women. It makes a great deal of sense, however, to reverse this seemingly obvious equation betwen the environment and behavior and to suggest that the environment itself is a symbolically constructed phenomenon (Goffman, 1977). There are, after all, countless ways in which an environment could be organized by persons in different societies. In American society biological differences between males and females are singled out as "essential" when numerous other attributes unrelated to gender could just as easily be selected. This should sensitize us to the fundamentally symbolic character of all forms of social differentiation.

GENDER TRACKS: BECOMING MALE AND FEMALE

In the last few pages we have been presenting a view of sex roles that emphasizes the socially arranged nature of female and male identities. We now turn our attention to the different life paths traversed by men and women in our society. Just as we earlier argued that society provides us with time tracks by which we can gauge our "on-timeness" in participating in socially expected activities, so too does society provide us with what we might call gender tracks. Babies are defined as boys or girls right at birth and then slotted into social tracking systems that continually emphasize time tracks in the sense that men are expected to be doing certain things at particular points in their life, while women are expected to be doing something else at those same life points.

In suggesting that society provides us with gender tracks, we are not arguing that persons are merely puppets pushed around by forces over which they have no control. Unlike physical objects, persons think, construct meanings, and transform their environments. We do not simply act out in a reflex-like fashion the roles society provides us. We all experience choice and discretion in our everyday lives. It would be misleading, however, to minimize the significance of the constraints within which we must act. The dramas of daily life occur within larger historical and institutional settings. Because we are born into a world that is itself a product of the actions of previous generations, many areas of social existence have already been staked out for us. There are understood limits on our behavior, enforced by moral caretakers such as the police, judges, and so on, who are entrusted with the responsibility to maintain society's moral boundaries.

Human behavior, we suggest, must be seen as neither only the product of the social structures enveloping persons, nor solely a matter of individual will and choice. There is a dynamic interplay between society's expectations for us and our own responses in situations. The nature of the relationship between individuals and social structures is beautifully captured in Wendell Bell's following statement:

> Some persons, unlike rats in a maze, view the social structure as tentative and approximate. They proceed more like the psychologist himself, experimentally testing to learn what parts of the system are subject to manipulation. At the extreme, such persons may decide that the social structure, the maze itself, is subject to some extent to their will and may decide to shape it, as best they can, to suit themselves...Usually in cooperation with others, some people try to manipulate the real world to conform more closely to their images of the future: push out some walls, add some new openings, widen the passageways, create some new opportunities (1968:163).

Early Socialization Experience

Many of you have no doubt been present in a hospital shortly after the birth of a child. The scene of parents proudly viewing their newborns through the nursery window is a common place event. That society wraps little boys in blue blankets and little girls in pink ones seems perfectly sensible. We should note here, however, that right from the outset the world responds quite differently to the person in the blue blanket than it does to the one in the pink.

Until recently there has been very little research on the preconceptions held by parents concerning their newborns. A study by Rubin, et al. (1974) sheds some interesting light on this question. These researchers interviewed thirty pairs of parents in the Boston area (15 of whom had sons, and 15 of whom had daughters) within twenty-four hours of their child's birth. Interviews were conducted with each of the parents in which they were asked, "Describe your baby as you would to a close friend or relative." Parents were also asked to rate their babies in relation to a list of eighteen adjectives such as firm-soft, big-little, active-inactive, and so on. Objective scores of the infants' physical movements and characteristics, based on pediatric measures known as the Apgar scale, were also obtained from hospital records. Importantly, *there were no significant differences* between male and female babies in terms of birth weight, birth length, or Apgar scores taken at five and ten minutes after birth. Through these procedures the researchers were able to compare the subjective impressions of the parents with the more objective measures based on medical procedures.

Findings from this study indicated that daughters were significantly more likely than sons to be rated as softer, having finer features, little, and more inattentive. The authors conclude their research by stating the following:

> The central implication of the study, then, is that sex-typing and sex-role socialization appear to have already begun their course at the time of the infant's birth when information about the infant is minimal. The Gestalt parents develop, and the labels they ascribe to their newborn infant, may well affect subsequent expectations about the manner in which their infant ought to behave, as well as parental behavior itself (1974:519).

Names given by parents to their infants also reveal the way in which symbolic definitions operate in placing persons on society's gender tracks. Names given males are drawn from much more traditional sources than those conferred on females. Findings from a study conducted by Elaine Cumming (1967) of the names of over 4,000 children in first, third, and fifth grades in upstate New York public schools indicated the following:

> The biggest contrast between the sexes lies in the difference in the
> number of variations on standard names. Almost 38 percent of the girls
> are given those familiar variation names like Molly and Sherry and Mary
> Beth that have traditional roots but emphasize the uniqueness and in-
> dividuality of their bearers. In contrast, only about 10 percent of the boys
> bear variation names. Further, four times as many girls as boys have very
> unusual or unique names (1967:52).

We might suggest here that women are expected to exhibit their in-
dividuality through their names and their appearances, while men
are expected to play down their uniqueness in those areas. For men,
uniqueness is to be expressed through success and achievements in
work and other competitive activities, such as sports. These spheres
of life—work and sports—are social arenas in which being on the
team is a prerequisite for further advancement. All teams, we should
note, provide their players with standardized uniforms. In this
sense, then, names and appearances constitute for men the appropriate uniforms needed for continued participation in the team
activity.

The self-fulfilling character of naming practices is touched upon
by Bruning and Albot (1974) in their discussion of naming patterns
among the Ashanti tribe in western Africa. These tribal members
believe that a child's character is determined by the day of the week
on which it is born. Children are then given the name of that day as
their actual name. Examination of arrest and criminal records indicated that Ashanti boys "whose day names connoted quick
tempers, aggressiveness and troublemaking were guilty much more
often of offenses such as assault and murder than were children
whose day names suggested passivity" (1974:57). Believing the relationship between personality and time of birth to be an "obvious"
one, the Ashantis appear to socialize their young in ways that conform to this assumed connection.

A child's entry into the world, as we have seen, is immediately
overloaded with parental expectations about the meanings of being a
boy or a girl. What differences, we might now ask, have been found
concerning the socialization patterns of young boys and girls? As
historians of sex roles have observed (Dubbert, 1979; Stearns,
1979), American society evidences an almost obsessive concern with
displays of machismo, or exaggerated postures of masculinity. Pop-

ular culture heroes, such as John Wayne, Clint Eastwood, and Paul Newman, to name just a few, display in their appearances and emotional responses a conception of maleness that reflects the view that men are supposed to be ruggedly individualistic and emotionally invulnerable. The athleticism and physical toughness of such persons also indicate the importance attached to the idea that men should "grin and bear it," "tough it out," and "play under pain."

Expectations attached to images of masculinity, we should point out here, exact a heavy psychological toll on Western men. Forced to always prove one's toughness and masculinity, boys very early in life develop a real fear of and animosity toward anything remotely "feminine." Studies by the psychologist Daniel Brown (1956, 1957, 1958), for example, of sex role preferences of children, indicate that from kindergarten age onward, girls are much more likely to prefer masculine roles and objects (such as toys) than are boys to claim a preference for anything feminine. Girls aged 3½ to 5½ are about equally divided in their preferences, with about 50 percent preferring feminine roles and toys, and 50 percent preferring the masculine versions. Among similarly aged boys, however, 70 to 80 percent express masculine preference. His data indicate that these differences widen as children get older. Boys from six to nine years old become even more committed to masculine choices, while similarly aged girls make many more masculine than feminine choices.

In discussing such findings, Nancy Chodorow (1971) suggests that as boys and girls in our society get older, it becomes obvious to them that status and power attach to male roles and activities. As a result, boys exhibit an increasing nervousness about doing anything that might cause them to be labelled "effeminate" or a "sissy." Girls, by contrast may partake of male activities such as being "tomboys." Girls may also dress in male clothing, such as pants and blue jeans, without calling attention to themselves. Many women will talk fondly and nostalgically about their youthful days as tomboys. Few men, however, will proudly proclaim that early in life they were considered sissies. Women, in effect, gain in status by crossing over into male activities, while men decline in status by similar crossovers into the female world (Spradley and Mann, 1975). The differential demands on men and women later in life deriving from these early definitions of sex roles are also reflected in American attitudes toward male and female homosexuality. Male homosexuality appears to be a much more severely punished and unfavorably viewed activity than is the case for lesbianism. Individuals of lower status, such as women, it seems, are given a greater latitude to engage in certain sexually deviant activities.

Studies of touching behaviors between parents and children indicate that during the earliest months of life boys are more likely than girls to be touched, held, or rocked by their parents (Lewis, 1972). At about the age of six months, however, this pattern reverses and remains that way for the rest of childhood. Michael Lewis argues that "the major socialization process" for American children "in terms of attachment or social behavior, is to move the infant from a proximal mode of social interaction (i.e., involving physical contact — touching, rocking, holding) to a distal mode (i.e., one which can be performed at a distance — looking at, smiling, vocalizing to); the former is an *infant mode*, while the latter is an *adult mode* of interaction" (1972:234) (quoted in Henley; 1977:119; italics added). From very early in life, then, boys are plugged into a set of expectations that emphasize independence and aggressiveness while girls are being prepared for lives as the future emotional caretakers of others, especially children and husbands.

In concluding this review of the literature on early socialization, we should mention that the evidence is mixed concerning clear-cut differences in actual behaviors of boys and girls. Reviews by O'Leary (1977) and Maccoby and Jacklin (1974) of various studies do indicate, however, that boys are more physically and verbally aggressive than girls. Cross-cultural studies also show that "girls between six and ten are more often seen behaving nurturantly" (1974:36). While the data may not be conclusive concerning early male/female behavioral differences, differences become more evident and pronounced during adolescence.

ADOLESCENCE

In recent years social psychologists have used a variety of techniques to measure persons' self-concepts. A primary data source has been a technique called the Twenty Statements Test. The Twenty Statements Test is very much in keeping with the assumptions of symbolic interaction theory, since it taps the manner in which persons view themselves. To complete the TST, subjects are asked to make twenty different responses to the simple question "Who am I?" That is, they are asked to complete the sentence "I am _____" twenty times. Subjects are instructed to write their answers quickly, in the order they come to mind, and without worrying about the logic or importance of their responses.

Manford Kuhn (1960) employed the TST technique in order to measure persons' changes in self-attitudes according to their sex, age, and amount of professional training. For our purposes in this chapter, his findings concerning age consciousness are particularly relevant. His data revealed that only about one-quarter of the nine-year-olds identified themselves by age in response to the question of "Who am I?" From that age onward, however, the salience of age consciousness increased, with a peak reached among thirteen-year-olds, 75 percent of whom mentioned age in response to that question. Since the age thirteen marks a transitional point in American society as the entry into teenagehood, it would seem to be a period in persons' lives that evokes a great deal of mental attention. Kuhn also found that there were no significant differences in the extent to which grade school boys and girls mentioned their sexual identities in response to the TST. With the beginning of high school years, however, women were considerably more likely to answer "I am a female" to the TST than were men to answer "I am a man." Such responses call our attention to the importance of junior high school and later high school situations as important contexts for the sharpening of differing male and female life curves.

Studies of high school social patterns and the values adhered to by students demonstrate the extent to which "intellectuality" is a trait that women have been reluctant to exhibit, particularly in male-female encounters. James Coleman's (1961) classic study of several working-class and middle-class American high schools demonstrated marked differences between men and women in the degree to which they wished to be remembered by their peers as brilliant students. The important point here, however, is that there were *no* differences between boys and girls in the freshman years. The differences increased widely over the high school years with far more males than females wanting to be remembered as brilliant students. Coleman (1961) also found that the beginning of serious dating and a growing concern with being thought physically attractive led girls to place less emphasis on scholastic work during their sophomore and junior years.

A more recent study of an upper middle-class suburban high school reveals some interesting continuities and differences with Coleman's earlier study (Larkin, 1979). In this high school, unlike any others noted in the sociological literature, there is a social circle known as the "intellectuals" that is actually part of the elite group in the school, along with the "politicos" and "jock/rah rahs" (1979:72). Women do participate as members of this intellectual group. It should be pointed out here that the group as such only contains about twenty-five members out of a total school population of two thousand students. Interpersonal relations between males and females, however, still reflect the operation of the same kind of "double standard" found earlier by Coleman:

> Thus, the major effect of the sexual revolution on students at Utopia High School has been the increased circulation of sexual commodities. The situation has improved for women in *absolute* terms vis-a-vis the 1950s, but their relative situation with men is unchanged. The *fundamental* relationships of the sexual marketplace have not changed, and sexual relationships between male and female at Utopia High are still male initiated and male dominated (1979:110; italics in original).

An emphasis on physical attractiveness by the adolescent girls studied by Coleman, in what still remains the most exhaustive study yet done on American high schools, was intimately related to their perceptions about what attracted boys to girls and what it took to be "popular." Such an orientation on the part of these girls may have been a response to their lack of opportunities to excel in other areas open to men, such as athletics. Popularity and physical attractiveness, then, became compensating factors, or readjustments to a "blocked opportunity structure." For the girls in the schools studied by Coleman there was "no clear-cut dimension in which they can 'star' as can boys in athletics. The nearest equivalent for girls is social success — being sought after by boys. In some of the schools, a girl who is popular with the right boys has a special position, envied by other girls and fought over by boys. In a sense, this is a dimension of achievement just as is athletics. It contrasts sharply with a situation in which family background determines the leading crowd" (1961:90).

Studies of male and female satisfaction with various bodily characteristics reveal some interesting data about the meanings of physical appearance in American society. Calden and his colleagues

(1959) found that the students in their sample expressed varying degrees of dissatisfaction with their bodies. Men expressed dissatisfaction with their height — wanting to be taller — while women wished to be lighter. Compared to the men in this study, the females expressed greater dissatisfaction with the attractiveness of their bodies. General findings indicated that "females desire changes from the waist down and wish for smallness and petiteness of body parts (except for bust). Males are dissatisfied with body dimensions from the waist up, desiring bigness of body parts" (1959:378). From this study, it would appear that these young males wished to possess the traditional macho image of masculinity — strong and big — while women aspired to the supposed feminine ideal — small and thin.

A later study of adolescents between the ages of eleven and nineteen also indicated that there was a "strong tendency for females to be relatively less satisfied, or more critical, of aspects of their bodies, than are males" (Clifford, 1971:82). Females in this study expressed particular dissatisfaction with five bodily dimensions: height, weight, bust, waist, and hips. Another study of adolescents also found that about 50 percent of the boys and 80 percent of the girls expressed anxieties about their physical appearances (Frazier and Lisonbee, 1971).

A concern with physical appearance among adolescents also calls our attention to the critical importance of the *body* and its transformations as a barometer for our sense of aging. The meanings that we confer on certain biological changes that our bodies undergo, particularly in adolescence, serve as sensitizing benchmarks for our movements through the life cycle. We must stress, however, that it is not the biological changes per se that are crucial, but rather the *responses* we make to such changes.

In thinking about the meanings persons attach to various bodily changes during adolescence, it is most unfortunate that few studies exist in this area. Most studies, such as the previously cited ones on body satisfaction, deal with the issue solely in quantitative terms, designed with the aim in mind of establishing appropriate levels of statistical significance. Such studies are helpful, of course, in sensitizing us to the broad dimensions of the problem. In seeking to understand the *experiences* of persons over the course of their lives, however, the works of writers and journalists offer a richness of data concerning the experiential aspects of aging generally lacking in more statistically oriented research reports. Drawing from these works we now examine how adolescents deal with the occurrence of particular bodily changes, such as menstruation and the development of breasts in young girls.

Data from the studies on body satisfaction of adolescents revealed, as we already noted, that young women generally express more dissatisfaction with their bodies than do men. The importance that young girls place on their physical appearance is a response to both blocked opportunities to achieve in other areas and also a realization on the part of young girls of the importance that boys attach to a woman's appearance (Rubin, 1973). Knowing that attractiveness is what men want and expect, young women are forced to conform to male definitions of female beauty and appearance in order to "succeed" in a man's world. The traditional fear among women that they won't appear as attractive in male eyes if they do compete and achieve in traditional male activities, such as sports and business, has tragically prevented women from living up to their fullest potential. Psychologists have referred to this phenomenon among women as the "fear of success" (Horner, 1972).

The ways in which young girls respond to the onset of menstruation reveals how male images of femininity have shaped women's perceptions of their bodies. In Western society, with its origins in the Judeo-Christian religious tradition, menstruation has historically been viewed in very negative terms. The *Old Testament* states ". . . if a woman have an issue, and her issue in her flesh be blood, she shall be put apart for seven days: and whosoever toucheth her shall be unclean until the even" (Lev. 15:19). Popular slang terms like "the curse," "she's on the rag," and "falling off the roof," also illustrate the unfavorable images of menstruation in Western society. As Virginia O'Leary (1977:24) states, "No matter how biologically sophisticated a young girl may be, it is unlikely that she views the onset of menses with unbridled enthusiasm." In reviewing a number of studies dealing with menstruation, O'Leary calls attention to the influence of cultural expectations on our perceptions of the presumed effects of menstruation.

The writer Nancy Friday interviewed more than 200 women throughout the United States over a four-year period. While her data may be questioned in terms of its representativeness, her findings do provide a thought-provoking basis for further studies. The way in which knowledge of menstruation relates to notions of aging is aptly captured in Friday's statement about her own adolescence: "My friends and I knew all about those blue and white kotex boxes in our mother's bathroom. We knew they were *our future*" (1977:97). Menstruation marks the beginning of the young girl's emergence into the status of an adult, full-grown woman and in that sense, as a number of Friday's respondents indicate, it is looked upon as making possible a much desired break with childhood. Responses of girls to this event, however, reveal the way in which it poses a double-edged problem. As Friday states—

> It points us inexorably forward into womanhood. At the same time it turns us back, regressing us in its own unheeding manner to that earlier time when we were unable to control our bodies. Suddenly we are back in touch with emotions we haven't felt in years, the primitive shame that went with wetting our bed, bad odors, soiling our clothes. The humiliation of involuntary or untimely excretion has been so pounded into us by years of zealous toilet training that to avoid it we have learned absolute control, iron control, control so rigid that neither our bladder nor sphincter dare to let go even while we are asleep. Abruptly, we are back in the middle of all that (1977:118).

The onset of menstruation also brings the adolescent girl to a vivid awakening concerning her new status vis-a-vis her mother. The mother's "womanness" now becomes a very conscious realization for the daughter. In this regard, Nancy Friday writes—

> Until we begin to menstruate, we have some distance from mother. We identify with her, but we are not like her. It is a kind of freedom. The gulf allows us to ignore the facts of life we don't yet want to face. We ask questions, open doors, but when we bump into facts we aren't ready for, we close the door, forget what we just saw or heard, and go back to our childish games. But once we begin to menstruate, we can't look away. *Her life is ours.* Having to understand what the periodic cycle means to mother makes us unable to avoid any longer recognizing that mom is not merely the kindly, "pure," and totally unsexual being we had always assumed, but is as irrationally taken by the same erotic desires as we. She feels our emotions and knows the same excitements we do within our own bodies. It is disturbing. . . . She is not only our mother, she is a woman too. And a rival (1977:117, italics added).

Another important bodily indicator of one's movement through the life cycle concerns young girls' attitudes toward the development of their breasts. In American society, males have succeeded in promoting an image of feminine beauty that emphasizes thinness, slim waists, and firm, well-developed breasts. Women who lack such characteristics often undergo a good deal of anxiety about their failure literally to "measure up" to male expectations. Previously cited data, you will recall, indicated that dissatisfaction with bust size was one of five bodily dimensions about which young girls expressed particular dissatisfaction.

The contrast between the growth of one's breasts and the onset of menstruation for young girls is beautifully captured in the writer Nora Ephron's reminiscences about her own adolescence. She writes —

> I suppose that for most girls, breasts, brassieres, that entire thing, has more trauma, more to do with the coming of adolescence, with becoming a woman, than anything else. Certainly more than getting your period, although that too was traumatic, symbolic. But you could see breasts; they were there; they were visible. Whereas a girl could claim to have her period for months before she actually got it and nobody would ever know the difference (1976:365).

Ephron's essay also illustrates the extent to which she and other young girls regarded the physical developments of their friends as criteria by which to gauge their own "on-timeness" or "off-timeness" in their movements through the life cycle.

Although young boys may begin to look for the appearance of facial hair, the advent of adolescence for them does not produce physical changes as noticeably dramatic as breast development and menstruation. For boys, however, a growing sexual responsiveness of the body made possible through the ability to ejaculate becomes an important transitional marker into adolescence. A focus on physical height also becomes an important issue for boys in this life phase. Two earlier cited studies (Calden, 1959; Clifford, 1971) both indicate a desire on the part of young males to be physically taller.

Adolescent boys' concern with physical growth and the *meanings* of height for young males in American society are sensitively chronicled in the writer Leonard Gross' (1980) autobiographical reflections "Short, Dark and Almost Handsome." Gross points out the ways in which one's height was used as a constant measure of the masculinity of young boys. The schools also reinforced a feeling of inadequacy on the part of the shorter boys by continually calling attention to the issue of physical size through official policies such as having students line up in single file with the shorter ones in front and the taller in back. Traditional male–female dating patterns also involve expectations about males being stronger and taller than their female partners. Men are expected to "lead" both on the dance floor and in the wider society. And, indeed, in terms of dating patterns, high school dances pose a serious question of strategic interaction for shorter males. Such boys must search around for appropriately shorter female partners with whom to dance.

As in the case of Ephron's reflections concerning the physical developments of her age mates, Gross indicates how the concern with height among teenage boys also involved a continual monitoring of the growth of one's age mates. Thus, he writes —

> In each new grade the scramble was on to establish a pecking order. First, I'd eye the two or three kids in my size league to make certain they hadn't sprouted six inches over the summer the way all other kids did, then I'd affect a swagger to browbeat them into my assertion of being taller. "No, you're not," one might shriek..."Measure!" So back-to-back we'd be, a clenched fist warning the judge not to notice heels off the floor (1980:62).

ADULTHOOD

In the previous section we discussed the significance of the meanings conferred by adolescents on bodily characteristics and physical appearances. Teenage involvements with such issues do not evaporate overnight, replaced by a calm feeling that the problem has been settled once and for all. Rather, a concern with physical attractiveness appears to last well into the mid-life period, although its intensity ebbs and flows over the course of the life cycle.

A recent study by Ellen Berscheid, Elaine Walster, and George Bohrnstedt (1973) of persons' attitudes toward their bodies provides one of the few available large data sets on how persons of different ages view their bodies. Their analysis is based on 62,000 reader responses to a questionnaire sent out by *Psychology Today*. After stratifying their total of 62,000 responses in such a way as to reflect the national distributions by sex and age, 2,000 questionnaires were selected for examination. While most of the respondents were generally satisfied with their bodies, women exhibited slightly more concern than did men with their appearance throughout the life cycle. Women over forty-five, in particular, were far more likely to have a "below-average body image" than were similarly aged men.

In evaluating the long-term effects of being attractive or unattractive, these investigators found that being beautiful as a child had little relationship to how happy persons saw themselves as being later in life. One's perception of oneself as attractive in adolescence, however, had a more lasting effect on future happiness. Even here, though, the effects of teenage beauty on personal happiness levels evened out by mid-life. Those who saw themselves as beautiful as teens were no happier than their less attractive age mates once they passed forty-five. These authors did not present any male–female differences here; so it is not possible to compare men and women on the issue of youthful attractiveness and later personal happiness.

In an interesting comparison of various male and female age groups, Carol Nowak (1977) examined the relationship between persons' definitions of *attractiveness* and *youthfulness*. She found that the mid-life period, and particularly the years between forty-five and fifty-five, are a time in which women exhibited a greater concern with facial attractiveness than at any other point in their lives. Surprisingly, women over sixty-five were the *least* concerned with looking old and unattractive of all three age groups (young adults, middle adults, and later adults) studied. As Nowak states —

> The midlife woman who has begun to notice a new wrinkle or sag begins to worry about things like "not being up on what's happening today," "being rather boring and unexciting lately," "having doubts about her husband's interest in her," and "not getting out and involved as much as she probably should." She is often too ready to write off her youth along with her looks....In short, while women under 45 are more concerned with their attractiveness but seldom see this affecting their youthfulness, and while women over 65 worry in just the opposite direction, middle-aged women clearly worry about both (1977:61).

Middle-aged males emerged from this study as the one group that was perceived as being the most attractive by all age groups. Her subjects found middle-aged males to be at the "epitome of their looks and vigor" (1977:63).

While concerns about physical attractiveness and body images are, as we have argued, important symbolic dimensions of the aging process, it would be a serious mistake to see such concerns as comprising the totality of what persons in adulthood are both confronted with and challenged by. The issue here concerns the question of whether or not most persons' experiences at mid-life accurately reflect the notion, continually suggested by the mass media, that middle age is a period of traumatic "crisis." Indeed, we may think of the research studies dealing with middle age as falling into two categories, a crisis pile, and a no-crisis pile (Stevens-Long, 1979: 252).

The crisis view of mid-life is largely based on studies written by psychiatrists and clinical psychologists. In reviewing studies of this genre, specifically the works of Gould (1972), Vaillant and McCarthy (1972), and Levinson (1978), Judith Stevens-Long writes —

> Three studies, three different samples, three groups of researchers all reach strikingly similar conclusions. All three point to the importance of the period between thirty-nine and forty-three specifically. All three make note of an acute awareness of mortality and aging, of people confronting the finiteness of time. All three emphasize the conscious questioning and conflict of values during this transition. All three repeat the themes of reassessment and self-evaluation (1979:256).

Research studies of mid-life that take a "no-crisis" position present evidence challenging the supposedly traumatic character of events, such as the female menopause, the empty nest phase of the family life cycle, and the question of job satisfaction. Work by Bernice Neugarten (1963) and her colleagues on responses of women of varying ages to the onset of menopause reveal that most of the middle-aged women interviewed agreed that "menopause creates no major discontinuity in life" and that "except for the underlying biological changes, women have a relative degree of control over their symptoms and need not inevitably have difficulties" (1963:148). Such sentiments certainly run counter to the crisis literature compiled by clinicians who see it as a precipitator of middle-age upheaval.

In the Neugarten et al. (1963) study, women between twenty-one and thirty had the most negative feelings about menopause, testifying to the way in which culturally shaped conceptions affect their anticipation of events thought to be unpleasant. The "saving grace" in human life, however, is that through our symbolic ability to interpret and, more importantly, to reinterpret our lives, we can alter our preconceptions in the light of the actual lived experience itself. This is precisely what appears to happen to middle-aged women undergoing the actual menopausal situation. These women compared to their younger counterparts view menopause in a much more favorable light.

The phase of the family life cycle termed the empty nest period has often been viewed as a stress inducing time for parents, particularly for mothers. Available studies, however, cast doubt on such assumptions. Marjorie Lowenthal and Daniel Chiriboga, researchers affiliated with the Adult Development Research Program at the University of California, conducted in-depth interviews with a number of men and women who were approaching the empty nest phase of parenthood. These researchers found that most of their respondents were favorably anticipating the departure of their children. They believed that this new phase in their lives held out the possibility for engaging in a less complicated life-style. Lowenthal and Chiriboga conclude their research report by pointing out that the empty nest period "is only rarely a low point or even a turning point of any kind in their lives and when it is, the impending empty nest is not one of the reasons cited. . . . Viewed in the context of the past and the anticipated future, the present period appears to be a favorable one for both men and women" (1972:14).

Particularly revealing data on the empty nest phase is presented by Norval Glenn (1975) in his analysis of evidence from six national U.S. surveys. Married women whose children had left home indicated a greater happiness and enjoyment of life than similarly aged women with a child or children still at home. Glenn's study also showed that the findings of parental versus empty nest phase reports of satisfaction were not very consistent for the fathers in these samples. Based on the data, he argues that a "net loss in psychological well-being, as a result of their children's leaving home, seems somewhat more likely for fathers as a whole than for mothers, but it is not likely that any such loss is substantial" (1975:108).

How, we might ask, did the notion of an "empty nest syndrome," thought to be experienced by all women, come to be so deeply rooted in our taken-for-granted assumptions about reality? The sociologist, Lillian Rubin (1979), suggests that the very language itself evokes an image of a woman who anxiously hovers over her "brood," like a little bird watching over its nest. When the "birds" leave home the mother is portrayed as a "lonely, depressed woman clinging pathetically and inappropriately to a lost past — a woman who has lived for and through her children, a woman incapable of either conceiving or desiring a 'room of her own'" (1979:14).

The actual experiences of the 160 middle-aged women interviewed by Rubin reveals once again that women's responses to this phase of life stand in sharp contrast to the negative images of it created by the ideology of motherhood in Western society. The follow-ing statement by one of her respondents serves as a representative view of sentiments expressed in this study: "To tell you the truth, most of the time it's a big relief to be free of them, finally. I suppose that's awful to say. But you know what, most of the women I know feel the same way. It's just that they're uncomfortable saying it because there's all this talk about how sad mothers are supposed to be when the kids leave home" (1979:28).

While Rubin did not interview the husbands of the women in her study, the comments of wives revealed that their husbands seemed to be expressing *more* distress over their children's departure than they were. For the woman, the child's leaving is part of what Rubin suggests is a "developmental sequence" in which the woman as mother has been the main participant in the child-rearing process. For the father, however, the empty nest phase constitutes a sudden rupture in the fabric of family life—a break in one's taken-for-granted notions about reality. The father's involvement in his work takes him away from a total concern with family matters and child rearing. As a result, the father is generally—

> ...not there when his children take the first step, when they come home from school on that first day. He's not there to watch their development, to share their triumphs and pains. Then, suddenly, one day it's too late. One day they're gone—gone before he ever had a chance really to know them.
>
> For him, indeed, it must seem sudden—one day infants, the next they're grown and gone. There's nothing natural about the process. He hasn't watched it, hasn't shared in it. One can almost see him passing his hand over his eyes wearily, wondering, "How did it all happen so fast?" (Rubin, 1979:36).

Since success at work has been the traditional avenue by which males have established their status in the Western world, it is in-structive to examine studies of job satisfaction in mid-life. John Clausen (1976) recently reviewed data concerning the experiences of middle-aged men and women in two long-term life history projects conducted by the Institute of Human Development. These projects were known as the Guidance Study and the Oakland Growth Study. Participants in these studies were almost all middle class in terms of SES characteristics, with many having upper middle-class charac-teristics as well. Satisfaction with one's job was quite high among these respondents, with only about one-fourth expressing any degree of dissatisfaction (1976:102). Clausen does not present any data on the job satisfaction of the female respondents, about one-half of whom were working. He did find that life satisfaction was most affected by whether or not a woman was doing what *she wanted to* — working or not working — rather than the mere fact of whether she worked or not. He does note, though, "The women now working receive the most favorable ratings on many of those attributes relating to personal effectiveness and are seen as significantly more productive, more autonomous and as having a higher level of aspiration than the women of each of the other groups" (1976:105).

Finally, a very recent study by Richard Cohn (1979) of work satisfaction among various age groups indicated a very high degree of job satisfaction among thirty-five- to forty-four-year-old male and female workers. Indeed, over three-quarters of these middle-aged workers said that they would continue working even if there were no financial necessity for them to continue doing so (1979:266, Table 1). Significant drops in level of work satisfaction start occurring among those in the forty-five to fifty-four age category, although even here more than 65 percent of the persons interviewed expressed high satisfaction with their jobs. The lowest levels of job satisfaction were found among those in the fifty-five to sixty-four age category. Data on work satisfaction also seem to challenge the inevitability of a mid-life crisis affecting one's entire range of life activities.

In this section we have examined a wide range of studies dealing with various aspects of mid-life. Some studies present data affirming its "crisis" dimensions, while others provide evidence challenging such notions. How, then, should we "see" the mid-life period? At the current time it is simply not possible, we believe, to argue for one position or the other as "the correct" position.

Given the recent historical emergence of this age category, as described in Chapter 2, it is not at all surprising that so little consensus has been achieved among social scientists about the exact nature of what men and women experience during this phase of life. After all, we have just "discovered" this age category. Perhaps, like Columbus' discovery of the "New World," it will take a while before we can really become familiar with the "natives!"

THE LATER YEARS

In discussing the life situations confronting the elderly, several social scientists have stressed the importance of financial issues to older persons. In the United States income increases with age up to the fifties when income begins to decrease with increasing age. Bureau of Census (1974) data indicate that the median income for families headed by someone over sixty-five was only $7,298 compared to a median income of $12,836 for all other families.

As Table 5-I reveals, compared to persons twenty-two to sixty-four, men and women over sixty-five are almost twice as likely to be living in conditions of poverty. Among males sixty-five or older, 12.4 percent live in poverty compared to 5.8 percent between twenty-two and sixty-four. Comparable figures for older women are 19 percent compared to 9.7 percent between twenty-two and sixty-four. The figures for older persons living as unrelated individuals — single persons, widows, widowers — are 27.1 percent for men and 33.5 percent for women.

Table 5-I   Percent of Men and Women in Poverty, 1973

Age	Men	Women
Total age 16 or older	7.4	11.6
16-21 years	10.4	13.2
Family head	13.2	75.6
Other family member	8.3	9.3
Unrelated individual	38.1	49.6
22-64 years	5.8	9.7
Family head	4.6	33.4
Other family member	5.7	5.2
Unrelated individual	15.2	22.8
65 or older	12.4	19.0
Family head	9.5	16.8
Other family member	8.0	8.0
Unrelated individual	27.1	33.5

Source: U.S. Bureau of the Census, 1975.

Figure 5-1 indicates that the retirement benefits category, consisting of all forms of governmental assistance plus private pension plan funds, accounts for 49 percent of the total income of elderly persons. As Russell Ward (1979:57) notes in discussing this issue: "Although the aged also receive some tax benefits, including nontaxation of

Social Security income, doubled personal exemptions, and property-tax reductions, the general picture remains of substantial economic deprivation for older people, certainly greater than the general population."

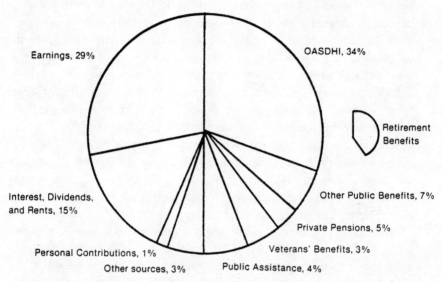

Figure 5-1. Sources of Money Income for Persons 65 and Over (Including Their Spouses), 1967. From Lenore Bixby, Income of people aged 65 and over, *Social Security Bulletin*, p. 10, April, 1970. Reprinted by permission.

Widowhood

The contrasting life curves of men and women in American society are dramatically revealed in the statistics concerning widowhood and the likelihood of older men and women remarrying. About 95 percent of the women who are widowed after age fifty-five will *never* remarry (Cleveland and Gianturco, 1976). Most widowers, however, *will remarry* if they are under seventy. Available data also reveal the following: only about 9 percent of males between sixty-five and seventy-four are widowed compared to 42 percent of similarly aged women (Bureau of Census, 1976:46).

Significant differences in male–female remarriage rates in older life are partly based on greater female longevity. More important,

however, are the cultural expectations attached to dating and marriage patterns in the Western world—phenomena that illustrate
what Susan Sontag (1972) has called "the double standard of aging."
As we noted earlier in this chapter, the "normal" arrangement between the sexes in the Western world is one in which women are expected to date and marry men who are physically taller and older.
This "architecture of intimacy," if you will, is constructed from the
cultural building blocks of age and size, dimensions of social life in
which males are expected to be more dominant and powerful. As
men and women age, then, the older man has an increasingly larger
"pool" of available younger women to date and marry. His similarly
aged female contemporary is faced with a declining supply of eligible
men her own age or above, while simultaneously being socially inhibited from marrying men much younger than herself. The male
emphasis on female attractiveness, it should also be noted, is very
much associated with notions of female youthfulness, and this factor
also creates difficulties for older women in the "remarriage market."

Additional support for our argument may be found in a recent
study by Norval Glenn (1980) in which he reviews data concerning
male and female perceptions of happiness. The data is based on national surveys conducted during the 1946–1974 period in the United
States. Glenn (1980:632) states "the data indicate that any negative
age effect on happiness is greater for females than for males." He
hypothesizes that the "double standard of aging" may account for
this difference since "aging from young adulthood to middle age
leads to a greater loss in resources and in the basis of self-esteem for
females than for males" (1980:633). We see here once again that the
aging process is inextricably bound up with cultural expectations
and power differentials between men and women having very little
to do with biology. From a social–psychological perspective, aging
has a great deal to do with the ability of one group to create a definition of "normal" aging that is experienced as binding by other
members of society.

A useful way to think about the situation of elderly widows in
American society is "to conceive of them as being very much like a
'minority group'" (Lopata, 1971). The life circumstances of these
women bear similarities to other "stigmatized" (Matthews, 1979)
minorities. Let us briefly examine some of the ways in which this
group might be seen as differing from the majority group. First, as

Helena Lopata (1971) notes, widows are prevented from participating in many leisure time activities with others because they lack a male companion, thereby creating "strains" in their interactions with couples. Second, there appears to be a "conspiracy of silence" concerning death and grieving in American society (Maddison, 1968; Parkes, 1972). Widows are thus prevented from openly engaging in "grief work." Third, as women in a male-dominated society, widows also suffer from the second-class status of women in general. Being generally older than the rest of the population, widows also suffer from the broader discrimination against the elderly. Their age makes it difficult for them to find employment. If they lack previous career training, as many widows do, they are particulary ill-equipped to compete in the job market. The fact that older widows are often foreign-born and members of racial and ethnic minority groups as well, creates additional difficulties. As Lopata (1971:69) states, based on interviews with widows in the Chicago area, "The older widow is also likely to be a homeowner in an old neighborhood and is the person left to experience the 'invasion' of people with other cultures or racial characteristics." The poverty situation of elderly widows coupled with their low level of formal education makes it difficult for them to participate fully in the larger society.

In a more recent work, Lopata (1979) puts forth an intriguing hypothesis on the role played by the "sanctification of the husband" in the grieving process; that is to say, the heightened idealization of one's former mate by the living spouse. She suggests—

the sanctification process is an effective means by which the widow can continue her obligation to the husband to remember him, yet break her ties and recreate herself into a person without a partner. Over time, with the help of mourning rituals and associates, she purifies the husband of mortal jealousies and demands for continued attention. He becomes saintly, safely out of the way in daily life and noninterfering as she goes about rebuilding her support network. Sanctification moves the late husband into an otherworldly position as an understanding, but safe and distant observer (1979:126-7).

The establishment of neighborhood networks, as recommended by Lopata (1979), would be an important aid to elderly widows in American society. There is currently a serious absence of devices to bridge the gap between the isolation of the widowed and the social resources of the community and the society at large. Lopata's proposal that federal funds be directed to the hiring of network coordinators is an important idea that has the potential for significantly improving the lives of widows and widowers.

Lynne Caine's (1974) account of her responses to the onset of widowhood makes clear in a very personal, experiential way many of the points discussed earlier. She points out how the loss of a husband raises significant issues for the ongoing nature of identity maintenance:

> Our society is set up so that most women lose their identities when their husbands die. Marriage is a symbolic relationship for most of us. We draw our identities from our husbands. We add ourselves to our men, pour ourselves into them and their lives. We exist in their reflection. And then...? If they die...? What is left? It is wrenching enough to lose the man who is your lover, your companion, your best friend, the father of your children without losing yourself as well (1974:1).

The transition from wife to widow also brings into prominence questions about one's identity as a woman. Going through the agonizing ordeal of watching her husband die from cancer, Lynne Caine was troubled by her ambivalence about sexuality. She saw herself as a highly sexual being and had always enjoyed sex with her husband. During the last few months of her husband's life, however, she had little interest in or energy for sex, while still remaining conscious of her own sexuality. As her husband approached death she notes that "...I hated the thought that men would no longer see me in sexual terms, but only as a widow. And I hated myself for this initial infidelity of thought. No man stirred my passions. Martin was my love. And yet I wanted men to see me as a woman" (1974:31).

Reflecting on her painful working-out of a new identity, Lynne Caine's memoir testifies to the resiliency of persons, to our ability to construct new meanings out of traumatic situations. In discussing her feelings about the kinds of relations she now desires with men, she writes —

> I did not need a man for my own self-esteem any longer. And in a very strange way, this made me much less lonely. I no longer worried about whether or not a man — or a woman — liked me. My concern was with how I liked them, how they affected me, what kind of people they were. I no longer sought approval. I discovered that I was happy enough alone, governing my own life. And I've modified that purposely. I am not "happy." But I am "happy enough." I am often lonely. I know what I am missing, but I can cope with life now. I find more pleasure in solitude. I am becoming a more serious woman. I want to write. I want to savor my children. I seek delight, but my delights are different now (1974:156).

While gerontologists have conducted much systematic research on widows (*see also* Adams, 1968), there is much less literature on widowers. As Lillian Troll and her colleagues (1979:76) note in this regard, research on widowers is "long on speculation and short on systematic research." There are some data available, however, that do provide informative contrasts on the life situations of widowers vis-a-vis widows.

A recent study by Robert Atchley (1975) of 900 men and women aged seventy to seventy-nine presents important comparative data. Atchley proposes a research model that, if pursued, would result in a considerable improvement in our knowledge of this issue. Atchley's findings indicated that certain dimensions of widowhood were "stressful" for both men and women while other dimensions were not. Widowed persons reported themselves as feeling older and more lonely than did their similarly aged counterparts. There were few significant differences, however, between the marrieds and the widowed in the following areas: sensitivity to criticism, anxiety, anomie, job commitment, self-esteem, self-stability, depression, attitude toward retirement, and job deprivation (1975:177).

Among the working-class segment of his sample, widowers were more likely to define themselves as old compared to similarly aged widows. Widows in this group were more likely than the widowers to report feelings of anxiety and lower degrees of job commitment. Among the middle-class respondents, widows and widowers only differed significantly in the area of job commitment, with the widowers reporting a higher degree of commitment.

Concerning the social impact of widowhood, Atchley's findings indicated that widowers were generally better off in terms of social involvements in clubs and organizations than were widows. Widowers in both the working-class and middle-class groups were more likely to have stepped up their levels of social involvement, but the differences were greatest in this regard among the working-class respondents. Most significantly, in view of our earlier remarks concerning finances, Atchley found that widows were more likely than widowers to have inadequate incomes.

These findings challenge Felix Bernardo's (1970) contention that widowers are confronted with greater stresses and problems of readjustment than are widows. Atchley's data calls attention to the significance of economic supports in the life circumstances of the elderly. As he states, "These data suggest that males have economic supports which for the most part tend to offset the effects of other social and psychological factors" (1975:178). The importance of financial concerns is also evidenced in interviews conducted by Ira Glick (1974) and his colleagues with widows and widowers during the first year of bereavement. These researchers found that "Widowers seemed to be distinctly less likely than widows to be worried about how they would manage their financial situation. Widows, even though they might be financially secure at the moment, recognized that they would in the future have to manage on a severely reduced income" (1974:271).

Atchley proposes a research model (*see* Figure 5-2 below) that highlights the significance of automobile driving as a crucial link in the social participation rates of elderly widows and widowers. Based on sex and social class as measured by industry group, a certain level of income adequacy or inadequacy is attained in widowhood. Men are more likely than women, for example, to reach a level of income adequacy in widowhood. The likelihood of having and driving a car is affected by income adequacy, and car driving in turn directly affects the level of social participation. The twofold combination of income inadequacy and low social participation operate to produce psychological anxiety in widowhood, with more severe effects on women than men.

Atchley's work has wide-reaching implications for mass transit policies. If it is the absence of transportation, particularly the private auto that is in fact the crucial link between the individual and social groups, then certainly governmental policies could be formulated to provide cheap, efficient, and safe modes of public transport for the elderly. Additionally, various kinds of van-pooling arrangements could be worked out with both public and private agencies so that elderly widows and widowers could drive themselves and their age mates to social functions. Apart from its social service implications, however, Atchley's theory serves as a fruitful way to organize and direct future empirical studies in this area.

Responses to Retirement

Common sense stereotypes and images conveyed by the mass media portray retirement as a stress-provoking, crisis-laden period

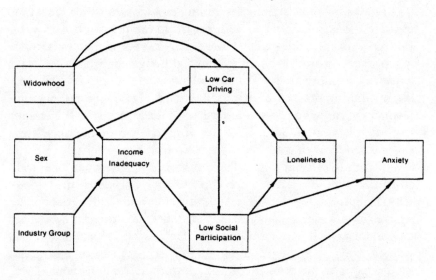

Figure 5-2. Impact of Widowhood. From Robert Atchley, Dimensions of widowhood in later life, *The Gerontologist*, *15*:178, 1975. Reprinted by permission.

in persons' lives. Recent findings, however, raise serious questions
about the accuracy of such views. In reviewing a large number of
studies dealing with retirement, Russell Ward concludes, "The overall impression to be gleaned from the many studies of retirement is
that most people adjust favorably to it and find it a relatively satisfying experience" (1979:199). He goes on to note that gerontologists
may have overemphasized the centrality of work in persons' lives
while underemphasizing our capacity to respond to new situations in
untraumatic ways. In this regard, social psychology makes an important contribution to our understanding of personal biography by
constantly alerting us to the ways in which persons reevaluate and
reinterpret their lives as they move through the various phases of the
life cycle.

Earlier studies of older men and women, as Robert Atchley
(1976) notes, have failed to separate out sex differences from the effects of numerous other variables. In a study designed to do precisely
this, he was able to report on male–female comparisons that have
been statistically controlled for the effects of age, marital status,
education, and income adequacy. His study was based on questionnaires filled out by 3,630 retired men and women.

Perhaps the most significant finding of Atchley's study concerned the *absence* of sex differences with regard to the importance of work. Retired women in this study were as likely as retired men to "seriously embrace job success as a life goal," although the women did take longer in reaching an adjustment to having left their jobs. This finding on the importance of work for women challenges earlier arguments in gerontology by Cumming and Henry (1961) and Donahue and his colleagues (1960). In terms of psychological characteristics, this study found that retired women were more likely than men to exhibit negative symptoms. Their response to questionnaires indicated that they were more likely to be lonely, anxious, unstable in self-concept, highly sensitive to criticism, and highly depressed. Atchley's work alerts us to the need for retirement programs oriented to women as well as men. Given the fact, as his data indicate, that women are also highly committed to work, counseling programs should focus on the problem of women workers' readjustment as well as those of males.

We should stress here that the findings from this study cast a very favorable light on the retirement experience. More than 80 percent of Atchley's respondents liked retirement. In addition, almost half of his sample adjusted quickly to their new situations. Even though, as just noted, older women were more likely than men to exhibit negative psychological symptoms, the prevalence of such characteristics was quite low for the sample as a whole.

The ways in which married couples respond to the retirement situation are nicely illustrated in other studies (Dressler, 1973; Parron and Troll, 1978). David Dressler interviewed thirty-eight working-class couples in the New Haven, Connecticut area. His findings indicated that there was little overall change in marital relationships as a result of retirement. His respondents expressed a high degree of marital satisfaction.

Parron and Troll's (1978) pilot study of twenty-two golden wedding couples — couples married at least fifty years — also showed evidence of high marital satisfaction. Data reported here provide little support for the presumed stressful effects of this period. This study also calls attention to an important issue, namely, the historical context in which relations occur. The couples interviewed by these researchers have lived through several historical crises, such as The Great Depression and at least one world war. Parron and Troll suggest —

The experience of accommodating to these trials can have led to their minimizing the importance of everyday irritations in conjugal living. In fact, many of the couples in Parron's study were so preoccupied in discussing the Depression that they paid little attention in their narration to the effect upon their marriage of the birth of their children: "I had two children by then. You know, we really had to work together then — we just had to make ends meet, so to speak." (1978:461).

Another recent study (Peretti and Wilson, 1975) helps to clarify our understanding of the conditions under which retirement will not be stress-provoking. Interviews were conducted with 140 working-class men in the Chicago area who had been retired from two to three years. These researchers found significant differences between those men who had retired *voluntarily* compared to those retired *involuntarily*. The voluntarily retired differed from the involuntarily retired in the following ways: They were more emotionally satisfied; they felt more useful; they had a higher self-image; they were more emotionally stable; and they had a greater number of interpersonal relations (1975:134-135). With respect to the involuntarily retired men: "Data, especially from interviews, suggested these men had an identity crisis in which they didn't seem able to reconstruct their roles in terms of their present status of retirees. It was as if they found it almost impossible to reconcile themselves to a retirement role. In such a state, their identity, self-esteem, and positive self-image are threatened" (1975:137).

The likelihood of stress for men and women in retirement, then, as suggested by research studies, results from a combination of two factors: (1) the voluntary or involuntary character of the job departure and (2) the person's ability to exert some control over his or her life circumstances in the retirement period. In the case of the second point the question of financial adequacy is a crucial variable, and it is in this area that older women are more likely than men to experience serious problems.

CONCLUSION

In discussing the different life curves of men and women we examined the social arrangements underlying the social construction of male and female identities. We explored the ways in which society's gender tracks provide the contexts in which men and women are socialized throughout the life cycle. Persons' concerns with physical appearance and bodily changes call our attention to the significance of these characteristics as symbolic, temporal benchmarks for our passages through the life cycle.

In reviewing studies dealing with middle age and the later years we described the reinterpretations that persons engage in when confronted with such changing life circumstances as menopause, the empty nest, and retirement. In the last chapter of this book we examine the significance of the current historical situation, and particularly the emergence of a *therapeutic state*, as the larger context shaping the contemporary aging experience.

REFERENCES

Adams, B.: The middle class adult and his widowed or still-married mother. *Social Problems, 16*:51-59, 1968.

Atchley, R.: Dimensions of widowhood in later life. *The Gerontologist, 15*:176-78, 1975.

Atchley, R.: Selected social and psychological differences between men and women in later life. *Journal of Gerontology, 31*:204-211, 1976.

Bell, W.: The city, the suburb, and a theory of social choice. In S. Greer et al. (Eds.): *The New Urbanization*. New York, St. Martin's Press, 1968.

Bernard, J.: *The Future of Marriage*. New York, Bantam, 1972.

Bernardo, F.: Widowhood status in the United States. *Family Coordinator, 17*: 191-203, 1968.

Bernardo, F.: Survivorship and social isolation: The case of the aged widower. *The Family Coordinator, 19*:11-25, 1970.

Berscheid, E., Walster, E., and Bohrnstedt, G.: The happy American body: A survey report. *Psychology Today, 7*:119-131, 1973.

Bixby, L.: Income of people aged 65 and older. *Social Security Bulletin, April*:10, 1970.

Brooks-Gunn, W., and Matthews, W.: *He and She*. Englewood Cliffs, Prentice-Hall, 1979.

Brown, D.: Sex role preferences in young children. *Psychological Monographs, 70*: 1-19, 1956.

Brown, D.: Masculinity-Femininity development in children. *Journal of Consulting Psychology, 21*:197-202, 1957.

Brown, D.: Sex role development in a changing culture. *Psychological Bulletin, 55*: 232-42, 1958.

Bruning, W., and Albott, J.: Funny, you don't look Cecil. *Human Behavior, 3*:56-57, 1974.

Caine, L.: *Widow*. New York, Bantam Books, 1974.

Calden, G.: Sex differences in body concepts. *Journal of Consulting Psychology, 23*:378, 1959.

Cath, S.: Individual adaptation in the middle years. *Journal of Geriatric Psychology, 9*: 19-40, 1976.

Chodorow, N.: Being and doing. In V. Gornick and B. Moran (Eds.): *Woman in Sexist Society*. New York, Mentor, 1971.

Clausen, J.: Glimpses into the social world of middle age. *Aging and Human Development, 7*:99-106, 1976.

Cleveland, W., and Gianturco, D.: Remarriage probabilities after widowhood. *Journal of Gerontology, 31*:99-103, 1976.

Clifford, E.: Body satisfaction in adolescence. In R. Muus (Ed.): *Adolescence: Behavior and Society*. New York, Random House, 1971.

Cohn, R.: Age and satisfaction from work. *Journal of Gerontology, 34*:264-272, 1979.

Coleman, J.: *The Adolescent Society*. New York, The Free Press, 1961.

Cumming, M., and Henry, W.: *Growing Old: The Process of Disengagement*. New York, Basic Books, 1961.

Cumming, E.: The name is the message. *Transaction, 4*:50-52, 1967.

Donahue, W., Orbach, H., and Pollack, O.: Retirement: The emerging social pattern. In C. Tibbets (Ed.): *Handbook of Social Gerontology*. Chicago, University of Chicago Press, 1960.

Douglas, A.: *The Feminization of American Culture*. New York, Avon, 1978.

Dressler, D.: Life adjustment in retired couples. *Aging and Human Development, 4*: 335-349, 1973.

Dubbert, J.: *A Man's Place*. Englewood Cliffs, Prentice-Hall, 1979.

Ephron, N.: A few words about breasts: Shaping up absurd. In J. Blankenship (Ed.): *Scenes from Life*. Boston, Little, Brown and Co., 1976.

Fontana, A.: *The Last Frontier: The Social Meaning of Growing Old*. Beverly Hills, Sage, 1977.

Fox, G.: Nice Girl: Social control of women through a value construct. *Signs, 2*: 805-817, 1977.

Frasier, A., and Lisonbee, L.K.: Adolescent concerns with physique. In R.E. Muus (Ed.): *Adolescent Behavior and Society*. New York, Random House, 1971.

Friday, N.: *My Mother/My Self*. New York, Delacorte, 1977.

Glenn, N.: Psychological well-being in the postparental stage. *Journal of Marriage and Family, 37*:105-109, 1975.

Glenn, N.: Values, attitudes, and beliefs. In O. Brim and J. Kagan (Eds.): *Constancy and Change in Human Development*. Cambridge, MA, Harvard University Press, 1980.

Glick, Ira, Weiss, R.S., and Parkes, M.: *The First Year of Bereavement*. New York, Wiley, 1977.

Goffman, E.: The arrangement between the sexes. *Theory and Society, 4*:301-331, 1977.

Gould, R.: The phases of adult life. *American Journal of Psychiatry, 129*:521-531, 1977.

Grambs, J., and Waetjen, W.: *Sex: Does It Make a Difference?* North Scituate, MA, Duxbury, 1975.

Gross, L.: Short, dark, and almost handsome. In A. Arkoff (Ed.): *Psychology and Personal Growth*. Boston, Allyn and Bacon, 1980.

Gubrium, J.F. (Ed.): *Time, Roles, and Self in Old Age*. New York, Human Sciences Press, 1976.

Gutmann, D.: An exploration of ego configuration in middle and later life. In B. Neugarten and associates (Eds.): *Personality in Middle and Later Life*. New York, Atherton, 1964.

Hendricks, J., and Hendricks, C.: *Aging In Mass Society*. Cambridge, MA, Winthrop, 1977.

Henley, N.: *Body Politics*. Englewood Cliffs, Prentice-Hall, 1977.

Horner, M.: Toward an understanding of achievement-related conflicts in women. *Journal of Social Issues, 28*:157-176, 1972.

Jacobs, R.: *Life After Youth*. Boston, Beacon Press, 1979.

Kuhn, M.: Self-attitudes by age, sex, and professional training. *Sociological Quarterly, 1*:39-55, 1960.

Larkin, R.: *Suburban Youth in Cultural Crisis*. New York, Oxford University Press, 1979.

Leavitt, R.: Women in other cultures. In V. Gornick and B. Moran (Eds.): *Woman in Sexist Society*. New York, Mentor, 1971.

Levinson, D.: *Seasons of a Man's Life*. New York, Knopf, 1978.

Lewis, M.: Parents and children: Sex-role development. *School Review, 80*:229-40, 1972.

Lopata, H.: Widows as a minority group. *The Gerontologist, 11*:67-77, 1971.

Lopata, H.: *Women as Widows*. New York, Elsevier, 1979.

Lowenthal, M., and Chiriboga, D.: Transitions to the empty nest. *Archives of General Psychiatry, 26*:8-14, 1972.

Lowenthal, M., Thurner, M., and Chiriboga, D.: *Four Stages of Life*. San Francisco, Jossey-Bass, 1975.

Maccoby, E., and Jacklin, C.: What we know and don't know about sex differences. In E. Morrison and V. Vorosage (Eds.): *Human Sexuality*. Palo Alto, Mayfield, 1974.

Maddison, D., and Viola, A.: The health of widows in the year following bereavement. *Journal of Psychosomatic Research, 12*:297-306, 1968.

Matthews, S.: *The Social World of Old Women*. Beverly Hills, Sage, 1979.

Mead, M.: *Sex and Temperament in Three Primitive Societies*. New York, Mentor, 1950.

Neugarten, B., and associates: Women's attitudes toward the menopause. *Vita Humana, 6*:140-151, 1963.

Nowak, C.: Does youthfulness equal attractiveness? In Lillian Troll et al. (Eds.): *Looking Ahead*. Englewood Cliffs, Prentice-Hall, 1977.

O'Leary, V.: *Toward Understanding Women*. Belmont, Wadsworth, 1977.

Parkes, C.M.: *Bereavement*. New York, International Universities Press, 1972.

Parron, E., and Troll, L.: Golden wedding couples. *Alternative Life-styles, 4*:447-464, 1978.

Peretti, P., and Wilson, L.: Voluntary and involuntary retirement of aged males and their effects on emotional satisfaction, usefulness, self-image, emotional stability, and interpersonal relationships. *Aging and Human Development, 6*:131-138, 1975.

Rubin, J., Provenzano, F., and Luria, Z.: The eye of the beholder: parents' views on sex of newborns. *American Journal of Orthopsychiatry, 44*:512-519, 1974.

Rubin, L.: *Women of a Certain Age*. New York, Harper and Row, 1979.

Rubin, Z.: *Liking and Loving*. New York, Holt, Rinehart, 1973.

Sontag, S.: The double-standard of aging. *Saturday Review, Sept. 23*:29-38, 1972.

Spradley, J., and Mann, B.: *The Cocktail Waitress*. New York, Wiley, 1975.

Stearns, P.: *Be A Man*. New York, Holmes and Meier, 1979.

Stevens-Long, J.: *Adult Life*. Palo Alto, Mayfield, 1979.

Stone, G.P.: Appearance and the self. In A. Rose (Ed.): *Human Behavior and Social Processes*. Boston, Houghton Mifflin, 1962.

Troll, L., Miller, S., and Atchley, R.: *Families in Later Life*. Belmont, Wadsworth, 1979.

United States Bureau of Census: *Vital Statistics of U.S., 1970, Vol. II, Mortality*, Part A. National Center for Health Statistics, Washington D.C., 1974.

United States Bureau of Census: *Characteristics of the Low Income Population: 1973*. Current Population reports P-60, No. 98, Washington D.C., 1975.

United States Bureau of Census: *Demographic Aspects of Aging in the Older Population in the United States*. Current Population Reports: Special Studies Series P-23 (59): 46, 1976.

Vaillant, G., and McCarthy, C.: Natural history of male psychological health. *Seminars in Psychiatry, 4*:415-427, 1972.

Walum, L.: *The Dynamics of Sex and Gender*. Chicago, Rand McNally, 1977.

Ward, R.: *The Aging Experience*. New York, Harper and Row, 1979.

Weitz, S.: *Sex Roles*. New York, Oxford University Press, 1977.

Chapter 6

THE THERAPEUTIC STATE
AND THE PROBLEM OF AGING

IN earlier chapters we used historical data to demonstrate how our taken-for-granted views of aging relate to particular cultural and historical circumstances. Every generation, due to its unique historical situation, experiences the world in somewhat different ways than its predecessors. Not having participated in the creation of its social world, each generation is likely to confer new meanings on old, familiar objects. Whatever the historical conditions into which persons are born, however, one problem remains constant: Human beings must have a coherent framework of meaning for their lives. In some historical periods the traditional meanings transmitted from one generation to the next adequately perform this function. In other epochs, however, such meaning coherence is not so easily established. The current historical period in the Western world appears to be one in which many individuals experience particular difficulty in understanding themselves. In the following pages, we want to explore why this is so. More specifically, this chapter considers the general social trends that have been shaping recent history and our consciousness of the aging process. If the modern era is marked by a general and deepening concern about personal identity, a major aspect of this "collective search for identity" (Klapp, 1962) relates to how we view aging. Ever more frequently in modern society an answer to the question "Who am I?" demands consideration of the age categories we fit into at different chronological points in our lives.

To preview briefly the general line of thought we will follow in the pages to come, we argue that aging has increasingly come to be viewed as a troublesome, problematic aspect of identity for many individuals in contemporary society. Persons today worry and concern themselves about age-related aspects of the life cycle that simply were not part of the day-to-day concerns of persons in simpler societies. As we shall see, this is, in large measure, one of the consequences of the rapid and pervasive growth of a "therapeutic society" during the twentieth century.

In this chapter we align ourselves with John Kitsuse and Malcolm Spector (1977) who maintain that the distinctive subject matter of the sociology of social problems is "the process by which members of groups or societies define a putative condition as a problem" (1977:415). Different groups may "prospect" and "lay claim" to areas of social life that they define as problematic and that require their intervention. On the following pages we describe the processes through which psychological and medical experts have contributed to the unique contemporary definition of aging as a problem to be solved.

As several observers of the contemporary social scene have noted, the behaviors of persons in today's "postindustrial" society are dominated by "experts." Experts advise us on virtually every aspect of our lives. Today, experts follow us throughout the life course. · They are there when we are born and follow us each step along the way, right down to our graves. Many have come to feel reliant on experts to tell them how to maintain their health, how to become educated, and how to raise their children. Experts have become indispensable for repairing the range of technical paraphenalia, TVs, autos, phones, for example, without which we believe it would be impossible to live. More important to us in this chapter, experts now tell us when our bodies and our "selves" need repair and the proper procedures for doing it. We agree with Eliot Freidson's evaluation of the importance of the enormously expanded role of professionals in our daily lives when he says the following:

> Due to the increased complexity of the technological, economic, and social foundations of our society, we are on the brink of changes in the structure of our society which will have a massive effect on the quality of the lives of the individuals who compose it. *The relation of the expert to modern society seems in fact to be one of the central problems of our time, for at its heart lie the issues of democracy and freedom and the degree to which ordinary men can shape the character of their own lives* (Freidson, 1970:336; italics added).

Our present task is to analyze how our conceptions of the aging process are formed in a society where persons feel obliged to listen to and rely upon the pronouncements and procedures of a growing army of psychological and medical experts. There are important connections to make between the increasing bureaucratization of the modern world, the corresponding growth of professionalism, the intrusion of experts into all areas of social life, and the imageries that influence our experience of the aging process. In order to specify fully the relationship of these social processes to aging, we need to consider the origin and prominence of identity questions in the modern world and the conditions giving rise to a "therapeutic culture" in which experts create our understanding of the meanings of the life course.

THE CONTEMPORARY CONCERN WITH SELF AND THE PROBLEM OF IDENTITY[1]

While the awareness of death has been present among members of all societies throughout human history, persons in tradition-oriented cultures are somewhat insulated from the trauma of death-consciousness. In such societies an overarching religious ideology helps to explain life's mysteries. Individuals may know that they are going to die, but they also believe that they know why they are destined to die and where their death will take them. Members of nonindustrial, tradition-oriented societies are also fairly secure in the knowledge of who they are. The anxiety occasioned by identity questions is siphoned off, if you will, by the importance accorded ascribed status characteristics. In such societies, persons' family status pretty well envelops them and dictates nearly all life experiences.

> In societies with a very simple division of labor, identities...are socially predefined and profiled to a high degree.... Put simply, everyone pretty much is what he is supposed to be. In such a society identities are easily recognizable, objectively and subjectively. Everybody knows who everybody else is and who he is himself. A knight is a knight and a peasant is a peasant, to others as well as to themselves. There is, therefore, no problem of identity. The question "Who am I?" is unlikely to arise in consciousness, since the socially defined answer is massively real subjectively and consistently confirmed in all significant social interaction (Berger and Luckman, 1967:164).

Persons in contemporary American society are confronted with a very different set of life problems. In the modern world, under the impetus of democratic ideologies, industrialization, and science,

---

[1]The discussion in the following two sections of this chapter draws on and sometimes quotes directly from David A. Karp and William C. Yoels, *Symbols, Selves and Society: Understanding Interaction*. New York, Harper and Row, 1979.

many areas of life previously accepted as natural are now viewed as subject to human volition and action. For example, persons no longer passively plead for charity; now they expect and demand that governments engage in social welfare activities. Were contemporary Western governments not to do so, large segments of their populations would view it as an injustice. When people come together and collectively act on their definitions of injustice, a social movement is born. In Ralph Turner's (1969:491) words, "A movement becomes possible when a group of people cease to petition the good will of others for relief of their misery and demand as their right that others ensure the correction of their condition." Turner argues that we are presently in the midst of a major social movement whose dominant theme is that advanced industrial societies deny their members a sense of personal worth, that such societies do not foster "an inner peace of mind which comes from a sense of personal dignity or a clear sense of identity" (1969:395). In short, ". . . the phenomenon of a man crying out with indignation because his society has not supplied him with a sense of personal worth and identity is the distinctive new feature of our era. The idea that a man who does not feel worthy and who cannot find his proper place in life is to be pitied is an old one. The notion that he is indeed a victim of injustice is the new idea" (1969:395).

The social movement that characterizes the contemporary period articulates a new definition of injustice, one much broader than the earlier demands for full political participation and freedom from material want. Today, alienation, previously seen only as a work-related phenomenon, has a much broader connotation. In the present era, "the new meaning (of alienation) refers to a deeply psychological state. It has been transformed into the designation for a psychological or psychiatric condition. . ." (1969:396). It is in the context of such alienation that, as Phillip Rieff (1966) has put it, the therapeutic state has triumphed.

THE TRIUMPH OF THE THERAPEUTIC STATE

To indicate the extent to which a more personalized conception of alienation has taken root in today's society, consider the influential role played by psychiatrists, psychologists, and such advice columnists as Dear Abby and Ann Landers. The increasing prominence accorded "mind tinkerers" who become nationwide celebrities such as Doctor David Rubin or Doctor Joyce Brothers attests to pervasive anxieties about questions of identity and psychological well-being. These experts are constantly invading our homes via television talk shows and dispensing "correct" recipes for the achievement of proper mental health and a satisfying life. One need only look at publications like the *National Enquirer*, with circulations in the millions, to get an immediate feel for today's widespread concern with "normalcy" and happiness.

Preoccupied with their dis-ease, large numbers of persons in today's society purchase the time and expertise of professionals in order to discover more about themselves. With the aid of the helping professions that have emerged as a major cultural force (Back, 1972) in the last few decades (among them psychiatrists, psychologists, therapists, and social workers), an increasing proportion of the population has set out to feel better, "to get their acts together," "to get their heads straight." We are in an era that has been variously characterized as the *age of narcissism*, the *me society*, and the *psychological society*. It seems a fair characterization that persons in contemporary American society are, in contrast to other cultures and historical eras, uniquely concerned with themselves. In an unsympathetic treatment of the growth of the helping professions, Martin Gross (1978:6) comments, "What the psychological society has done is to redefine normality. It has taken the painful reactions to the normal vicissitudes of life... despair, anger, frustration — and labelled them as maladjustments. The semantic trick is in equating happiness with normality. By permitting this, we have given up our simple right to be both normal and suffering at the same time."

We should point out that the mental health experts constituting the core of the therapeutic culture are complemented by other self-oriented, self-discovery movements in the twentieth century. For example, the huge increase in Americans' involvements in different fundamentalist and Eastern religious groups also provides a vehicle for the contemporary search for self. In the broadest sense, these "new" religions stand as a reaction to the ever increasing penetration of science and bureaucratic rationality into the innermost preserves of our everyday lives. The interest of many in astrology is another good example. In a world in which science and technology have portrayed the universe as barren and bereft of meaning, with humans like pebbles on a vast beach, the infusion of personal life forces, as provided for in astrology, gives many persons a sense of cosmic significance that is otherwise lacking in their lives. What is distinctive, however, about the various forms of psychotherapy available to today's pilgrims journeying into the self is that they attempt to harness the methodologies and perspectives of behavioral *science* to uncover the intuitive, emotional aspects of personal identity.

Among those who have analyzed the emergence of a therapeutic state and the burgeoning role of experts in shaping our self-images, the historian Christopher Lasch has been especially vocal and articulate. In one book entitled *The Culture of Narcissism* (1978) and in another entitled *Haven In A Heartless World* (1977), Lasch concerns himself with the importance of experts' intrusion into family life. Contrary to much sociological theorizing on the matter, Lasch does not view the modern family as an oasis of privatism. Instead, he shows how the family has come under the close scrutiny of the state.

Lasch argues that the therapeutic state composed of doctors, psychiatrists, guidance counselors, child development specialists, and the like has not arisen simply through the impersonal workings of historical forces. He reads these developments as part of a political process of *social control*. His interpretation of nineteenth century history is that the ascendancy of the professions, and of medical professionals especially, exposed the family to a system of social control based on systematic observation and surveillance. By bringing sexuality, child rearing, and other family practices under ceaseless technocratic intervention, professionals simultaneously wrested control over domestic life from the family itself. In this respect Lasch interprets the rise of the therapeutic state as a political event that allowed greater bureaucratic control over any dangerous socialistic energies that an unsupervised family structure might potentially create. According to these views, Sigmund Freud is one of the great stabilizers of liberal capitalism because his ideas gave rise to a psychiatric apparatus that governs society by prescribing the standards that define normality.

> Doctors, criminologists, . . . and other members of the learned professions to which in the twentieth century were added social workers, psychiatrists, educators, marriage counselors, child development experts, pediatricians, parole officers, judges of the juvenile courts, in short the modern apparatus of resocialization — governed society not "by right but by teaching

technique, not by law but by normalization, not by punishment but by control" (Lasch, 1980:28).

Whether or not we agree with Lasch's political interpretation of history, one thing is clear. The development of a society that is highly dependent on experts of all sorts, but particularly therapeutic experts who have collectively come to define the normative boundaries of our daily lives, is unique in human history. Along with Lasch we consider this an historical development having powerful consequences for the general ordering of society and for virtually every aspect of individuals' daily lives. We will discuss how these same events have created the context for today's consciousness of the aging process.

EXPERTS AND THE CREATION OF AGE CATEGORIES

The way we think about the world depends upon the categories available to us for ordering our perceptions. Classic works in the social sciences have a revolutionary character because they give persons a new vocabulary, new images, or a new set of concepts, for viewing their lives. This is surely true of the writings of Sigmund Freud, Karl Marx, and Adam Smith, to name a few. In this regard theories in the social sciences, compared with those in the natural sciences, have a unique status. They change the phenomena that it is their object to explain. Theories about some feature of the physical world, e.g. theories about the behavior of molecules, do not change the phenomena; they describe and explain. On the other hand, theories about the social world, once voiced and given credence, have the potential to transform and re-form what they purport to explain. In this respect it is hard to separate social scientists' theories about the world and the causes of social change itself. Consider, as an example, the profound effects that the prescriptions for child rearing found in Benjamin Spock's early book on the subject had on the socialization practices of a whole generation of parents.

We make the point about the interconnection of social theory and human consciousness because we think that it is precisely in these terms that the psychological society described in the last section has had its impact on our sense and experience of aging. It is not that any one theory or theorist has dictated contemporary experiences of the aging process. Taken together, however, one result of the constant analysis of self emanating from various sectors of the .psychological society has been an enormous expansion in the nature of the age categories that structure the way we define ourselves and others.

In Chapter 2 we made the case that the meaning of such age categories as childhood and adolescence have varied during different historical periods. To this we should add that the *number* of categories used to think about our positions in the life course has also changed over time. We define our aging selves in terms of an expanded number and more finely grained set of age categories than ever before. Americans speak of infants, toddlers, babies, children, preteens, teens, adolescents, young adults, adults, the middle-aged, and the elderly. To these categories, one social scientist (Neugarten, 1975) has now added the labels, the young-old and the old-old. Persons in their everyday discussion also make distinctions between early middle age, middle age, and late middle age. Because of advances in medical technology the terms *perinatal* and *neonatal* are now slowly entering the public's vocabulary. Our own thinking is influenced by those whose professional lives are dedicated to the "discovery" and analysis of age categories, which are then .used to highlight the distinctive problems and processes posed by the life course. The very fine distributions in age or life cycle categories that become the basis for scientific theorizing on the matter is nicely illustrated by studies such as Daniel Levinson's (1978).

The Seasons of A Man's Life

We see in Figure 6-1 that Levinson names several developmental stages each of which, he argues, presents its unique difficulties, problems, and prospects. Let us point out that each of the phases described covers only a period of a few years and that the categories focus only on early and middle adulthood. Were his descriptions to cover childhood, adolescence, and late adulthood, the number of categories or stages would easily double in number! Within each of the periods described, Levinson, in his text, makes further distinctions about the process individuals typically follow.

To the extent that descriptions and theories of the life course, such as Levinson's, become adopted and used by large numbers of therapeutic experts, and also filter down to the public at large, they exert a substantial influence on us. In short, psychological experts by attempting to understand the structure of our lives end up, in fact, structuring our lives.

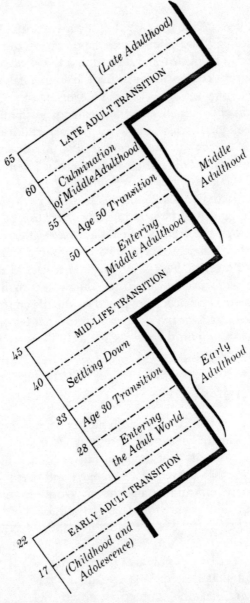

Figure 6-1. Developmental Periods in Early and Middle Adulthood. From Daniel Levinson, *Seasons of a Man's Life*, 1978. Courtesy of Alfred A. Knopf Co.

As suggested in an earlier chapter, ideas such as the "mid-life crisis," which originate in the research efforts of social scientists, become incorporated into the rhetoric many now use to anticipate, predict, and explain their own and others' responses to the middle years. As a result such a notion actually shapes the way many experience life in their early to mid-forties. The point of our exposition is that an important aspect of life in the therapeutic culture is that we are encouraged to analyze in ever greater detail the kinds of life exigencies and experiences we will have at a number of discrete chronological points during our progress through the life course.

The prescriptive/normative focus of much of the developmental psychology that has entered the public domain has mixed value. Consider once more the impact of experts on child rearing. On the one hand, parents who routinely seek out the advice of child development experts in the various media can be comforted upon learning that the "odd" or "bizarre" behaviors of their children are actually quite "normal." Equally, however, parents who constantly look to child experts for guidance sometimes become alarmed when their child's behaviors do not conform to what they are expected to do at their age. It is because they have access to and believe in the pronouncements of experts that contemporary parents recognize certain childhood "problems." There is, for example, the curious paradox that psychotherapy in its various forms appears in a significant degree to create the illnesses it treats. In general, the more life cycle experts there are, the larger will be the number of age categories we use to describe and evaluate ourselves, and the more will age connected problems be diagnosed and treated. The case of child psychiatry nicely illustrates this point:

> Child psychotherapy is epidemic in the Psychological Society. A National Institute of Mental Health survey showed that 772,000 youngsters under eighteen were in psychological care at some clinic facility. Added to private patients, the number rises to over one million. Parents who think therapy is the path to happiness routinely send their children to a psychiatrist or child guidance center for such complaints as school phobias, headaches, bed-wetting, truancy, behavior problems, aggressiveness, low school achievement, even the time-honored fear of animals (Gross, 1978:6).

One could argue endlessly about the general utility and truth value of the age-related categories and concepts that emerge from the writings of experts on the matter. Indeed, surveys of the literature yield no consensus in the important categories, stages, or benchmarks constituting the life cycle. This does not surprise us. Such unanimity is impossible since, as we have argued throughout this volume, the experience is vastly different for persons situated at different points in a society. In fact, if the literature reveals any pattern at all, it is that the life categories named by one set of scientists have often been constructed in response to the perceived inadequacy of the life stages named by another "camp" of theorists. The categories presented as describing the aging process are frequently the product of debates between persons advocating different theoretical positions. As an example, *humanistic psychology* arose partly as a response to the Freudian conceptions of normal human development. The response has been to challenge the validity of Freudian descriptions of development and to replace them with what its proponents believe to be a more adequate description and analysis. And so in this way, the formulation and reformulation of life stage categories expresses the ongoing endeavor of life cycle professionals to refine their understanding of aging.

From our viewpoint, the truth of the categories named is less important than the fact that the naming is going on. Our argument has been that the close scrutiny by experts of the aging process is part of the ambience of the therapeutic state that encourages a culture and its people constantly to psychologize about themselves. It is a culture that fosters a deeply introspective self-consciousness about the proper, normal behaviors associated with different ages.

What does all of this add up to? Perhaps the single most dominant and significant alteration of the consciousness produced by the existence of a therapeutic state has been the view that aging, in several of its specific aspects and in general, is a problem. The languages and conceptual apparatuses of the therapeutic state, informed especially by a medical model of disease, lead to a conception of aging as a process to be changed, slowed down, and some hope, even stopped. In the next section we shall consider more closely the implications of what may be termed the *medicalization of the life cycle*.

THE MEDICALIZATION OF THE LIFE CYCLE

The movement toward an all-embracing concern with psychological health and personal identity has been accompanied by a corresponding transformation in our "vocabulary of motives," or explanatory schemes of human behavior. When someone today acts in a deviant manner, our first impulse is to question their mental health and probe their psychological makeup. Is the person normal? Why is he or she doing that? Behaviors such as alcoholism are typically couched in a *sickness* vocabulary rather than the earlier *sin* vocabulary. Watching the greasy man with the waxed mustache tie the beautiful blonde on the railroad tracks as the train approaches, we now ask, "What would make a person do something as *sick* as that?" Our grandparents, however, would have had little difficulty in understanding such behavior. For them, the man was simply evil.

Coincident with the adoption of a sickness vocabulary is the generally expanded role of the medical profession into nearly all spheres of our daily lives. The medical profession has played a key role in the rise of the therapeutic society. The history of medicine has been one of ever greater numbers of behaviors falling under the aegis of the "medical model" (Conrad and Schneider, 1980).

The medical model begins with the easily accepted assertion that normalcy is preferable to abnormalcy. However, normalcy then becomes a synonym for *health* and abnormalcy a synonym for *pathology*. Health and pathology, in turn, are defined in terms of the presumed scientific, objective, unbiased standards originating from experimentation and laboratory research. Because it is better to be healthy than to be sick, the medical model implicitly supports physicians' decisions, whether requested or not, to provide health for the patient. No other profession, we might add, has the extensive access to a person's body and self as do both physical and psychiatric medicine. By defining certain aspects of the human condition as "illness," and therefore in need of cure, physicians also provide themselves the right to explore every part of the human anatomy, to prescribe a myriad of curative agents, and frequently, to compel treatment.

As Thomas Szasz (1961), Ronald Laing (1967) and Erving Goffman (1961), among others, point out, the term *healthy*, as used in the medical model, can be replaced by the word *conforming*. In societies where it predominates, the medical model is often used in lieu of the law or religious sanctions to legislate behavior. Whereas "peculiar" individuals were once viewed as "possessed," or as agents of the devil, now they can be classified as emotionally ill. An earlier religious model was explicitly moral. The medical model disclaims any moral stance. In the name of science it is used in the courts to deal with acts that are *not* defined as crimes. It is used to "treat" both children and adults whose behaviors do not conform to the expectations of or impinge on the moral sensitivities of others. Recent examples of the medicalization of deviance include the expansion of medicine to deal with hyperactive children (Conrad, 1976) and child abuse (Pfohl, 1977).

The medical model is used to support the political reality created by a coalition of physicians, teachers, judges, and other health professionals. Peter Berger and Thomas Luckman (1967) refer to this coalition as "universe maintenance specialists." These specialists from different disciplines set the norms defining proper and improper behavior, deviant and conforming behavior, normal and pathological behavior, sick and healthy behavior. Speaking about the social control role of psychotherapy, Berger and Luckman write the following:

> Therapy entails the application of conceptual machinery to ensure that actual or potential deviants stay within the institutionalized definitions of reality.... Since therapy must concern itself with deviation from the "official" definition of reality, it must develop a conceptual machinery to account for such deviations and to maintain the realities thus challenged. This requires a body of knowledge that includes a theory of deviance, a diagnostic apparatus and a conceptual system for the "cure of souls" (1967:112).

In this way, moral and scientific judgments become inextricably entangled in a society where the medical model operates to define behaviors as troublesome and then to explain their causes.

As Peter Conrad and Joseph Schneider (1980) point out, it is not very surprising that the expansion of medical jurisdiction over various human behaviors would occur at a particularly rapid rate in the United States. In a general sense, "the American values of experimentation, newness, humanitarianism, pragmatism, and individualism have all contributed to a nurturing crucible for medicalization, for the medical perspective on deviance contains elements of all these values" (1980:263). Americans who believe deeply in the values of technology and science for creating progress and solving human problems are easily drawn to a medical model that views human problems in disease terms and provides, therefore, for the possibility of rational, technical, scientifically based "cures." And so, in the hospitable American context, such diverse human behaviors as drunknenness, delinquency, and various forms of criminality come to be defined as manifestations of illness states and thus properly under the auspices of the medical profession. In each case mentioned, the change has been from a definition of the behavior as "bad" to its definition as "sick."

If it is not altogether clear, the redefinition of a behavior from bad to sick is not merely a semantic issue. These labels have critical political implications for the treatment received by those so labelled. The treatment, for example, that homosexuals will face in a society depends greatly on whether homosexuality is viewed by the society as an evil state, as a sickness condition, or as a legitimate sexual life-style. The political character of these decisions and the powerful role played by physicians is revealed in the American Psychiatric Association's decision that homosexuality is a *life-style* rather than an *illness*. This decision was arrived at *by taking a vote at a professional meeting*! As another example, acceptance of the idea that behaviors such as violence are products of disease states legitimizes a range of medical interventions to "cure" violent persons. Psychosurgeons, with National Institute of Mental Health funding, have urged psychosurgery for violence-prone individuals as a measure to prevent ghetto riots. And California authorities have begun to implement psychosurgery with noncompliant prisoners (Chavkin, 1978). Plainly, the labelling of behavior as illness is very much a political process with great policy and moral implications.

An examination of the history of medicine reveals that like the universe, the medicalization of human behaviors seems an ever expanding phenomenon. The medical profession takes an active role in "discovering" new illnesses, and then begins to intervene with "appropriate" medical treatment. We might say that physicians are constantly ready to find new problems to medicalize. Medical research frequently has the effect of creating new definitions of normality and new categories of illness. Eliot Freidson comments —

> Medicine is active in seeking out illness. The profession does treat the illnesses laymen take to it, but it also seeks to discover illness of which laymen may not even be aware. One of the great ambitions of the physician is to discover and describe a "new" disease or syndrome and to be immortalized by having his name used to identify the disease. Medicine then

is oriented to seeking out and finding illness, which is to say that it *seeks to create social meanings of illness where that meaning or interpretation was lacking before* (Freidson, 1970:252; italics added).

In recent years a new medical specialty, family medicine, has come into existence. We predict that in order to legitimize its place among other more established medical specialties, practitioners of family medicine will provide scientific reasons for treating a range of common family problems, such as alcoholism, drug abuse, violence, and sexual difficulty. It is worth noting that persons with nearly any domestic problem are encouraged, via TV public service spots, to seek out their physicians as often as a social worker or a clergyman. The growth of family medicine presages the likelihood of increased medical influence into all spheres of family life.

We have been describing how the medical profession has accrued to itself the right to treat more and more human behaviors. As Zola (1975) has argued, this process has proceeded to the point where we can properly talk about "the medicalization of everyday life." Medicalization has expanded virtually to the *entirety of life*. Nearly all aspects of the life cycle—birth, puberty, menopause, old age, and death—are conceived of as problems requiring medical intervention. Once we view the life course as requiring alteration by medical intervention, we have fundamentally transformed its meaning. "Just as at the turn of the century all men were defined as pupils born into original stupidity and standing in need of eight years of schooling before they could enter productive life, today they are stamped from birth as patients who need all kinds of treatment if they want to lead life the right way" (Illich, 1976:195).

Aging as a Disease

The medicalization of the life course creates havoc with our conceptions of health and "normal" aging. The norm for physical health presented in the mass media is of persons like the Olympic champion Bruce Jenner who are at the very height of their physical capabilities. The implication drawn from such media images is that uncompromised health is something that few fully possess. The standard has, indeed, been set high. This perception is, of course, not simply to be attributed to the efforts of physicians who constantly tell us what we must eat, how we must live, what exercises we must do, what stresses we must avoid, and what drugs we should take to safeguard our fragile health. The view that any body discomfort, however slight, is a problem to be eradicated if possible, is a natural for exploitation in a capitalist economic order.

Any drugstore displays row upon row of tablets, liquids, lozenges, creams, lotions, powders, and pastes for every imaginable blemish, wrinkle, or body discomfort. This indicates clearly the number of businesses that profit from the medicalization process we are describing. The more illnesses discovered, the more new products and services there are that can be sold to the public. From a Marxist perspective, one could say that the economic order stimulates the search for new illnesses. Here we note that the phenomenal growth of the pharmaceutical, health insurance, and medical technology industries parallels the medicalization process. Various sectors of the economy now have a substantial investment in persuading the public, through advertising, that its collective health is ill.

The use of prescribed drugs dramatically illustrates how far the medicalization of the life cycle has proceeded. It has been estimated (Zola, 1972) that in the United States, within a given twenty-four- to thirty-six-hour period, up to 80 percent of the adult population takes one or more medically prescribed drugs. Turned around, this statistic suggests that, at most, only 20 percent of America's adult population could be described as fully healthy. Indeed, the percentage of fully healthy persons would dip even further if we could know how many of the drug-free 20 percent suffer from ailments not treatable with medication. Plainly, living is injurious to one's health!

Disease is, in large measure, a social construct. The progressive discovery that aging is a disease is not occurring in the same way that smallpox or cancer have been labelled diseases. For example, decisions that aging is "premature" reflect more our changing *attitudes* toward aging than new evidence of abnormal physiological dysfunction. When we say that "he is in good health for a man of eighty," or that "she is prematurely old for a woman of forty," we are offering prescriptive judgments about the way aging ought to proceed.

As medical technology advances, there is a corresponding transformation in our expectations about what our bodies ought to be capable of at different ages. In turn, there is a transformation in our ideas about when medical innovation is appropriate to slow down or postpone aging. ". . . When a society as a whole wishes a different range of abilities than is statistically expected at a particular age, raised expectations are likely, forcing questions whether aging is a disease or whether debilities associated with growing old. . . should be disease states. . ." (Engelhardt, 1979:187).

As continued illustration for the point of view we are taking, we will briefly consider how three points in the life cycle—birth, the mid-life period of women, and death—have been medicalized. We want to examine how these natural life events have come under the jurisdiction of professionals, have been defined as medical problems, and then have been responded to as illnesses.

The Medicalization of Birth

During the last decade increasing numbers of pregnant women have been attending classes to prepare for "natural" childbirth. This is an interesting phenomenon when we stop to consider that women must be trained to bear children naturally. This surely evidences the extent to which medical technology and ideology have distanced women from this normal life event and have distanced women from their own bodies.

Beginning with the seventeenth century invention of forceps to hasten slow deliveries, and then with the rise of obstetrical practice and the use of anesthesia, childbirth moved from the home to the hospital. The success of medical experts in annexing childbirth as their professional responsibility is reflected in the fact that today it is illegal in most states for midwives to deliver babies. Scholars of the history of medicine have documented how "normal" births disappeared along with the female midwife and all births came to be treated as potentially pathological (*see* Scully, 1980; Erenreich and English, 1978; Arney, forthcoming). Feminist scholars describe how the growing profession of obstetrics, viewing midwives as a social, political, and economic obstacle to its own development, waged a successful political campaign to solve the "midwife problem." In short, the capturing of childbirth by the medical profession was as much a social and political achievement as it was a scientific one.

Feminist critics also argue that increased technology applied to the process of pregnancy and childbirth have unnecessarily intruded into a period of life that need not be treated as a medical problem. Ann Oakley, for example, has commented that "the process of medicalization has accelerated particularly in the last ten years as pharmacological and technical innovation has been introduced to obstetric work on the untested assumption that more means better" (Oakley, 1980:97). In her book *Immaculate Deception*, Suzanne Arms (1975) argues that the technological childbirth, invented by Western medicine to provide safer childbirth, may actually contribute to infant mortality in the United States. Rather than having the safety and comfort of the prospective mother uppermost in mind, she contends, the labor room has become a theatre in which a variety of technological apparatuses are the central props. The birth itself is then transformed into a medical drama starring the physician. Brigitte Jordan, an anthropologist, concurs in her description of childbirth as a "culturally produced event." In American society, the event has been constructed in terms of—

> a complex of practices...justified on medical grounds as being in the best interests of mother and child...induction and stimulation of labor with drugs, the routine administration of sedatives and of medication for pain relief, the separation of the laboring woman from any sources of psychological support, surgical rupturing of the membranes, routine episiotomy, routine forceps delivery, and the lithotomy (supine) position for delivery to name just a few (Jordan, 1974).

Still other researchers (*see* Guillemin, 1981) have documented a large increase in the use of the cesarian section procedure in recent years. Between 1968 and 1977 the rate of cesarian sections in the United States has increased by 156 percent. The national rate has risen from 5 percent in 1968 to 12.8 percent in 1977, with some institutions reporting rates as high as 25 percent. We should note that this sharp increase has been at the very same time that birth rates decreased by 12 percent. Although justified in terms of decreasing infant morbidity rates, evaluations of the procedure call into question any causal connection between cesarian sections and decreasing infant morbidity rates. One uncharitable interpretation of obstetrical practice is that obstetricians have, in order to sustain their incomes in the face of declining birth rates, turned to a surgical procedure that is approximately three times more costly than vaginal deliveries.

While the mother is normally defined as the patient during pregnancy and childbirth, increasingly the unborn fetus and newborn infant have been cast into the patient role. This is most plainly seen in the burgeoning of another new medical specialty, neonatology. Several hospitals now have Neonatal Intensive Care Units (nicus) which treat infants that until recently would, in all likelihood, otherwise have died. These are infants with extremely low birth weights and/or multiple congenital abnormalities.

Immediately, this new direction in medicine seems deserving of our applause. Many infants who would previously not have survived now have a chance to live. At the same time, the development of nicus raises a host of new and puzzling questions, both scientific and moral. In order to train doctors and to advance their techniques, neonatologists seek out the worst cases; the most damaged babies, many of whom the physicians know will die even with their intervention. In a forthcoming book based on several months of research on nicus, Jeanne Harley Guillemin and Lynda Lytle Holmstrom[2] make this observation: "...Often the most resources are spent on the least viable cases. These cases are not called experimental, but in fact, since their (the infants') chances of survival are so small, they constitute latent experiments." The phrase used by nicu staff is "being on the frontier"; that is, on the edge of knowledge. One factor that perpetuates the latent experiment is that this frontier keeps moving. Guillemin and Holmstrom go on to describe this case: "Perhaps the most striking case was the admission of a 480 gram (about one pound) baby referred to the unit at 36 hours of life. The baby died after 9 days in the nicu and one attending physician commented that it was an accomplishment just to keep the baby alive that long."

The frontier keeps moving! That pretty well sums up what we have been describing. Just as earlier generations pushed across America's geographic frontier, physicians have inexorably, bit by bit, pushed across and "colonized" the territory from birth to death. Having accomplished that technological and political feat, physicians are now turning their attention to another frontier; that extending from the moment of conception to just after birth.

---

[2]Jeanne Guillemin and Lynda Lytle Holmstrom kindly shared drafts of their book, currently in progress.

Women of a Certain Age: The Medicalization of Mid-life

If the medical and other helping professions have exerted increasing control over many areas of social life, this process appears still more pronounced if we focus on particular groups of persons, at particular points in the life cycle. It is a matter of common sense that control is most easily gained over those groups having the least power in society. Groups will differ in their degree of participation in those institutions, social circles, and professions where definitions of reality are created, including, of course, definitions of the human conditions constituting illness. Groups traditionally with little power in American society, blacks, lower class persons, children, and women, have least control over the decisions that will affect their treatment by medical personnel—how much medical care they will receive, when and under what conditions they will receive it, and for which illnesses or conditions.

In recent years women have come to understand more fully how the medical system controls them, and through such publications as *Our Bodies, Ourselves* (1974) have moved to *de*medicalize certain aspects of their lives. Still, the decisions about the aspects of women's lives requiring medical intervention continue to be made largely by physicians.

In this section we will argue that decisions about the conditions sometimes euphemistically labelled "women's troubles," especially for middle-aged women, are often products of prevailing sex role stereotypes and the relatively powerless position of women in American society. Much of what is labelled as requiring treatment reflects a number of unstated, taken-for-granted assumptions about what it means to be a woman. Physicians, like everyone else, are subject to historically created and deeply institutionalized images about the behaviors, dispositions, and emotional states of women.

In a recent article, Linda Fidell (1979) draws upon a number of surveys to illustrate how sex role stereotypes influence women's patient behavior, physicians' expectations of their female patients, and thus the interaction between women and their physicians. Consider the following:

• Physicians expect women to be less stoic than men during illness (Mechanic, 1965).

- Physicians prescribe more mood modifying drugs to housewives than to other categories of persons based on the belief that they can always sleep and need not be mentally alert to perform their jobs around the house (Brodsky, 1971).
- One survey of Canadian physicians asked them to describe "the typical complaining patient." In 72 percent of the cases the doctors spontaneously adopted the pronoun *she* in their descriptions. Only 4 percent referred to a man. Twenty-four percent referred to the patient without reference to gender (Cooperstock, 1971).
- The labels *crock* or *turkey* used by doctors to describe and identify patients most likely to provide unreliable information, are applied with much greater frequency to women than to men (Millman, 1977).
- In one survey, 87 percent of the physicians surveyed judged the daily use of minor tranquilizers as legitimate for housewives, but only 53 percent considered even occasional use as legitimate for students, with yet lower percentages for a variety of other situations (Lynn, 1971).

Before proceeding further, we should make plain that physicians do not unilaterally impose unwelcome definitions of illness onto women. The process is more subtle than that. For example, as Coser (1975) points out, women are trained to be social–emotional experts within the family and are, therefore, expected to monitor more closely than men their own and others mental and physical symptoms. As one result, women more frequently than men present to physicians symptoms of a psychological character. Women are more likely than men to seek help for complaints that physicians often categorize as unexplained, psychsomatic, or of neurotic origin. Such gender-linked behavior bolsters physicians' images of their women patients and influences their mode of treatment. The women, in turn, who have sought treatment for their discomforts, have their own "ill" view of themselves confirmed when treatment is offered by society's experts on illness. And so, a self-fulfilling system of illness definition, creation, and treatment is generated. It is a system based less on solid scientific evidence than on prevailing, but unstated assumptions about the role of women. These assumptions are held by *both* women and their physicians and are sustained and strengthened through their interactions.

To see how stereotypes translate into treatment, consider the distribution and use of psychotropic drugs. Among the range of drugs prescribed by physicians, one group, psychotropic or mood altering drugs are used disproportionately by women. Women use psychotropic drugs twice as often as men (Rogers, 1971). To understand why this is so, we need to see how sex role stereotypes are used by drug companies in the advertisements they place in medical journals.

Drug companies play a substantial role in broadening definitions of ill health. The availability of new drugs has so expanded in recent years that physicians frequently decide to use these drugs based on broad and often vague descriptions provided by drug company salesmen or by advertisements. The following advertisement is typical of many found in psychiatric and medical journals:

WHAT MAKES A WOMAN CRY? A man? Another woman? Three kids? Wrinkles? You name it....If she is depressed, consider Pertofrane®.

Such advertisements redefine normal problems of living as medical problems to be solved by drugs. In advertisements like the one above, symptoms of depression (here, crying) and the conditions that cause them are defined so broadly that *every* woman would at some point be an appropriate candidate for drugs like Pertofrane.

Because of their reproductive capacity, women stand in a particularly special relationship to medicine. For reproductive health care, women are dependent upon obstetricians/gynecologists, approximately 91 percent of whom are men. A study of twenty-seven gynecology texts written from 1943 to 1972 shows that gynecologists, society's official experts on women's health, have traditionally held faulty stereotypes about their patients. As late as 1970, the following version of female sexuality could be found in a gynecology textbook: "The frequency of intercourse depends entirely upon the male sex drive....The bride should be advised to allow her husband's sex drive to set their pace and she should attempt to gear her's satisfactorily to his. If she finds after several months or years that this is not possible, she is advised *to consult her physician as soon as she realizes there is a real problem*" (Scully and Bart, 1972:1048; italics added). Among other stereotypes found in gynecology texts are these: The male sex drive is more powerful than the female drive, women are more interested in sex for procreation than for recreation, and vaginal rather than clitoral orgams represent a "more mature" sexual response.

The clearest example of how these and other stereotypes influence the medical treatment of women and the medicalization of a natural biological event is medicine's response to women at mid-life. It is by looking at the period of menopause, and such medically related procedures as hysterectomies, that we see most fully the interplay of biological events, cultural expectations, social roles, and the medical treatment of symptoms. During the 1950s and 1960s especially, the "feminine-forever" concept led to thousands of women being put on hormone treatments to delay aging and the effects of menopause. These treatments brought with them a large increase in hormone-induced uterine bleeding as well as large increases in hysterectomies among middle-aged women. Today, hysterectomies are still viewed as a quick and easy way to end the "nuisance" of menstruation and to relieve many of the emotional problems of middle age.

Data on hysterectomies reveals perhaps most clearly how persons' relative power, their gender, and their location in the life cycle intersect in the medicalization process. Approximately 800,000 hysterectomies are performed each year at an estimated cost of 450 million dollars and 2,000 deaths (Blair, 1981). Next to the removal of tonsils, hysterectomies are the most frequently performed major surgery. While gynecologists maintain that hysterectomies performed on middle-aged and older women solve many more problems than they create, critics claim that as high as 40 percent of these operations are unnecessary (Budoff, 1980; Denney, 1979). One critic (Rogers, 1975) notes, interestingly, that while prostate cancer causes approximately the same number of deaths in men as uterine cancer in women, preventive prostate surgery is performed far less frequently than preventive hysterectomies.

Claims that only medical criteria influence physicians' decisions to recommend hysterectomies seem contradicted by the following facts (Rogers, 1975):

- On a nationwide level, the number of hysterectomies performed for insured persons is double that for the uninsured.
- In prepaid health plans run by unions, where peer review discourages unjustified surgery, rates of operations are as much as a fourth lower than in fee for service plans like Blue Cross–Blue Shield.
- Hysterectomies are performed two and a half times more often in the U.S. than in England and four times more often than in Swe-

den, where, because medical care is state paid, doctors stanu gain little for performing more hysterectomies.

These group, class, and national variations surely cannot be accounted for by group, class, regional, or national variations in actual rates of gynecological problems.

To see how extensively the mid-life period of American women has been medicalized, we can look at the meanings given to menopause and the mid-life period of women in other cultures. From anthropological evidence we learn that many cultures put wholly different emphases and meanings on physiological changes occurring over the life cycle. Consequently, members of different cultures experience quite different levels of stress when faced with these biological changes.

To understand the nonbiological origins of stress felt at different life points, we must examine where persons are located in a social structure at a given point in the life cycle and the kinds of socially determined status transitions they typically undergo at that point in their lives. It is no accident, as Bart (1970) has noted, that in our society depression most often occurs among middle-class, middle-aged, married women, after their children have left home. As pointed out in Chapter 5, available evidence is quite mixed on the significance to women of the empty nest period. In contrast to many investigations, Lillian Rubin (1980), in her study of mid-life women, offers evidence that many women are relieved rather than distressed when their children leave home. Women, however, who have exclusively identified themselves within the traditional role of wife and mother may find themselves at mid-life in an existential void of sorts. It is a period of transition during which women are obliged to create new identities, but many may have great difficulty doing so. Mid-life depression experienced by women, contrary to many generally held beliefs, may have quite little to do with the biological event of menopause. Menopause may simply coincide with a moment in women's lives when they are grappling with difficult identity questions.

In a fascinating study of an Italian village, Sydel Silverman (1975) provides evidence that the points in the life cycle generating greatest stress for women vary greatly across cultures. Her data on the life cycle of the women in the community of Colleverde (a pseudonym) indicate greatest stress during their transition to married life. The courtship period leading up to marriage and the months immediately following marriage were times of expected and experienced anxiety and stress. Marriage was the key point of transition both in the life of the women and the life of the society. It was also during this period in the life cycle that mental breakdowns were highest among the women of Colleverde. Silverman's work points out that two moments in the life cycle experienced with a great deal of stress in American culture — adolescence and menopause — are insignificant stress points for the women of Colleverde:

> In Colleverde... adolescence is a rather peacable time, during which girls speculate about courtship rather than actively engage in courtship activities: they communicate with boys only tentatively and sporadically, in groups. Their activity involves the development of marriageable assets — learning housewifely skills, beautifying themselves, and preparing their dowries. As for possible crises surrounding the menopause period, the evidence was negative; not only was there little indication of stress or even concern, but the matter was of little interest to anyone (1975:314).

Plainly, different societies "schedule" differently the points of major life transitions. Depending upon the particular contingencies faced by members of a culture at different points in the life cycle, different life moments will be considered problematic. We might well imagine that healers in Colleverde would not be able to comprehend the medical management of menopause in American society. Yet, in their own society, they would have no trouble justifying medicalization of the period just prior to marriage and shortly thereafter. Moreover, were doctors to identify this period as one with unhealthy consequences, the women of Colleverde would, in all likelihood, be socialized to accept this definition and to see themselves as "patients."

The Medicalization of Death

Thus far, we have discussed the medicalization of the beginning and middle of the life cycle. The sophistication of modern technology has also transformed the experience of dying. The most striking characteristic of the current "American way of death" (Mitford, 1963) is that a majority of persons now die within institutions. Well over half of the annual deaths in the United States occur in hospitals rather than in the home (Glaser and Strauss, 1968). Just as we have turned other features of our lives over to experts, we have given the responsibilities for the management of death to physicians, nursing home personnel, and funeral directors. As in previous chapters, to see how the process of dying and the event of death itself have come to assume unique meanings in the modern era, we must adopt a broader historical perspective.

Today, dying often takes place within a "closed awareness context" (Glaser and Strauss, 1965); that is in a situation where family and physician studiously conceal from the patient the fact of his or her impending death. In addition, many today experience a social death prior to their actual biological death. Dying in bureaucratic institutions, isolated from family and friends, patients often are treated as objects, as nonpersons. This is most especially true of those who die in large, public, urban hospitals or nursing homes (Sudnow, 1967; Gubrium, 1975). In contrast, Phillipe Aries (1975) points out that persons in the late Middle Ages and the Rennaissance period actively participated in their own dying process. Dying was an open, public, and collective community process:

> As soon as someone "was helplessly sick in bed," his room filled with people—parents, children, friends, neighbors, fellow guild members. The windows and shutters were closed. Candles were lit. When passersby in the street met a priest carrying the *viaticum* (the Christian Eucharist given to a dying person), custom and piety demanded that they follow him into the dying man's room, even if he was a stranger. The approach of death transformed the room of a dying man into a sort of public place (Aries, 1975:137).

> The leading role went to the dying man himself. He presided over the affair with hardly a misstep, for he knew how to conduct himself, having previously witnessed so many similar scenes. He called to him one by one his relatives, his friends, his servants. . . . He said farewell to them, asking their pardon, gave them his blessing (Aries, 1975:138).

Persons living during the historical periods described by Aries greatly feared a sudden death that would rob them of the opportunity to author this "last chapter" (Marshall, 1980) of their lives. Today, with medicine's capacity to prolong the life of chronically ill persons, it is a long, drawn out, often painful death that is feared. Now, an increasingly larger proportion of persons eventually die after a "lingering death trajectory" (Glaser and Strauss, 1968). Death has shifted from being a moral, religious event to a technological event. In North America, most notably, "death is a technical matter, a failure of technology in rescuing the body" (Cassell, 1974:31). This historical transformation has been described by Ivan Illich (1976).

Illich describes six historical stages corresponding to changes in the imageries held of dying. The first stage, which he labels the *dance-of-the-dead* image, appeared during the fifteenth century. During this stage, death was an occasion to celebrate life, often by dancing on the tomb as an affirmation of the joy of life. Later, during the Rennaissance, this image was replaced by one which saw the end of life as marking the beginning of eternity. "Now death becomes the point at which linear clock-time ends and eternity meets man" (Illich, 1976:189). According to Illich, one indication of the switch to the stage he labels the *danse macabre* (taken from the title of a sixteenth century Hans Holbein picture book on death) was the proliferation of clocks symbolizing a new time-bound consciousness. *Bourgeoise death,* the third stage, emerges with the appearance of a bourgeoise class that could begin to pay physicians to delay or to keep death away. This image, in turn, set the stage for physicians' promulgation of a *clinical* image of death based on the idea that death was the result of a disease that could be fought. By the 1900s, the image of clinical death had been further transformed into the notion of *natural death* in which doctors were expected to prevent any deaths occurring from disease. Finally, our imagery of death evolved to the current view that "unnecessary" deaths are to be prevented at any cost through a vast armament of medical technology. This Illich terms "death under compulsory care."

In sum, Illich finds that our image of death has been changed from death as part of nature to death as a force of nature that makes the event *untimely*, and finally to an image of "unnatural" death against which total war must be waged. Although a natural and inevitable part of the living process, death is viewed today as an evil adversary that must be defeated regardless of how heroic the technological measures required. The contemporary treatment of death has, as we all know, created a range of new moral and legal questions about prolonging life beyond its "normal" course with a range of technical devices.

Our conception of ourselves as patients and the life cycle as a proper sphere for medical intervention begins, we have been suggesting, even before birth. But this is just the beginning. From there on, a series of quite natural functions spanning the life course fall under the scrutiny of medical experts. A range of professionals now offer advice to help persons "get through" the problems of childhood, adolescence, menopause, and old age. We have seen how medical specialties such as neonatology, pediatrics, and medical gerontology have arisen specifically to deal with particular age-related "problems." From the beginning we are subject to a medical definition that says we cannot get through life without the constant attention of doctors, psychiatrists, and other mental health experts. Although our discussion has focused on the way our society defines and treats the beginning, middle, and ending of life, other points along the life cycle could also have served to illustrate the same point. It is that the therapeutic culture, unique to our historical era, has, by treating many life processes as problems, made the aging experience more central to our identities and self-conceptions than in any previous society in human history. Ivan Illich nicely sums up several of our points with his following statement:

> Once a society is so organized that medicine can transform people into patients because they are unborn, newborn, menopausal, or at some other "age of risk," the population inevitably loses some of its autonomy to its healers. The ritualization of stages in life is nothing new; what is new is their intense medicalization.... For rich and poor, life is turned into a pilgrimage through check-ups and clinics back to the ward where it started. Life is thus reduced to a "span," to a statistical phenomenon which, for better or for worse, must be institutionally planned and shaped. This life span is brought into existence with the pre-natal checkup, when the doctor decides if and how the fetus shall be born, and it ends with a mark on a chart ordering resuscitation suspended (Illich, 1976:73).

CONCLUSION

Throughout this book we have tried to convey the idea that our experience of the aging process depends upon where we stand in society. Persons living out their lives as members of different social classes, races, and ethnic and occupational groups perceive their life cycles in subjectively distinctive ways. One of our messages has been, it follows, that we too much oversimplify the aging process if we think of it only in chronological and biological terms. It is worth restating that age carries no intrinsic meaning. Human beings in communication with one another attach meanings to age. Our feelings about growing up, older, and old are formed by the values of the society at large and by those of the particular groups we belong to. In this book we have given special attention to the importance of our several "places" in the world; our gender, our place in the family life cycle, our rung on the occupational career ladder, and more broadly still, our place in history. By this point, you can understand how significantly these social locations shape the way we conceive of the world.

Certainly we have meant to present some of the significant research in the burgeoning area of aging. Description of research findings alone, however, has not been our purpose. In previous chapters we have been making a theoretical statement as well. We have reviewed and synthesized available literature with the aim of highlighting the subjective, personal dimensions of the aging process — dimensions that have been given scant attention by other writers on the subject. In this respect, we view ours as a work of revision. We have not claimed available aging theories to be incorrect. Our task has been the more modest one of amendment and specification of existing theoretical explanation. The theoretical perspective informing our inquiry — symbolic interaction — required responses to the question, How do persons give meaning to, adapt to, and make intelligible their passage through the life course? This global question, in turn, supposes a number of additional assumptions concerning the way to understand aging.

Human beings are not simply objects in nature, not simply passive receptacles for biological processes associated with the passage of time. Rather, human beings shape the aging process by thinking about it, interpreting it, defining it, categorizing it, labelling it, and attaching values to it. Too, these mental activities have critical consequences for our actual behaviors. In this book we have followed through on the simple truth that chronological age is a symbol and consequently subject to continuous human definition and redefinition. Our inquiry has centered on the interplay of social structure, biological change, human beings' definitions of situations, and their actual behaviors. These connections define the substance of the *social psychology* of aging.

REFERENCES

Aries, P.: The reversal of death: Changes in attitudes toward death in western societies. In D. Stannard: *Death in America.* PA, University of Pennsylvania Press, 1975.

Arms, S.: *Immaculate Deception*. Boston, Houghton-Mifflin, 1975.

Arney, W.: *Preserving Childbirth: Power and the Profession of Obstetrics*. In press.

Back, K.: *Beyond Words*. New York, Russell Sage Foundation, 1972.

Bart, P.: Mother Portnoy's Complaint. *Transaction, 8*:69-74, 1970.

Berger, P., and Luckman, T.: *The Social Construction of Reality*. New York, Doubleday, 1967.

Blair, B.: Women's Medicine: The deadly cure. *The Detroit News, August 23*:1C, 13C, 1981.

Boston Women's Health Book Collective: *Our Bodies — Our Selves*. New York, Simon and Schuster, 1974.

Brodsky, C.: The Pharmacology system. *Psychosomatics, 11*:24-30, 1971.

Budoff, P.: *More Menstrual Cramps and Other Good News*. New York, G.P. Putnam, 1980.

Cassell, E.: Dying in a technological society. In P. Steinfels and R. Veatch (Eds.): *Death Inside Out*. New York, Harper and Row, 1975.

Chavkin, S.: *The Mind Stealers: Psycho-Surgery and Mind Control*. Boston, Houghton-Mifflin, 1978.

Conrad, P.: *Identifying Hyperactive Children: The Medicalization of Deviant Behavior*. MA, D.C. Heath, 1976.

Conrad, P., and Schneider, J.: *Deviance and Medicalization*. St. Louis, C.V. Mosby, 1980.

Cooperstock, R.: Sex differences in the use of mood modifying drugs: An Exploratory Model. *Journal of Health and Social Behavior, 12*:238-244, 19__.

Denney, M.: *Second Opinion*. New York, Grosset and Dunlap, 1979.

Engelhardt, H.: Is aging a disease? In R. Veatch (Ed.): *Life Span: Values and Life-Extending Technologies*. New York, Harper and Row, 1979.

Erenreich, B., and English, D.: *For Her Own Good: 150 Years of the Experts' Advise to Women*. Garden City, NY, Anchor Press, 1978.

Fidell, L.: Sex Role Stereotypes and the American Physician. *Psychology of Women Quarterly*, 1980.

Freidson, E.: *Profession of Medicine*. New York, Harper and Row, 1970.

Glaser, B., and Strauss, A.: *Time for Dying*. Chicago, Aldine, 1968.

Glaser, B., and Strauss, A.: *Awareness of Dying*. Chicago, Aldine, 1965.

Goffman, I.: *Asylums*. New York, Anchor Books, 1961.

Gross, M.: *The Psychological Society*, 1978.

Gubrium, J.: *Living and Dying at Murray Manor*. New York, St. Martin's Press, 1975.

Guillemin, J.: Babies by cesarean. *The Hastings Center Report, 11 (3)*:15-22, 1981.

Guillemin, J., and Holmstrom, L.: *Life Ventures: The Medical Management of the New Born*. In press.

Illich, I.: *Medical Nemesis*. New York, Pantheon Books, 1976.

Jordan, B.: *The Cultural Production of Childbirth*. Unpublished Ph.D. thesis. Department of Anthropology, Michigan State University, 1974.

Karp, D., and Yoels, W.: *Symbols, Selves, and Society*. New York, Harper and Row, 1979.

Klapp, O.: *The Collective Search for Identity*. New York, Holt, Rinehart, and Winston, 1969.

Laing, R.: *The Politics of Experience*. New York, Ballantine, 1967.

Lasch, C.: Life in the Therapeutic State. New York Review of Books, June 12:24-31, 1980.

Lasch, C.: The Culture of Narcissism. New York, W.W. Norton, 1978.

Lasch, C.: Haven in a Heartless World. New York, Basic Books, 1977.

Levinson, D.: The Seasons of a Man's Life. New York, Knopf, 1978.

Lofland, L.: The Craft of Dying: The Modern Face of Death. Beverly Hills, CA, Sage Publications, 1978.

Lynn, L.: Physicians' characteristics and attitudes toward legitimate use of therapeutic drugs. Journal of Health and Human Behavior, 12:132-140, 1971.

Marshall, V.: Last Chapters. CA, Brooks/Cole, 1980.

Mechanic, D.: Perceptions of parental responses to illness. Journal of Health and Human Behavior, 6:253-257, 1965.

Millman, M.: The Unkindest Cut. New York, William Morrow, 1977.

Mitford, J.: The American Way of Death. New York, Simon and Schuster, 1963.

Muller, C.: The overmedicated society: Forces in the marketplace for medical care. Science, 176:488-492, 1972.

Neugarten, B.: The future and the young-old. The Gerontologist, February:4-9, 1975.

Oakley, A.: Women Confined: Towards a Sociology of Childbirth. Oxford, Martin Robinson, 1980.

Pfohl, S.: The "discovery" of child abuse. Social Problems, 24:310-323, 1977.

Reiff, P.: Triumph of the Therapeutic. New York, Harper and Row, 1966.

Rogers, J.: Rush to surgery. New York Times Magazine, September 21:34-42, 1975.

Rogers, J.: Drug abuse: Just what the doctor ordered. Psychology Today, September: 16-24, 1971.

Rubin, L.: Women of a Certain Age. New York, Harper and Row, 1980.

Scully, D.: Men Who Control Women's Health: Education of Obstetricians and Gynecologists. Boston, Houghton Mifflin, 1980.

Scully, D., and Bart, P.: A funny thing happened on the way to the orifice: Women in gynecology textbooks. American Journal of Sociology, 78:1045-1050, 1972.

Silverman, S.: The life crisis as a clue to social function: The case of Italy. Toward An Anthropology of Women. New York, Monthly Review Press, 1975.

Spector, M., and Kitsuse, J.: Constructing Social Problems. CA, The Benjamin/Cummings Co., 1977.

Sudnow, D.: Passing On. NJ, Prentice-Hall, 1967.

Szasz, T.: The Myth of Mental Illness. New York, Hoeber-Harper, 1961.

Turner, R.: The theme of contemporary social movements. British Journal of Sociology, 20:390-405, 1969.

Zola, I.: In the name of health and illness: On some socio-political consequences of medical influence. Social Science and Medicine, 9:83-87, 1975.

Zola, I.: Medicine as an institution of social control. Sociological Review, 20:487-504, 1972.

INDEX